Seraffyn's Oriental Adventure

Seraffyn's
Oriental Adventure

by
Lin and Larry Pardey

PARDEY BOOKS

Copyright © 1996 by Mary Lin and Lawrence F. Pardey
All rights reserved.
Published by Pardey Books, Box 20, Middletown, CA 95461-0020; 800-736-4509, 1996.
Printed in the United States of America.
Cover design, Rob Johnson; editor, Allison Peter
The text of this book is composed in Janson, with
display type set in Perpetua. Composition by ComCom
Manufacturing by Thomson Shore
Book design by Jacques Chazaud
Second Edition

Library of Congress Cataloging in Publication Data

Pardey, Lin.
Seraffyn's Oriental adventure.

1. Seraffyn (Cutter) 2. Voyages and travels
—1951–   3. Pardey, Lin. 4. Pardey, Larry.
I. Pardey, Larry. II. Title.
G490.P33   1983   910.4'5   82–14289

Originally published by W.W. Norton & Company, Inc.
New York, NY 1983
ISBN–0964036–3–2
1 2 3 4 5 6 7 8 9 0

To Betty and Ed Greeff,
Susan and Eric Hiscock

Their example gives us the promise of
another lifetime of sailing.

Contents

~~~~~

Acknowledgements

It's the people you meet who make a cruise so interesting. Unfortunately, since this book is about voyaging, we have had to leave out the stories about many of the wonderful people we met in our short sojourns onshore. Marcella and Bunny Cox, Michael and Judy Oliver, Nobby and Gloria Clark, Roger and Sam Fletcher. The list could fill two pages. Our thanks and wishes go out to them, and we'd like to know where they are now and what they're up to.

Bob and Shearlean Duke willingly took their time to read parts of this manuscript and add their comments to assure us we were on the right track. Bob edited every page and tried his best to convince me that *among* really should not have a *U* in it. Spencer Smith and Eric Swenson helped us find the information we needed on heavy-weather sailing. Patience Wales encouraged us to write about the storms we encountered and how we handled them, physically and emotionally. All of this assistance makes writing an exciting learning experience.

As typist and final coordinator for all of our writing projects I would like to take this time to thank my coauthor, Larry. He has been right beside me all the way, adding his suggestions as we discuss the shape and content of each chapter, putting up with my tantrums when I dislike one of his early-morning editing suggestions, accepting my impatience when he doesn't understand why I just have to include that story or delete another. After so many years of working together as a team, of discussing each idea, each event, it's often hard to remember whose words actually reach the final pages of anything we write.

Several of the chapters in this book have appeared in *Cruising World* and *Pacific Yachting*; the appendixes on heaving-to were used in *Sail* magazine. Our sincere appreciation goes to the editors of both. We often used their editing changes to improve our final copy.

A last word of thanks goes to Jim and Barbara Moore, who have always encouraged and helped us survive the projects we so readily jump into. Without their constant reminder that everything works better when it's greased with a little laughter, boat building, writing, and just plain living would have been a lot harder.

Introduction

~~~~~~

Larry made three statements when he was building *Seraffyn* that now make us smile and shake our heads.

"I'm building this boat to last the rest of my life."

"If we could find some way to leave here and cruise for six months or a year, I'd be satisfied."

"I have no desire to circumnavigate the world; I'd just like to wander along the coast of Mexico."

At twenty-one I was a complete novice: boats, cruising, even life. I was just a pair of wide-open, wondering eyes. So I accepted Larry's words. How could I disagree with someone who had already owned four sailboats and made two ocean passages on an eighty-five-foot schooner? As I worked along with Larry, learning to build *Seraffyn*, I agreed, building one wooden sailboat seemed like enough work to last a lifetime. For three years every extra penny we had went into that project. Some months our grocery allowance was cut in half so that we could buy that extra sixty board feet of teak for the cockpit and cabin sills. Our social life wrapped into a tight, pleasant cocoon surrounded by other boat builders and sailors who pot lucked and shared gallon bottles of red mountain wine. When *Seraffyn* was finally launched, she seemed like the boat of a lifetime.

But a year and a half later we began to laugh at Larry's young dream of being satisfied with six months of cruising. We'd sold out, set sail, and after a year of exploring Mexico were on our way south to Costa Rica. We'd found ways to earn money and keep on going. We loved the freedom of our unplanned cruising life.

For almost eight years we wandered on, exploring the southern Caribbean, getting to know the Chesapeake, taking the plunge across the Atlantic. Then England and Scandinavia filled our lives. We'd work three or four months each year, delivering yachts, writing, doing boat carpentry or repairs. Then we'd excitedly set sail for a new adventure. I think it was during our seventh year of cruising, as we headed toward the Mediterranean, that Larry's first conviction began to fall by the wayside. He never found fault with little *Seraffyn*. In fact, he often defended the choice he'd made as a twenty-five-year-old. "She's a terrific boat, does everything we ask her to, sails well." But I noticed two distinct changes in his attitude. He'd look on in dismay as I ruthlessly went through all of our belongings and acquisitions each spring and discarded his shaggy spare sweaters, a bruised, leaking fender, scraps of wood we might use someday. Then he'd lament, "We never planned to live on her for more than six months or a year. I sure wish we had a bit more cargo space." At the same time, our casual investigation of boat-building yards in each of the ports we visited began to be earnest searches for new ideas. Each time we'd be invited on some well-built custom boat, Larry would ferret through its innermost recesses, scrutinize the rigging or deck layout, then come home and say something like "I wish I'd known about bronze floors when I was building *Seraffyn*."

I think I was the first to realize that Larry had to build a new boat. *Seraffyn* had been the work of a cautious young craftsman constrained by lack of experience to the most conventional and conservative of construction methods. Now, as he was a more mature, more experienced sailor and boat builder, Larry's inner desires to try and do it better were forcing themselves to the surface.

It took us almost a year to convince ourselves that we were not being disloyal to *Seraffyn* when we talked about a new, larger, more scientifically built boat. Yet even after we'd received the preliminary drawings for our future boat, we still put off the decision to give up cruising for three years while we not only built the boat but also earned the money to pay for its materials and equipment.

"Let's head toward California. It's time we revisited our old friends and got to know our families again. When we get there we'll either build a new boat or just set off cruising on *Seraffyn* again. Either way, its a nice goal to shoot for, a leisurely cruise back home. It could take us another eight years to get there," I suggested as a way of not really making a decision. This was in Malta, exactly halfway around the world from where we started if we followed the prescribed sailing routes.

And that is what caused Larry's final statement to fall by the wayside.

On every list of pros and cons we made as we tried to decide which way to sail, one item always had to be added to the argument in favor of the east-about route: that way we'd circumnavigate. West-about was technically the easier way: familiar waters, trade winds to carry us across the Atlantic, the friendly, well-regulated Panama Canal, 14,000 miles by way of Honolulu. East-about was all new to us. The Suez Canal had been reopened that year. Horror stories of the heat, pirates, and currents of the Red Sea ran rife among the cruising fleet, fanned by maybe half a dozen voyagers who'd fought head winds and frustrating bureaucracy to leave the Indian Ocean and enter the Med. The North Pacific presented a 4,500-mile passage that neither of us really looked forward to. This way was only fifty or a hundred miles longer than the west-about route. We listed the newness of this course as its main attraction. But in our minds even before we made the final decision was the prestige of joining that limited number of voyagers who could say, "I circumnavigated the world."

Then we got caught up in a completely new kind of voyaging. No longer were we cruising; we were passage making. No longer did we choose our next destination by a flip of the coin or plan our goals by the wind direction or someone's description of fine lobster hunting, interesting jobs, or neat islands. Our route and schedule were determined solely by the seasons. To avoid the typhoon season in one area we had to leave a favorite anchorage before we'd drunk our fill of its beauty, diversions, and peace. To have a chance of fair winds for the longest passages we had to avoid the distractions of new island groups just sixty miles off our course.

The last two and a half years of our voyaging on *Seraffyn* were in many ways the most difficult of an eleven-year cruise. But at the same time they offered us glimpses of one of the most unusual parts of the world we'd come to call our own. The Orient proved to be as mysterious as childhood adventure books had lead us to believe. We spent over two hundred days at sea during the year and a half starting when we left Malta. Those thousands of hours alone together showed me the depths our relationship had developed. As we worked together to accept the weather, the calms, the storms, I learned the value of the partnership we'd forged.

So, now we smile and shake our heads at dicta made and broken during our first eleven years together. But now both of us look back at the last two and a half years of our cruise as the time when we grew up and realized that nothing is forever and the course of our future will always be a question mark.

Seraffyn's
Oriental
Adventure

CHAPTER 1

~~~~~~~

Where
Does the Time Go?

I t was late afternoon when we ran up the wide channel between Sivota and Corfu, the tree-covered northernmost islands of the Ionian Sea. As soon as we rounded Cape Sidero, the old Venetian fortress and gold-stone buildings of Corfu Town came into view. I was eager to be onshore, exploring the alleys and tiny streets we could see from the waterfront. But when we sailed through the tiny harbor where local fish boats competed with a dozen charter yachts for the only spaces available, we found there wasn't room left, even for a boat as small as *Seraffyn*. Larry wasn't too concerned. "Everyone in Malta talked about a beautiful bay only three miles north of here. Let's sail up there and I'll come into town tomorrow to clear our papers. It's Sunday; no one will mind."

But I wasn't so sure. Some customs and immigration officials could be pretty touchy if you didn't play the game by their rules. We'd gotten into trouble in Yugoslavia by not clearing into a proper port of entry as soon as we arrived. So I convinced Larry to tie alongside a fish boat for the night. He was grumbling when he left with our passports and ship's papers. I stayed on board in case the fish boat's owner came back.

I hadn't even finished coiling up the halyards when Larry came running down the dock yelling, "We're free. Hoist the mainsail. Let's get going."

"But, but . . ." I started to say.

"Come on, Lin, we've only got an hour before it's dark. I don't want to spend the night here. Too noisy, too crowded. Look at that oil on the sea walls," Larry said as he threw our papers down below and started untying our mooring lines.

"What about customs inspections?" I asked as I steered through the

twenty-five-foot-wide opening into the ferry harbor, then out past the breakwaters.

"Customs inspection, hell, they don't even care if we're here. I went into the port office and all three officials were watching the World Cup playoffs on television. Didn't even look at our papers, just stamped our passports, then invited me to join them. If that's the way Greek officials are, I'm going to like cruising here."

The southerly breeze was growing lighter as we headed toward Gouvia. There were no navigation lights to guide us past the shoals at the entrance, so we packed on every bit of canvas we could as the light faded into a pink and gray sunset. It was almost dark when we lined up to sail between a tree-covered point and a low, sandy spit with a tiny stone building on its end. Even though the shoals were completely unmarked, there was no cause for concern as we trickled into the bay after dark. There was absolutely no swell; the water was flat and calm; the bottom, soft mud. So, even if we ran aground it didn't really matter.

I coiled the lead line, then heaved it, chanting, "Four fathoms, four fathoms, three and a half fathoms." Larry steered along the bearing that led to a safe, protected part of the bay. I enjoyed the feeling of the lead line, the slight pull as each mark slid through my fingers. I leaned against the starboard shrouds and heaved, let the lead settle, and waited until *Seraffyn* slid alongside the line. When it stood perpendicular to our deck, I'd note the knots or pieces of rag nearest the waterline, call the depth, and jerk the line to pull it free of the bottom mud and coil it carefully to keep the lead from banging our topsides. In the light shed by our stern oil lamp, this ancient seaman's ritual seemed to suit the quiet bay. Only a few lights filtered through the trees onshore. We could hear crickets or frogs calling across the water. The only other sound came from *Seraffyn*'s tiny bow wave, then our quiet discussion when my line showed two fathoms. "We'll round up now. You drop the anchor, I'll get the sails down," Larry said. "Then let's eat that spaghetti you cooked up this afternoon."

Once again we enjoyed that end-of-the-voyage feeling, a feeling that never seems to grow old. Anchor down in good holding ground, boat secure for the night, hot food and a bottle of wine on the table, and no watches to stand. But this time we had a special treat. When we climbed into the cockpit after dinner to enjoy the quiet evening sounds, a firefly flew out from shore. It was the brightest one I'd ever seen, and it chose Larry's hair as its landing field. Bright flashes filtered through Larry's curly hair like the flash from a lighthouse beacon welcoming a weary sailor from a storm-tossed sea. Onshore we could see the pinpoints of light as other fireflies flitted from bush to bush. But that lone long-range dot of living light made us feel especially welcome. Larry was reluctant to brush him from his hair until we were ready to go below and climb into our warm double bunk.

It was the end of April 1977, just over eight years from the day we first set sail from California. But now there was a worrisome intrusion in the casual, easygoing life-style we'd worked hard to promote and protect all these years. No longer were we cruising with absolutely no schedules or long-range plans. During the past winter we'd spent long, careful hours discussing the merits of continuing our comfortable, easy life-style or giving it all up for the much harder challenge of finishing our voyage and building a new, slightly larger boat so that we could try a different sort of cruising. All winter long we'd tossed the question around. Neither of us really likes making decisions. Maybe it's because we both sometimes take ourselves too seriously. Once we argue through to any final decision, we feel we are morally obligated to stick by it, no matter how small the decision is, no matter if no one but ourselves has heard a word of our plans. Let me falter and want to turn back, and Larry reminds me of our goal, shores up my resolve, or offers to carry some of the extra load. If it's Larry who backs away, then it's my turn to step into the lead, encouraging and sympathizing with him.

Now we'd arrived in Gouvia with a firm personal commitment to sail either east- or west-about toward Vancouver, Canada, and eventually Southern California, catching the seasons to make the North Pacific leg of our voyage in the summer of 1978. Whichever way we chose, we had to be headed for the Suez Canal or Gibraltar by August.

When I climbed out of our companionway the next morning I was assailed with the dilemma presented by trying to see and enjoy the Greek islands in less than four months. In the daylight, Gouvia Bay made this even more difficult to resolve. Rugged hills thrust rocky boulders into the blue sky; pines climbed down the slopes and marched toward the shore to meet the flowering shrubs that lined the water. The sand spit we'd skirted in the dark cut the mile-long bay into two distinct halves. The tiny stone building that crowned its outermost tip was a small, open chapel. North of this lay a natural enclosed basin with a dozen small boats bobbing gently at anchor. South of us lay the stone piers of a marina that had never been finished, with half a dozen foreign yachts now tied there. We lay anchored right in the middle of the bay; not another boat was within a quarter mile of us. Right ahead a tiny freshwater stream bubbled across smooth rocks and seeped into the bay. This anchorage was the type of place we loved best, a place to make our cruising headquarters. We could have our solitude when we wanted, or we could join the partylike atmosphere at the concrete piers simply by sailing over and tying at one of the two dozen empty spaces. We could sail into Corfu to go shopping or walk a quarter mile to the main road and catch the bus. There were a dozen islands and anchorages to explore within three or four hours of sailing, and we could return from each one to this safe, secure anchorage to restock and retrench.

Larry echoed my thoughts when he climbed on deck. "I could spend months in a place like this. Come on, let's row ashore and have a bath in that stream."

We launched the dinghy, loaded our spare water jugs and some towels, then rowed over to a sandy patch next to the stream. Even though that water was shockingly cold at first, we were soon sitting in the crystal-clear stream right at the edge of the beach. Tiny saltwater breakers curled over our feet; the midmorning sun warmed our backs. *Seraffyn* bobbed to her anchor chain two hundred yards away, her Canadian flag lifting to a slight breeze.

"What do we do now?" I asked Larry. "How are we going to pack it all into four months? How do we stop cruising and get moving and still enjoy this?"

"Forget seeing it all. We'll just play it by ear. If we want to sit right here for the next four months, we will. On your birthday we'll set sail and start moving. But until then let's just enjoy each day."

I'm glad he said that, because the next six weeks went far differently than I'd have expected. That same afternoon we heard a familiar voice calling from the beach. Marybelle and Will Bulmer, Larry's favorite Canadian cousins, stood on the beach waving. Their two girls, Shannon and Kelly, played in the water chasing crabs and small fish. This was probably one of the most relaxed and enjoyable rendezvous we'd ever had during our cruising years. When Marybelle wrote to us to say, "We're coming to Europe for a few months to buy a camper van and explore. Love to meet up with you somewhere in Italy and Greece," I'd immediately started worrying. How could we plan a date or an exact rendezvous? We never could keep to schedules, since our engineless state meant that the weather dictated our lives more than it does most people's. But Larry's suggestion worked, and it is a plan we'll follow in the future. "Just write and say we'll try to be near Corfu Town during the first two weeks of May. If we know we can't get there for some reason, we'll send them a letter at the main post office." This took the pressures off all of us. Instead of worrying about being a day or two late, we had two weeks to work with. Instead of feeling responsible for someone else's whole vacation, we were just an additional part.

For the next week we were part of a big family, riding around the island in Will's van, teaching the girls to sail our dinghy, sharing family news. Larry and Will took off for a day of fishing on *Seraffyn* and brought back only fish stories to the campfire Marybelle and I had built on the beach.

By being with Marybelle and Will we learned about a good solution to one of the flaws of a cruising sailor's life. It has always seemed wrong to sail across an ocean to get to a new country, then see only the ports and seacoast, especially around Europe, where the inland areas have so much to offer. Many cruising people try to remedy this by taking two or three day trips by bus or train. But traveling more extensively using public transportation soon becomes a drag. There is another way to go. It seems that the street in front of the American and Australian embassies in most European capitals has become a sort of unofficial clearing house for camp- ers, vans, and motorcycles. Travelers who fly into one part of Europe often find themselves at the far end when it is time to leave for home. They can't sell their vehicle to locals, because customs duties and reregistration away from the country of purchase would make the price prohibitive. So, these vans are sold to freshly arriving foreigners who can get a six-month regis- tration permit for free. Marybelle and Will said they'd had a choice of six or seven vans within two days of arriving in London. When they sold theirs almost a year later, it took only two days, and they got most of their money back, even though the van had the added mileage of a journey that included Spain, Italy, Greece, France, and Morocco.

After Marybelle and her family left, we forgot about time and just enjoyed the relaxed atmosphere of Corfu. We did a bit of varnish work in the mornings and found the local restaurant, where the menu was a walk through the kitchen guided by the cook, who opened each pot and directed the planning of our meal. Charter skippers whom we knew from Malta stopped by while they lay at anchor one last night before picking up their first charter of the season in Corfu Town. Almost every skipper we talked with cursed the rubber-duck fleets that they claimed were killing the real charter business.

One afternoon, when the last crewed charter boat had left Gouvia, we rowed into the quiet lagoon behind the chapel and said hello to the young

Larry stripping the forehatch, then putting a one-inch radius on its corner so that the varnish stays nicer.

man who was obviously the caretaker for thirteen identical twenty-seven foot fiberglass boats, obviously called, the rubber-duck fleet. He laughed when we told him about the resentful skippers on the larger charter boats. Then he described the way this group of boats worked. The *flotilla*, as it is called, was a direct challenge to the regular charter trade. Some enterprising travel agent in England had bought four fleets of identical boats, then arranged a package tour that flew people out from England, provided them with their own private boat, and then had an extra boat go along with a couple who acted as tour guides, party organizers, and trouble shooters. These two-week charters were a real bargain. They gave neophyte sailors a chance to see the Greek islands in the most romantic way possible with no worry about breakdowns or navigation. The disadvantages were small. For seven days of the charter you had to stay with the fleet. But the routes and harbors chosen for this fleet sailing were planned so that people got to visit the nicest anchorages in the area. The fleets did clutter up some of the best cruising spots when they arrived, but they stayed for only one night out of every two weeks.

Within a few days we got to know several of the multinational young couples who handled these fleets so professionally. Somehow this led to our smallest ever delivery job. Six new boats had just arrived in Brindisi, Italy, trucked in overland from England. Someone had to go and sail them across the Adriatic to Corfu. The fee we were offered to be part of this team was too little to really add to our cruising kitty. But it did justify an excursion both of us wanted to make. So, we moored *Seraffyn* among the Gouvia rubber-duck fleet and took the ferry to Brindisi to spend the next five days traveling in a rented car, exploring Pompeii, Napoli, and the wonderful Sorrento peninsula. We ended up at a beautiful old hotel in Positano where our balcony hung over orange trees that clung in steep terraces right at the edge of the sea. We enjoyed the room service and the quiet of this ancient village, where it is against the law even to shout across the streets or otherwise disturb the peace. As we spent the last of our delivery fee on a final, real Italian dinner, I laughed at the memory of Larry's words. We'd played it by ear and almost six weeks had fled pleasantly. But we still hadn't seen any of the Greek islands except Corfu.

CHAPTER 2

～～～～

Our Kind of Cruising

I used to wonder why people always chose to tell the horror stories about their cruising life instead of relating tales of the best times, when life flowed as it should. Then I started trying to write about the almost perfect cruising we had when we left Corfu to explore the Ionian Sea. The spring weather was warm and sunny; days were growing longer, so every landfall came before nightfall. Winds blew in at 0800 almost always from the north or northwest at eight to twelve knots. So, each small voyage was either a reach or a run over one-foot wind waves. The water in each bay was warm and inviting for afternoon swims overboard. Each anchorage we visited was peaceful and quiet, with the warm, friendly people we'd always found in island societies. But not one exciting, really noteworthy thing happened while we cruised over a zigzagging 300-mile course from Corfu, through the Ionian and on to Kithira.

I remember anchoring in two fathoms of aquamarine water at the village of Lakka, on Paxos, diving overboard for a swim, then going ashore to watch the sponge fishermen power into the rickety wooden pier at the foot of a small village. We sat on a pile of fishnets and watched while the two men tried to compress each freshly caught sponge into the overloaded hold of a thirty-foot cargo boat. One miscalculation would send a dozen soggy sponges springing out from under the hatch coamings at the same time as the man on the far side of the tiny hold squeezed six more sponges into an imaginary empty space. We couldn't control our laughter when the two sponge divers tried to get the lid on the hold. Even when we volunteered our weight to press down the recalcitrant sponges, it was impossible to get the hatch even close to its latches. In fact, I almost expected the sides

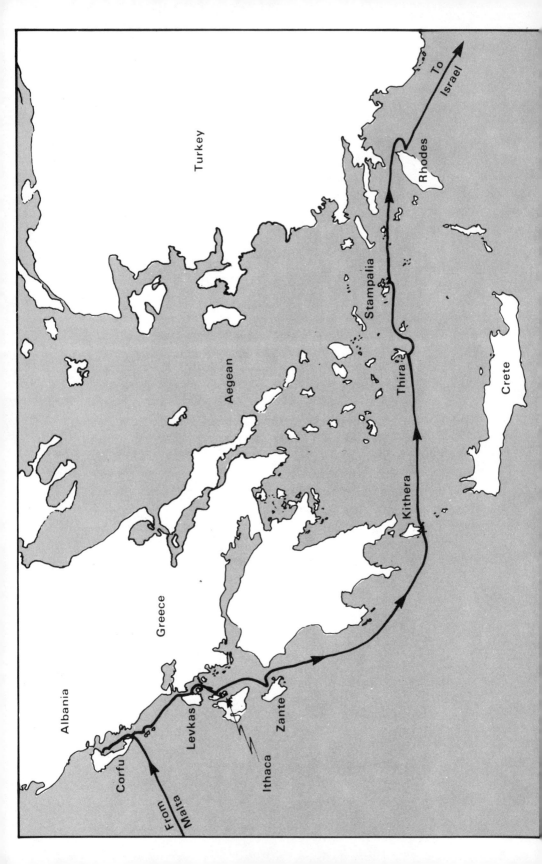

of that rough-looking old boat to burst from the pressures. Finally the sponge divers gave up and used a fishnet to secure down the bulging load. Then they offered us a drink of ouzo while all four of us sat quietly on the edge of the dock watching the sun go down. We were locked in silence by our language barrier but joined by our seafaring lives.

Just sixteen miles south of Lakka we tied stern to a tiny road that led into the village of Gayo. Our anchor held us firmly away from the rocks. The island of Paxos wrapped around us, and at night it was so quiet it seemed as if we were anchored in the middle of a farm instead of across the road from dozens of chickens, sheep, goats, and a pair of donkeys.

There are four small restaurants in Gayo. Their trade comes mostly from the tour boat that runs from Corfu three times a week. We weren't a bit disturbed by the tourists, who stayed for only two or three hours. In fact, one came by and told us that Spiro's restaurant had some of the finest food he'd ever tasted in three months of touring Greece.

So, that evening I put on my new, hand-embroidered gauzy Greek blouse, a long skirt, and high heels. Larry trimmed his beard and got out his carefully stowed favorite shirt. We ferried ourselves along the endless

Lin securing a new mast boot as we prepare for the voyages that lie ahead.

Some of the Greek fishing vessels we came to know.

towline we'd rigged for *Rinky Dink* and carefully climbed ashore, then towed *Rinky* clear of the rocks to sit and wait for us just behind *Seraffyn*.

We walked along the water's edge, listening to the late-evening sounds of this tiny island community. There were no other yachts tied along the edges of the protected bay. The five small shops were already closed; oil lamps glowed in the windows of two dozen fishermen's homes. But when we came to where all four restaurants faced each other, there were at least two dozen people seated at small tables under the trees that grew in the center of the cobblestone plaza. Spiro fussed about us as we joined the Greek visitors from the mainland and an English artist who spent each summer in the back rooms of a small farmhouse a mile outside of the village.

The tart bite of iced local retsina contrasted with sweet slices of tomato, onion, and green pepper soaked in olive oil and oregano. Spiro's youngest son brought a perfect gardenia to sit next to each of our plates on the linen tablecloth. Two candles flickered in tall glasses next to the sweet-smelling flowers; they lent a quiet glow that didn't detract from the bright stars overhead. When we began eating marinated lamb on a bed of soft, dry rice, Spiro's wife came out and sat on the step of the restaurant, then softly strummed local melodies on a battered bouzouki. Just as we were finishing a plate of tiny island-grown apricots and plums, the owner of the restaurant across the hundred-foot-wide plaza came walking over with a portable battery-operated record player. He set it on a table, and soon the familiar-sounding strains of Greek dance music had half a dozen men on their feet. The slow, intricate movements of their dance fit perfectly into the mellow mood of this quiet evening. We tried to join them, but even Spiro's patient coaxing and demonstrations left us feeling clumsy. So, we sat and sipped hot, spicy tea while our host and his friends wove their spell.

It was close to midnight when we ferried ourselves out to *Seraffyn*. But both of us were reluctant to end the fine evening. Larry got out our cockpit cushions and poured me a cream sherry. Then we just relaxed and waited.

A lone man came down the dark road behind us, his small kerosene hand lamp lighting the packed-dirt path. We watched the lamp trace a line that led to the far end of the island. Then it stopped, and a few minutes later we saw the fifteen-foot-high navigation light on the point sputter, then glow. When the lamplighter came walking past *Seraffyn* we called hello. The Greek words for "good night" echoed over the still water. So, we climbed below for the night. Just before I dozed off I felt gentle rocking as a small cargo boat came through the narrow passage leading to the village. Somehow I felt as if I'd been part of a day that had been just the same for two thousand years. Nothing exciting ever happened on Paxos, and that was its special charm.

Our spinnaker was up and pulling when we spotted the Venetian fortress of Santa Maura, on the north shore of Levkás. We were moving at close to six knots, and even though our charts and guidebooks assured us that there was a well-marked channel leading into the Levkás Canal, I felt a bit nervous rushing straight down on what looked like a low, continuous, sandy lee shore. We kept checking our bearings on the fortress, and even Larry became a bit concerned when we were within a mile of the beach and still couldn't see any break to indicate the entrance. "Let's get this chute down now," he said. I was at the helm as he released our 1,000-square-foot spinnaker. It slid docilely onto the deck behind the blanketing mainsail as I steered toward the fortress. We were less than a quarter mile from shore when Larry spotted a ten-foot-high post topped by a small green light on the sand spot that protected the canal. The wind was from the west-northwest at about fifteen knots, so Larry set our small genoa, the one we call our lapper. *Seraffyn* heeled sharply when I sheeted in the sails. The canal entrance was far narrower than I expected, maybe a hundred feet wide between the buoys and the shoals our chart showed. A low, barge-type chain ferry was crossing between the fort and a road along the far side of the canal. For some reason I called to Larry, "I'll take her through myself."

"Okay," he said as he worked coiling halyards. "I'll just keep a watch."

There wasn't another vessel in the narrow, mile-long canal. I steered carefully to catch each small wind shift, easing off when the luff of the lapper started to pant, coming up toward the wind when the wool telltale on our windward cap shroud fell back. I had to take three short tacks to clear the pilings leading to the ferry. Each time I eased slowly through the eye of the wind, I let the sheet go quickly, then hauled the lapper in on the other side before it filled. Two or three cranks on the winch and I was under way on a new tack. Water lapped at the edge of our sharply heeled deck. I was just preparing for the final tack when Larry called, "If you tack now you'll clear the ferry." I gave him what I hoped was a withering glare as I pulled the tiller toward me and eased the lapper sheet. "Okay, okay," he said, laughing, "I'll keep my big mouth shut."

I was too busy watching for the wind shifts to say a word. I just steered down the long, narrow canal enjoying the live feel of our tiller as *Seraffyn* charged along on the flat water. I played the wind shifts carefully, luffing up just a bit on the stronger gusts to keep on the windward side of the canal, letting the sails fill completely when the wind eased off. I made the last half mile in one long tack. Half a dozen yachts lay stern to the seawall in front of the public gardens of Levkás village. We knew several of them from our winter in Malta and spring in Gouvia. I could feel the people on them watching as I checked the chart that lay enclosed in a plastic case at the forward end of the cockpit. When I'd chosen a spot for our bow anchor I told Larry my plan. We worked quietly as a team. Larry dropped the lapper and furled it in the jib net as I headed into the wind. Then I eased the mainsheet and shoved the boom out until the sail spilled all of its wind. *Seraffyn* slowed gently, then lost her way and began to settle slowly back away from the wind. "Let the anchor go," I called. The chain rattled over the bronze cathead, disturbing the quiet of the late afternoon. I walked forward to drop the mainsail while Larry began to unlash the dinghy. A German sailor we'd never met came rowing over. "Hand me your stern line. I'll row it in to shore for you," he said. When he'd secured the line to a big bronze bollard on the seawall, Larry put the end around the sheet winch and I eased the anchor chain until we rested five feet from the edge of town. Together we secured our lines, furled and tied our sails, then invited our assistant on board for a glass of wine. Another day had meandered away. Nothing exciting had happened. But that special warm feeling that comes from knowing we'd had a nearly perfect day of sailing was more than enough for me.

The islands south of the Levkás Canal seem to be a forgotten part of Greece. Small villages cling around protected bays; a few ferries bring supplies from the mainland. Some tourists come here looking for peace and quiet. But there are no big hotels, no night life, and almost no industry except on the southernmost island of Zante. Although this area was the home of Ulysses and the heart of ancient Greek mythology, history seems to have passed the Ionian Islands by for almost two thousand years. So, even now, only fishermen and farmers live scattered around the less rocky areas, growing grapes, raisins, and vegetables in tiny, carefully cultivated plots. It is this quiet, unhurried pace that makes these islands such a wonderful cruising area. Dozens of small natural harbors can be found, and even though we met seven different cruising boats on Levkás, once we headed south we did not see another foreigner for almost a month.

All of the islands in this area are high and rugged. We'd heard about the fierce williwaws that could knock even a sixty-foot boat flat when you sailed into the calm-looking lee of certain islands. The day we sailed into Ithaca, we felt these unexpected gusts ourselves. When we sailed south past Scorpios, the heavily wooded retreat islands owned by the Onassis family, the wind was blowing from the northwest at about twelve knots. We ran wing and wing with all working sail set, reading our Denham guidebook and enjoying the warm sunshine. Larry dropped our whisker pole when the Gulf of Mola opened up before us. Just three miles inside this safe, beautiful-looking gulf lay Port Vathy, the place historians felt was Ulysses' home and kingdom. I hadn't had time to sheet the lapper in on the lee side when the first williwaw came whistling down the 3,000-foot-high mountain that forms the northern side of the gulf. Two hundred yards ahead of us the water turned white. Even with the lapper flogging and the main eased out for a beam reach, *Seraffyn* staggered until her lee deck was completely awash. We headed into the gusty wind and dropped both sails. Then Larry hauled our hundred-square-foot staysail up, and we charged into the gulf at close to six knots, whitecaps chattering against *Seraffyn*'s side, spray flying from her bow wake. That wind must have been gusting at least forty-five knots.

We flew dead downwind into Port Vathy and rounded up behind the tiny island that lay just off the town. Roaring gusts raked through the harbor, sending two-foot-high white horses galloping down on the berths next to the town's seawall. But we had found good protection even though the island we were nestled behind was only about two hundred feet wide. So, we gladly dropped our anchor, paid out seven-to-one scope, and went below for iced drinks away from the pressure of that wind. By early evening the wind had died down, and we rowed ashore to see if our mail package had arrived. We found the post office and our package easily in this small town. In fact, the postmistress seemed to know what we were after as soon as we walked through the door of her tiny office. Our two-pound registered-mail pack was the only thing in the poste restante (general delivery) slot. We walked through half a dozen streets until we found a café that featured beautiful, large prawns. I laughed when the waiter rushed to remove four large rocks from our sidewalk table. He stowed the ten- or twelve-pound tablecloth holders against the front of his restaurant, then brought us our drinks while we opened the first letters from home. When we were leaving, we watched the waiter set the rocks back in position on the sturdy, three-foot-square table. We laughed then, but the next morning, soon after we'd rowed ashore, those gusts began again. The man who rented battered old Vespa motor scooters for five dollars a day spoke some English, and he told us this happened almost every day except when there was a storm.

"What happens when there is a storm?" I asked as I stuffed our bathing suits and towels into the saddlebag. "The gusts come from a different direction," he said in complete seriousness.

We were riding the only vehicle on the long, winding road that led to the top of the hills. We did pass a lone, black-clad woman leading a burro. The small animal was piled high with brush and twigs; a gangling baby burro frolicked alongside her. But otherwise we were alone as we explored the island and finally stood on the peak overlooking the Gulf of Mola. The wind up here blew at only about twelve knots; the sea outside the gulf was dark blue and smooth. But we watched the wind pile up against the hills behind us, then tumble down the mountainside and gather speed as it hit the water three thousand feet below us and turned it into a maelstrom of white lace. "I'm surprised Ulysses ever went to sea if the winds blew like this," Larry commented when we turned to head for the north end of the island. "But maybe that's why he went. Storms couldn't faze a man who learned to sail in gusts like these."

Port Vathy, Ulysses' home port. *Seraffyn* is anchored just behind the smallest island.

It was almost July when we headed out of Port Vathy early one morning before the first williwaws hit. We still hadn't decided which way to go to start our long voyage back toward California. Larry still wanted to play it all by ear, making our final decision on the first of August. But I have always been an organizer. I hate leaving ends dangling. "Come on, Larry," I insisted as we beat out onto the open sea. "Shall we start working toward the Suez Canal or head toward Gibraltar?"

"Let's not commit ourselves yet," he said. "Let's just go some places we've never been before." But when we reached Zante, Larry started talking about seeing some of the Aegean Islands. "I hear Rhodes is a great meeting place. Might be someone there who's just come up the Red Sea." As soon as he suggested shaping a course for the island of Kithira, on the southern tip of the Peloponnesus, I knew what our final decision would be. Larry, just like me, hates to backtrack. I knew then that we'd soon be headed for the Far East through some of the most worrisome waters in the world. When the Ionian Islands faded from view behind us, I tried to package up the last two months in my mind so that I could draw comfort and strength from those lovely days when nothing much happened. Days when we walked through quiet hills or worked on *Seraffyn*, tightening the caulking in her decks, repaying the seams, and casually getting her ready for the demanding ocean passages that lay ahead. Days when we swam and dove looking for our perfect fish dinners, and others when we sampled the local food at quiet tavernas. These past two months were what we wanted as cruising sailors. But as I said in the beginning of this chapter, they are also the hardest ones to share with you.

~~~~~

CHAPTER 3

Meltemi

W e normally stand round-the-clock watches of three hours on, three hours off whenever we are offshore. These are usually casual: "take a look around the horizon every ten minutes, then read a book" type watches. But as we neared the western approaches to the Aegean Sea, shipping traffic became so heavy that one of us stayed on deck all of the time, ready to change course or flash a light on our sails. Ferries, freighters, oil tankers, even two large charter yachts hustled past us bound to or from Athens, Istanbul, the Black Sea, and Turkey. We often had as many as a dozen ships' lights in view at the same time.

The crowded seas seemed to emphasize the barrenness of the land we sailed past. The hills lay brown and parched-looking, reaching inland toward rugged mountains. Our charts indicated a few small villages in the creases of the hills, but from the sea it seemed as if no one at all lived within sight of this rocky, indented coastline. For some reason I was surprised to see the navigation lights on Venetico Island, then Cape Matapan spring over the horizon right on cue. But even on the most forbidding, deserted islands of this wide-flung country, navigation aids were carefully maintained and easily visible.

It was close to midnight when we passed Cape Matapan and shaped our final course for Kapsali Bay on Kithira. A fresh, warm, northerly breeze would have kept us moving at over five knots. But there were no navigation lights shown on our detailed chart of Kithira, so we trickled through the night at only two knots with just our staysail set so that we could make our landfall right at dawn.

I was a little grumpy when Larry woke me. I squirmed to look at the clock. It was still at least an hour before my watch. "What's wrong?" I yelled out the companionway. "Nothing at all, just didn't want you to miss this. Come on up; you can take the rest of your off watch later," Larry answered.

I can't say I climbed out of the sleeping bag too eagerly. But when I'd pulled on a pair of shorts and a sweatshirt and climbed out into the rosy sunrise to see what had excited Larry, my grumpiness disappeared. He was right; I'd have hated to miss the rugged, shadowed mountains that surrounded Kapsali Bay. One range of hills reached toward the south like the paw of a sleeping leopard. At the head of the bay a massive Venetian castle crowned the 600-foot-high bluff; a white village clustered along its golden-colored stone walls. Denham's sea guide states, "It was the strength of the castle which so impressed travelers of the sixteenth and seventeenth centuries. Its one gate of entry was always guarded by twenty Italian soldiers, and no one might enter without laying their weapons down outside."

We were impressed too, and as we maneuvered to tie stern to the stone quay in the well-protected port, Larry commented again on the hilltop fortresses and towns we'd seen throughout the less populated parts of the Med. At first it had seemed odd that most of the villages were situated two or three miles from the ports. Usually the few buildings near the waterfront were fishermen's warehouses, a café, and maybe one or two small homes. But when we considered the maurauders, pirates, and armies that had plagued this sea as late as the 1900s, these hilltop towns made sense. Late that same afternoon, when the sun had lost some of its strength, we gave up diving for our dinner near the rocky entrance to the bay, put on good walking shoes, and set out along the winding road to the castle.

Seraffyn shrank to a tiny speck as we climbed the hill. Above us the ramparts of the fortress towered threateningly. We could imagine defenders rolling stones off the parapets to make this narrow road impassable. It took us almost an hour to reach the quiet town nestled against the castle. Two youngsters joined us with their pet goats to show us through the ruins of the old castle, and for the first time I understood the word *impregnable*. No army could have scaled the sheer cliffs that dropped away from the castle on three sides. No attackers could have sneaked across the whole island to climb the hills leading to the fourth side. I think it was as I sat on the edge of the walls of Kapsali that I realized for the first time what a protected world I'd grown up in. But before I could fall too deeply under the spell of these ancient walls, Larry started using his six new Greek words, and soon the two boys were leading us through the narrow, twisting streets of the village, bound for a café.

The village of Kapsali.

Kapsali butcher, complete with worry beads.

I had to laugh as we pushed open the heavy wooden doors of the unmarked café. Polished linoleum floors, oilcloth-covered tables, and pictures of soccer teams greeted us. A big Lyons International symbol covered most of the wall behind an ancient cash register. And of course the burly café owner spoke some English, from his time with the U.S. military. We dug into bowls of coffee-flavored ice cream accompanied by a complimentary glass of retsina while he told us about the fine raisins and currants that were the mainstay of the thousand people who lived scattered about Kithira Island. "Life doesn't change much out here," he told us. "The government strung wires across the ocean so we could have electricity. So now my children have ice cream and three hours of television each day. But still they play around the castle, go to school, grow up, and decide to live here where there is peace and not too much government."

Two days later we set sail bound across the Aegean Sea toward Rhodes. One of the most often discussed subjects among the cruising fleet in Malta the previous winter had been the best way to explore the Aegean in spite of the Meltemi. This blustery north wind starts blowing off the mountains of Yugoslavia and Bulgaria in early June and persists right through September. It usually blows at twenty to twenty-five knots, twelve or fifteen hours of each day. Sometimes it reaches gale force for a week at a time. Near the steeper, higher islands the Meltemi is known to cause gusts of close to seventy knots. So, most cruising sailors try to gain as much northing as they can by sneaking through the Corinthian Canal to arrive at the islands near Athens. Then they wait for any quiet days to head farther north into the Aegean. From their northernmost goal they can then reach or run with the Meltemi to the hundreds of anchorages scattered throughout this history-laden sea. We'd decided against trying to beat into the more populated parts of Greece, and when we cleared Kithira and felt the full blast of the Meltemi for the first time, I was glad we had. We dug out our wet-weather gear, reefed our mainsail, set the staysail, and secured everything for a heavy-weather reach across short, choppy seas.

I don't remember what started Larry and me arguing. Maybe it was the sloppy way I handled the mainsheet when we were reefing down, maybe it was the spray that caught him before he pulled on his wet-weather jacket, or maybe it was just the prospect of 300 miles of rough-weather sailing after two months of dreamlike cruising in the Ionian Sea. But we started sniping at each other until we had a full-fledged argument going that ranged from the way I sailed to the way he dressed. *Seraffyn* charged along oblivious to our rude words, the wind vane steering a straight, true course, the taffrail log spinning, marking over five knots through the water. I finally got so angry I said, "I'm getting off at the next place that has a ferry to Athens. I'm tired of living with you. I'm tired of sailing. I'm leaving!"

Larry yelled, "Good riddance!" Then he climbed below and got into the forward bunk with a book.

I settled into a corner of the cockpit to mope. I didn't really want to leave. This was my home. I resented my angry words but hated Larry for forcing me to say them. For an hour I sat there planning where I'd go from Athens, what kind of life I could start with half of our cruising kitty, which now seemed like a very small sum. In a way it was frightening to realize that all the two of us owned was a twenty-four-foot boat and maybe $5,000 cash. The boat was Larry's. He'd dreamed her up. He'd built her. I hated him lying up there in that bunk oblivious to my pain and frustration. But I'd never take his boat away. For an hour my thoughts ranged wildly. Then an owl flew right past my head, plopped on the side deck, struggled to regain its footing, hopped forward, and settled on the end of the bowsprit, one foot clutched around the head stay, the other digging into the top of the bagged jib. We'd often had land birds arrive on deck. Once we'd had a pigeon join us. But this foot-and-a-half-tall owl was our strangest visitor. And he sat glaring at me, bucked back and forth by *Seraffyn*'s motion, his feathers ruffled and tangled by the force-six winds.

"Larry," I called, "there's an owl out here!"

"Sure there is," he grumbled in complete disgust.

"Okay, the hell with you," I said in a quiet voice so that I wouldn't disturb our owl. Then I climbed below to get the camera. I slid slowly down the side deck to get a good photo, and then I started to giggle. Larry's curiosity couldn't be contained. I saw the front edge of the fore hatch lift just a bit. A dollop of spray hit Larry's fingers. He snapped the hatch closed, scrambled awkwardly through the boat, and tried to climb quietly into the cockpit. I felt him beside me and heard him whisper, "There really is an owl out here!" That seemed to break the spell of evil that had surrounded us both. Larry held out his hand to help me back into the cockpit. "We sure do have big problems, don't we," he said, laughing with tears in his eyes. I clung closely to him as we watched the owl take flight and circle the boat. Then that lovely bird set off downwind toward Crete, fifty miles to leeward. For the rest of that day and long into the night we talked about the big and small problems in our life together, the wonderful and fun things we had been able to do, the plans we hoped to bring to fruition. The confines of a small boat at sea can be a wonderful joining force. You have no place to run to, no one else to turn toward for sympathy, no distractions to hide behind when there are problems that should be faced. The only solutions lie right there before you and close to your grasp, as logic, caring, love, and the need for each other force you to talk things out. Our only real problems boiled down to my concern over heavy-weather sailing, and Larry's indecision over our plan to push across 15,500 miles of ocean during the next year, just to go back to the so-called rat race and build a new boat.

The Meltemi increased during the night and the barometer began to fall. So, by mid afternoon the next day we were glad to anchor in the lee of Thíra. We lay there for two days while the wind howled at thirty-five to forty knots. We probably could have launched the dinghy and rowed ashore to explore this blown-out remains of a volcano and its fabled ridge-top town. But we had too much to talk about, too many plans to scheme on. Neither of us wanted to break the close spell our owl had created.

When the barometer started to rise two days later, we set our reefed sails and headed farther east. Just to test my newfound resolve to enjoy

The owl.

heavy-weather sailing, I suggested beating north around Anaphi Island so that we could reach toward Stampalia. And, as Larry had promised, when I set my mind to enjoying the sport of getting the best-possible performance out of our little cutter, the thirty-knot winds became a joyful challenge. Together we adjusted the sail trim, tried easing sheets, tightening them, releading the staysail. *Seraffyn* seemed to love it, picking up a tenth of a knot, riding just a bit easier, throwing a bit less spray. We unclutched the vane and took turns steering, trying to gain every extra bit of weathering as we guided *Seraffyn* over and through the wind chop, easing her off to meet the higher waves, heading her up in the calmer patches. Then Larry came up with the idea of making waterproof canvas socks to cover our ventilators so that we wouldn't have to remove them, search for the proper caps, and shut them off completely each time we started to take on a bit of spray. So, we set the wind vane again, and the two of us sat together in the cockpit, protecting our thread and needles from the spray, stitching bits of Velcro to scraps of material from our rigging kit, twisting tarred marlin into grommets. When Larry slipped the two new covers over the ventilators, drew their drawstrings tight, and I went below and could report complete success, we felt like winners. By noon we'd made good our fifteen miles to weather, and I felt the finest reward a sailor can have. We eased sheets. *Seraffyn* seemed to gather her skirts and charge easily across the short, choppy seas as we flew toward Stampalia at close to six knots on a sunny, Meltemi-swept summer day.

It was growing late when we skimmed into the lee of the island. The wind was lighter here. We set the full main and lapper to beat toward the landlocked anchorage our chart showed nestled behind two small islands and around a hook in the southern side of Stampalia. I was a bit concerned about beating through a narrow pass in the dark. But a careful study of the chart showed absolutely no dangers and two fathoms of water as long as we stayed 100 feet away from the shore. So, even though we had no lights to guide us, our short tacks became a game. I stood on the foredeck with our six-volt, battery-operated high-power torch. As soon as its beam picked up the rocks on one side of the channel I'd call to Larry, "Time to tack." He'd bring the boat about, sheet in, and we'd slide along, heeled until water lapped at *Seraffyn*'s channels. Eight or nine minutes later my light would pick up the opposite side of the pass and we'd tack again.

Even in the seemingly complete darkness I could see the outline of the end of the second small island. I took bearings on it, set a course for the center of Puerto Maltazana, then got out the lead line. There were no lights

Lin fitting the Velcro quick cover on the ventilator.

onshore. The hills surrounding the bay could barely be seen, except that the stars stopped where their rugged summits formed a barrier. Yes, I was tense about sailing into the unknown with only a chart to guide us. I'd gone over my piloting logic with Larry, showing him the bearing I'd taken while he steered a careful compass course. As soon as my lead line found bottom at four fathoms I said, "Let's drop the hook here," even though the most perfect anchorage would have been closer to shore in two fathoms.

The water was absolutely calm. Only a light breeze filtered through the hills now. Our anchor grabbed securely, and as we put the boat to bed, we talked about this special thrill of sailing without an engine: the challenge of making calculated decisions, planning each tack, then handling the boat with only the sound of water and wind to fill your ears. Evenings like this gave us a great sense of satisfaction.

Stampalia turned out to be a place that rarely had any cruising visitors. We walked five miles along a twisting dirt road the next day and found a thriving little village in spite of the fact that we had seen only two farmhouses along the way. We'd become used to the very limited supplies available in most of the island villages. Local yogurt, feta cheese, a few vegetables such as onions, tomatoes, and peppers, plus ice cream, frozen pork, and fishermen's supplies usually were the only things on the shelves of the small shops. But here half a dozen shops had shelves laden with Dresden china, fine ceramics from France, elaborate Venetian glassware. It all seemed out of place on an island where the total population was less than 500 people. But when we sat down in the waterfront café next to half a dozen older Greek men who were deeply involved in a backgammon game, the café owner came over and explained it all. Stampalia is a free port and a center for a vigorous smuggling trade. People from Athens take an overnight ferry to come here and pick up household goods they order through brokers on the mainland. They save close to 50 percent of the cost for the same heavily taxed goods in the capital.

Early the next morning we noticed a small fishing boat pull up at the tiny wood pier in our quiet bay. We swam ashore to see the catch. It consisted mostly of foot-and-a-half-long, brown, fanlike shells. We'd seen these shells sticking up out of the sand around our anchor. Now we watched as the fisherman was joined by his wife to pry each shell open, then clean the mussel inside until they had a scalloplike piece and large brown strips like the skirts of a clam. The black-clad, chunky wife gave a pantomime of quick frying these bits. Then she gathered her husband's catch and walked toward the small farmhouse that lay a few hundred yards up a winding path. Before she was out of sight she called to us and indicated we could get fresh water to drink at her house.

Larry soon gathered a dozen of the fanlike shells from the sand below *Seraffyn*. His cleaning efforts weren't as neat as the fisherman's. But lightly fried in olive oil, then seasoned with garlic and lemon juice, the results were a fine taste treat.

When we decided to set sail two days later, Larry suggested getting some fresh water from the farmhouse. I'd cleaned *Seraffyn*'s lockers and had half a dozen empty two-pound coffee cans with plastic lids that really didn't seem worth saving, plus an almost new pair of leather sandals that persisted in giving my wide feet blisters. I took them along just in case. They surely made a hit at the carefully laid out little farm with its white-washed two-room stone house. The farm wife set us to work pumping the well to fill our five-gallon jugs. Then she ran into the house with our gifts. A few minutes later she came out with a small cardboard box for us. In it lay six perfect brown eggs, six rosy plums, and six sweet-smelling figs.

As we reached out of the bay and through the narrow channel we'd negotiated in the dark five nights before, I was mentally prepared for the Meltemi winds I knew waited just outside the lee of the island. They didn't worry me at all, because now the Meltemi would be on our beam to give us a sleigh ride past a dozen islands to the fabled capital of the Dodecanese, the pleasure isle of Rhodos.

~~~~~

CHAPTER 4

Rhodos

S ometimes small-boat sailors fall under a spell: solitary anchorages, days alone together at sea, occasional stops at tiny, friendly villages. Sailing into a real harbor with crowds, noise, and water that is too dirty for swimming turns into a frightening prospect far out of proportion to reality. I have heard of voyagers who hove to rather than complete their thirty- or forty-day passage and break this spell. Bernard Moitessier forsook a $15,000 cash prize and stayed at sea for another four months until he reached the quiet of Tahiti rather than risk the turmoil of a welcome in England. We too came under the same spell as we neared Rhodos, on the far edge of the Aegean Sea.

It was midday as we approached the northern end of the island. Resort hotels lined the west side of the point. Speedboats and sailing dinghies skittered along inshore of us. The Meltemi wind turned as it swept between the coasts of Turkey and Rhodos, so we ran wing and wing past the outskirts of the largest city we'd seen for over four months. As we reached toward Mandraki harbor, we could hear cars and buses honking. A factory whistle shrieked its end-of-lunch threat. And that gave Larry cold feet. "Let's keep on for Lindos. It's only twenty miles south of here. Ian told me it's a beautiful, quiet anchorage. Maybe four or five boats, a nice café onshore, daily bus connections to the city so we could get our mail and buy stores."

As the big ships' harbor opened in front of us, I started to agree with him. Two cruise liners dwarfed the fish boats and coastal freighters lining the stone seawalls. Another gleaming white liner lay at anchor and disgorged hundreds of tourists into bobbing shore boats. Then I remembered the empty spaces in my stores lockers, two months' worth of mail at the port captain's office, and a twenty-pound bag of dirty laundry. Our guide-book definitely mentioned a coin-operated launderette.

But Larry wasn't easy to convince. "We can bus in tomorrow, bring the laundry, get the mail. What we save on harbor charges we'll spend for a taxi to bring stores back to Lindos. Just think of the lovely quiet."

"You promised me a real night on the town," I said in my most persuasive tones. "Let's just tie in Mandraki for a night, then go to Lindos. Come on, let's just sail in and out for a look. If it's too crowded we'll have gone only a mile out of our way."

We got the harbor chart and checked the exact bearings of a sewage drainpipe other cruising sailors had told us about. It juts out past the stag-crowned entrance to Mandraki yacht harbor. This concrete drain had taken the life of a fine long-term Mediterranean cruising sailor a few years ago. Bobby Somerset was bringing a group of charterers from Turkey to Rhodos in the teeth of a southeast winter gale. The small red warning light that stood on the rocky point 200 feet behind this drain had been washed out by breaking seas. Driving rain, spray, and the confusion of shore lights caused Bobby to mistake the red flasher on Mandraki's breakwater for the missing warning light. His fifty-foot *Trenchemer* foundered on the pipe, and three out of the six people on board were drowned. We could imagine the horrid breaking seas that must have built around the just submerged pipe. Even now, with only fifteen knots of wind from the northwest, surf sucked and ebbed, one minute exposing the huge concrete-and-iron pipe, the next minute covering it in swirling, muddy water three feet deep.

We cleared the obstructions and reached between the handsome stone pillars of the 800-foot-long, 500-foot-wide yacht harbor and almost turned around and left. Close to two hundred yachts lined the seawalls, cheek by jowl, sterns close to the yellow rocks, bow anchors stretching toward the middle of the basin. In some places the boats lay two deep, tied bow to stern. Hundreds of people walked along the seawall. Cars and vendors lined the street on the inshore side. But we reached further into the harbor, just to look at some of the cruising boats flying French, American, Italian, and Australian flags.

"Hey, matey, slide right in heeya!" called a slim, balding man on an Australian sloop. The dark-haired man on the Australian ketch next to him repeated his words, climbed quickly into his dinghy, and rowed out. "I'll take your stern line. Get your sails down. Where you coming from?"

This warm welcome began to break our spell. We did drop our sails and set our anchor. Then we let our new friend haul our stern line to the huge bronze bollard on the seawall. Within three hours any thoughts of leaving for a quiet anchorage disappeared.

Both of our Australian neighbors had just arrived from a northbound transit of the Suez Canal. They were eager to trade charts and information. But first we were eager to see our mail package and a bit less eager to pay our harbor dues. Both were a pleasant surprise. The port captain was a charmer who explained that our first four days in his port were free; then fees gradually grew steeper to discourage overly long visits in the crowded port. The second week was seven dollars; the third, fourteen; the fourth, twenty-eight.

A young American couple was going through the mailbox set on the counter at the port captain's office. "Watched you sail in, nice boat," Jonathan Peter said. "Want to go to the hum mum?"

"The what?" I asked.

"Public bath house. Several of us are meeting there in twenty minutes," his girl friend, Lillian Jarmon, answered.

So we walked the half mile back to *Seraffyn*, got our towels and fresh clothes, then followed our new friends past the charter boat they ran, past the octagonal public market that lay only four hundred yards from our boat, then across the tree-lined moat and through the eighteen-foot-thick ramparts of the Venetian walled city. We met up with six more sailing crews seated at a sidewalk café under one of the largest banyan trees I've ever seen. Its branches spread over fifty feet from the huge, columnlike trunk. Almost two hundred chairs with maybe fifty tables crowded under the thick shade it provided.

All of us then headed through the narrow stone streets while we exchanged names and ports, "did you meet"s, and "where you going"s. Next to the far wall of the city we stopped at the small double entrance to an imposing marble-and-granite structure. Men were directed through one door, women through the other, by a gnarled old Greek couple who spoke no English but pointed, shook their heads at our noisy crowd, then took our fifteen cents each.

I was absolutely stunned by the interior of the 500-year-old Turkish bath house. Marble floors had been worn into hollows by thousands of feet. High overhead, skylights in an onion-shaped dome sent sunlight gleaming off pink-and-gray marble carvings. We left our clothes in small, raised cubicles in the anteroom, then came into the communal central hall to sit on marble blocks worn into rounded shapes by centuries of bathing women. Spotless marble founts held bubbling clear water, each at a different temperature. Seven dark-haired Greek women opened their circle when we four English-speaking girls walked in. For an hour we took turns pouring first hot, then cold water over ourselves and each other with small metal bowls. We washed each other's hair, scrubbed inaccessible spots on each other's backs. Eleven bare bodies ranging from the palest white of the slim, athletic young sailing cook from England to the golden glow of a rounded, fifty-year-old Greek matron gleamed wet in the filtered sunlight. Stone ducts pierced the walls around us and led to central fireplaces, where wood was burned to heat these massive rooms during the winter months. The walls echoed with our laughter and gossip as they'd echoed with the laughter and tears of all the women in this ancient city for over four centuries. Time stopped at the entrance to the hum mum. Rank and distinction faded as each lady shed her clothes in the anteroom. The solace of cool marble and cleansing water drained away any cares caused by the summer's heat.

Later, when Larry and I were wandering through the narrow streets of the old town, I commented, "This afternoon at the bath house, it was almost a sensual experience. I can understand women falling in love with each other. Did you feel anything, surrounded by all those bare male bodies?"

"Hell, no," Larry laughed; "we just got into a rousing water fight."

The next morning it was Larry's turn to get serious. We carried our Meditereanean charts over to *Shikama*, the forty-five-foot Aussie sloop. Max Vanderbent got out his Red Sea charts. A few minutes later we were joined by Ross Irvine, who brought another armful of charts from his thirty-foot ketch, *Girl Morgan*. Together they dispelled our last fears of leaving the Med by way of the Suez Canal. "Sure, it's a hard bit of sailing," Max said. "I've been racing around Fremantle for twenty years and never seen anything like it. But you're going the easiest way. You should have a following breeze in the narrowest areas, not like us. We had forty-knot headwinds most of the last five hundred miles and up the Gulf of Suez. Couldn't use the engine much because of all the sand in the water. It was so thick the engine overheated after an hour. So it was tacking for almost ten days. Ya, I'd go south down the Red Sea, but north? Never again."

Ross was even less reluctant about the Red Sea. "I loved it. I'm going back for sure. What fabulous skin diving, wonderful reefs. We watched camel caravans come into Suakin loaded with pottery and silver from Khartoum and the blue Nile. Never spent a night at sea, anchored behind coral reefs or tucked up into wadis [the indentations made by dried river washes]." Ross, his wife, Margaret, and their two sons had taken over two months to make their way up the Red Sea. Theirs was the most exuberant report we heard. Following a dictum we've come to depend on, we decided to base our plans on information from people who'd actually sailed in the area we were curious about, not on hearsay or even guidebooks, which could be as much as ten years out of date.

While Larry made notes along the margins of our new charts of each anchorage to be avoided or visited, I filled several pages in my notebook with hints from Margaret Irvine and Shirley Vanderbent. "Fill your boat to the brim right here," they both agreed. "Nothing's available in Port Said. Prices for canned food in Israel and Turkey are five times what they are in Rhodos. Take small-denomination American dollars to bribe the officials and pilots at the canal. That way it looks like they are getting a lot when you hand them a fistful of dollar bills instead of a single twenty. I think they care more for what their friends think they are getting then what the actual amount is," Margaret told me.

Larry is showing fourteen-year-old Simon, crew of *Girl Morgan*, how to do a wire-to-rope splice.

"Don't carry anything with Israeli labels. If you've visited Israel you can't legally go through the canal. But don't miss Israel. It's fantastic. The officials in Israel won't stamp your passports if you tell them you're going on to Egypt," Shirley added.

What had started as a morning of chart trading ended up as a dinner at the serve-yourself stands in the center of the public market. This seemed to be the favorite cruising sailors' meeting place, probably because a dinner of souvlaki (lamb ground with spices and roasted over an open fire) pita bread, fruit, and wine cost only two dollars. When some of the other sailors heard of our intentions, they started telling us about the Red Sea pirate stories they'd heard, always second- or third-hand, of course. This was ended abruptly when a husky, determined sixty-five-year-old man introduced himself. "These stories are all exaggerations. I know. They are mostly about me!"

Gus had purchased a Taiwan-built forty-one-foot ketch and was sailing toward the Med on his way to a retirement home he'd built in Sweden. Unfortunately, delays at the shipyard, then further delays caused by gear failures ate up the vacation time of the friends who planned to sail with him. So, Gus ended up single-handing his ketch west from Sri Lanka during the height of the southwest monsoon.

Gales and rough seas took their toll on the new, untried boat and its skipper. So, in spite of a cryptic warning in the *British Admiralty Pilot* which states, "Being exposed to both monsoons and having no harbors in which vessels can anchor at all times with safety, coupled with the unfavorable character of the natives hitherto born, Socotra is but little visited," Gus decided to heave to in the lee of Socotra Island, get some rest, then repair his broken backstay and try to start his reluctant motor before sailing into the Gulf of Aden. He slept through the night and late into the next day as his boat lay quietly. Then he started to carry out his rigging repairs. He saw a native boat with several turbaned fishermen approaching. He yelled at them to stay away, but they brought their rough thirty-foot dhow alongside in the choppy water and threw grappling hooks over Gus's rail to secure their boat. His only defense was to grab the broadcast microphone of his ham radio and pretend he was sending messages to rescuers who were just over the horizon. Gus hoped the Arab invaders wouldn't notice his aerial, which was part of his wayward backstay, lying useless on the afterdeck.

For some reason the Arabs decided to take Gus in tow, then proceeded to drag his boat slowly along toward the west end of Socotra. But just before dark they seemed to tire of this idea, or maybe they were worried about spending the night at sea. So they came back alongside, further damaging Gus's rails, climbed on board, and took most of his food, plus two pots and six coffee mugs. Then they left, waving as they went.

Gus didn't take any more chances. He set sail immediately to clear Socotra. He managed to make Aden six days later, hungry, tired, and quite shook up. "The most frightening thing was not understanding a word they said. The two that stayed on my boat when it was being towed kept jabbering at me and pointing. No, they never threatened me, but they didn't have to. They never pointed any guns at me. I never saw any guns. I just shouldn't have hove to three miles off Socotra."

Gus turned out to be correct. If we listened carefully to the pirate stories cruising sailors were passing around from Malta all the way east to Singapore—stories magnified by the sheer lack of information, since the canal had been open for only eight months—each story mentioned a forty-one-foot ketch, a sixty-five-year-old Swedish-American, pirates from Socotra, or all three.

Lindos harbor, twelve miles south of Rhodos. Lovely, peaceful, but it can become extremely dangerous during an easterly wind.

So, within two days of our arriving in Rhodos, our minds were firmly made up. We were bound for Canada and California by way of the Red Sea. We really had little choice now, since we'd traded away our complete set of charts of the Med west of Rhodos in exchange for anointed charts east to Singapore. Now we had one last decision to make. The best time for a passage down the Red Sea was between August 15 and September 15. That left us about a month for cruising. Tales of fabulous sailing among tree-clad islands with unexploited Venetian, Greek, and Roman ruins made Turkey inviting. Stories of warm, fast friendships made in Israel along with the lure of the old city of Jerusalem countered the charms of Turkey. Which should we choose for our last impression of the Med? We talked long into the night, weighing the advantages of visiting each country. Then Larry came up with the best reason to choose Israel. "No other country has had as much influence on history during the past decade. Even if we spend only two or three weeks there, we'll at least have some idea of what's behind the news reports we read."

With our plans fully set for the first time in over a year, we settled in to savor some of the joys of Greek civilization while we stocked up our stores lockers for the hard sailing we knew lay beyond Israel.

I've shaken my head hundreds of times as people listed the sacrifices they imagined we made to take up our cruising way of life. Space, stability, luxuries—not one of these was a real loss when we compared it to the fulfilling life we'd led for over eight years. In fact, up until an almost fated meeting in Rhodos, I was hard pressed to think of even one sacrifice worth a moment's thought. Within an hour of meeting Lillian in the port captain's office, I realized how much cruising could cut you off from deep outside friendships.

Lillian and I could have been sisters. We were the same age within days, grew up within five miles of each other, went to high schools only one district apart. Our mothers had used the same threats to try and keep us in line. We'd missed meeting back in our teenage years only because she chose to work on her school newspaper while I chose the debate team. Now we spent every spare moment together, giggling one minute, deep in serious discussions of consumer rights or people's liberation the next. Lillian had worked as an investigative reporter for Ralph Nader before she joined Jonathan to work for a summer as cook and crew on an English-owned charter boat.

Larry seemed to love our craziness. "You come back from an hour with Lillian bouncing like a new tennis ball," he teased. The night before we set sail for Israel we invited Lillian and Jon over for dinner. It was a soft, still evening. Max and Shirley sat on the rail of their boat talking with the four of us after dinner was cleared away. Two French sailors, an Italian cruising couple, and an Englishman we'd met in Corfu came walking along the seawall. "Hey, Lin, want to play the piano tonight?" Mark called. "Haven't got a piano," I yelled back. "Franco does, on his boat, come on. Bring everyone. We'll all squeeze in," Mark replied.

The six of us joined all five of them and boarded the forty-three-foot French ketch at the far end of the seawall. We crowded below and watched in amazement as a push of a button turned a hanging locker on one side of the main saloon into a spinet-type piano. "I wanted to learn to play for twenty years," our French host explained. "So I figured if I went sailing I'd finally have time. I searched for a boat that would hold this old traveling piano."

Retsina wine, oil lamps, and the tranquility of Rhodos harbor mellowed any mistakes I made with the Mozart sonatinas and Beethoven sonatas I tried to play from memory. Then our host took out a lovely, well-used guitar and sang the French love songs he'd played as a busker to pay his way through college. But Max made the evening. He remembered the chords and words to dozens of old sing-along favorites. He borrowed Franco's guitar, strummed loudly and roughly, and soon the boat rang with renditions of "Waltzing Matilda," "Yellow Submarine," and "When You and I Were Young, Maggie." One by one, tired voices dropped out as the clock struck first 0200, then 0230. Then Max strummed the chords

Jon Peter and Lillian Jarman.

for "Summertime." Lillian swung into a pseudo-bass rendition, I chimed in with soprano, and our host provided the rhythm section, drumming on the edge and side of the huge mahogany table all eleven of us sat around. Each time we'd come to the last verse, someone would call, "Again!" Lillian improvised a trombone passage, I harmonized as best I could, Max changed the tempo, and we all followed until our voices failed. Then no one said good-bye. We just climbed into the quiet night. Lillian and I hugged on the seawall behind *Seraffyn.* She had tears in her eyes too as she said, "It's been special."

When we set sail early the next day I was sorry to be leaving Greece with so many hundreds of harbors left unexplored. I was sorry to leave the fun evenings in Rhodos cafés. But I was saddest to find I was leaving a small bit of me behind with the special friendship that had bloomed so quickly. Larry understood well. As we ran wing and wing on a thirty-knot breeze toward Tel Aviv, he took me in his arms. "I guess there are some things women share that no men can understand," he said. "But please don't blame cruising for keeping you away from outside friends. How many times in your whole life have you hit it off with someone like Lillian? That was probably a one-in-a-million chance."

I thought about his words all during the morning as the Greek islands faded in our wake. Yes, an instant friendship like that was a one-in-a-million chance. My very good fortune was that I'd had two chances to savor the experience. The second one may have lasted only a week, but the first seemed able to last a lifetime, because the friend I'd found then was Larry.

~~~~~

CHAPTER 5

Israel

Our years in the Med had been filled with the persistent rumor that said, "You can't sail here without an engine; there's either too much wind or not enough." There had been times when we cursed the fickle winds that filtered through a dozen different mountain chains, deflected around every island, and lifted as they neared the African deserts. But we reached each goal we aimed for and learned more about our boat and our sails as we worked to catch each zephyr or rushed to pull in another reef. Now as we ran wing and wing over a smoothly rolling sea, the rambunctious thirty-knot wind seemed to be rewarding us for our persistence or maybe urging us to be on our way out of Homer's sea. Larry washed the shore dirt off our decks; I set to work on our pile of correspondence. Life seemed perfect on our fully laden floating pantry as the miles ticked off at a steady five-knot pace.

But we weren't going to be let off quite that easily. For no apparent reason, with absolutely no warning, we sailed right out of the wind halfway between Rhodos and Tel Aviv, even though we were over seventy-five miles from the nearest land. It was like hitting a brick wall. One minute there was wind, the next there was none, and we were being tossed around on a popcorn-machine sea so rough we couldn't stand on deck. The wind was still blowing only 100 yards astern of us, and all around the boat whitecaps decorated five-foot waves. I was furious as I fought to steady myself and think. Then, to make everything infinitely worse, I got seasick. I mean head-over-the-rail, wish-I-were-dead seasick.

Larry, with his cast-iron stomach, chuckled at my prone body as he took all of our madly slatting sails down. But when we realized that this was not a five- or ten-minute affair, he set to work rigging a flopper stopper.

He got out our canvas deck bucket and secured the lead line inside it, then rigged a line from the bucket to the spinnaker-pole end. He set the pole so that it was dead square to the boat with fore and aft guys holding it steady, then lowered the bucket until it was a few feet underwater when the boat was on an even keel. I was surprised to feel the effect of that weighted, water-filled bucket trying to resist the motion as it lifted and dipped twelve feet from our side. *Seraffyn* steadied so that instead of feeling like a bucking bronco, she was more like a horse galloping in place with one lame leg. My seasickness faded to discomfort, then disappeared exactly four hours later, when the same following wind filled in at almost the exact same strength. As soon as we set our main and lapper wing and wing, we were skimming along as if the popcorn-sea episode had been a figment of our imagination.

We had no official chart of Tel Aviv harbor. A friend in Malta had drawn a sketch that showed a frightening twenty-five-foot-wide entrance to a large, safe, manmade basin right at the foot of Israel's newest, tallest, and largest hotel complex. The sketch showed breaking waves only five feet from the shoal-encumbered entrance, rock groins sticking out across the approaches. All the sketch lacked was a sea serpent attacking a sailing ship. So, when we positively identified the stone breakwater after four days and 415 miles of sailing from Rhodos, Larry suggested heaving to about a third of a mile offshore. "We'll launch the dinghy and I'll row in and check out the entrance while you stay here and make sure *Seraffyn* keeps a safe offing," he said, and I remembered the English jingle "There are old sailors and bold sailors but very few old bold sailors."

We set to work dropping our small genoa, but before we could unlash the dinghy, a dark-eyed Israeli sailor came alongside in a twelve-foot dinghy. "Aren't you going to come into our port?" he called. "I don't have a good chart," Larry called back. "Just follow me," the enthusiastic, lean young sailor called. When Larry explained our preference for a personal look at the situation before we tried to tack into an unknown harbor, Yoni said, "Jump on board, I'll show you the channel. There's a neat wind shift if you hug the shallow side." So Larry sailed off in the dinghy and I started some lunch while I kept an eye on our position. *Seraffyn* lay comfortably under her full main, tiller tied to leeward as a fifteen-knot breeze held her steady. I'd just gotten out a book and our cockpit cushions when a Boston Whaler–type launch came roaring out from the breakwater. "Throw me a line, I'll tow you in," yelled the husky blond as he shut down his powerful outboard engine right next to *Seraffyn*. I explained that Larry was checking out the channel so that we could sail in. But the marina manager came right alongside without attempting to fend off. "Give me a tow line," he demanded. I resented his aggressiveness but held my temper and told him to talk to Larry, who was headed back, hiking out as our dinghy-sailing friend worked his skimming dish to windward.

The marina manager and Larry seemed to clash even worse. I could see hands flinging and pointing. Then the Boston Whaler zoomed off toward shore and disappeared behind the breakwater.

"Yoni says the wind always shifts to the southwest after lunch. So we'll wait till then and we can lay in on one tack. We couldn't do it now; it's dead to windward and that sketch Tom made us doesn't show the half of it. I checked the depths with Yoni's spinnaker pole, and there's only twenty-five feet of clear water right in back of seven-foot breakers. The channel has a long, shoal smack in the center only three feet of water on it. We tacked in and out several times and if we get just a ten-degree wind shift *Seraffyn* will make it okay. But I'm not letting any marina manager push me into doing something chancy. If his engine sputters for even a minute, we'll be in the breakers. I've got a lot more to lose then he has. He's not the one that spent three and a half years building this boat."

Yoni joined us for lunch in the warm, sunlit cockpit as we rose and fell on the wind-driven swell. He listened eagerly while we told of being talked into taking a tow in the harbor at Horta in the Azores. That harbormaster was trying to be helpful and friendly too. But he hadn't accounted for the windage in our rigging, and we'd had to cast off the towline and grab a nearby mooring to avoid being slammed into the harbor wall. In the Panama Canal, Larry had had to demand center lockage rather than tie up alongside a barge so that our pilot and line handlers could relax. Even I thought he was being too cautious and self-sufficient until I read a recent story about a thirty-foot cruising sloop being crushed like an egg and sunk in one of the locks at Panama when she was tied against a tugboat that got out of control leaving the locks.

Just when I was feeling a bit embarrassed about hurting the Tel Aviv marina manager's feelings, Yoni confirmed the wisdom of our cautious approach. "Three weeks ago a big Greek power yacht came here," he said. "The owner let the manager of the marina take charge because the entrance was frightening. Something went wrong. The yacht was in the breakers and wrecked in minutes. The salvaged engines and gear are in the shop in back of the club."

Yoni had to leave soon after lunch. "I go on duty patrolling the Sinai border in three hours. I'll come and see you if you are still here in a week, take you home to meet my wife, and have a real kosher dinner."

As Yoni had observed from a year of racing dinghies, the wind did shift slowly clockwise away from the sun, and two pleasant sunbathing hours later, *Seraffyn*'s bowsprit was pointing ten degrees more to the west. Larry sketched out our battle plan. "We'll close reach in toward that rock groin and as soon as we can lay in the channel, we'll tack. I'll take the staysail stay away to make things easier, because that's the important moment. If we don't tack smartly we'll be in the breakers. Then we'll lay close-hauled up the channel. We can bail out for a few minutes then if things don't look good, but once we get behind the breakwater there's a long, narrow shoal that cuts the entrance in half. If we go aground there it's no big problem, because we're inside the harbor. But I think we'll have room to tack, and when we're past the shoal there's lots of sailing room."

His whole description worried me, but when we headed right toward the rising, arching backs of breaking waves and I could see the sandy bottom only five feet below our keel and almost feel the roar of crashing water, I was scared. Only Larry's calm, deliberate sailing kept me from insisting we bail out. Our tack went smoothly, and *Seraffyn* eased smartly through the eye of the wind, then gathered speed on the glossy backs of swells that crumbled into seven-foot breakers only fifteen feet from where I sat almost paralyzed. Thank God, that tension lasted only minutes. The stone breakwater enfolded us, and in the calm of the harbor I felt so brave I stood on the foredeck and urged Larry to within inches of the sandy shoal before I called for a tack.

Half a dozen Israeli sailors helped us secure our mooring lines as we backed *Seraffyn* into a space between two local cruising boats. Each person who came down the dock to help us secure our lines apologized for their dangerous harbor entrance. "It needs dredging, but the government is using this truce period to rebuild the military. So, yacht harbors get low priority."

This volatile, war-zone air swirled around every moment of our month-long stay in Israel. The friendly customs and immigration officer insisted we come home and have dinner with him so that we could meet his heroic son. "He just came back from the raid at Entebbe airport and his head is swelled to double." I had my purse searched by an armed military guard when I went into any department store or post office in Tel Aviv. I shopped at the Carmel open market for meat, left my purchases for twenty minutes to run to a stationery store, and returned to find that a bomb blast had raked through the meat stall and killed seventeen people. When we were taken for a tour of the West Bank by an Israeli friend, Larry asked why each military jeep had a stout metal bar clamped to its front bumper and extending into the air like a rhinoceros horn. "That's to cut the piano-wire traps terrorists string across the roads at night. Those wires can decapitate a patrol."

Even the enthusiastic sailing activities around the busy yacht harbor were motivated by Israel's armed state. Israelis were buying any yachts they could from visiting sailors. In fact, four of the eight foreign yachts there had come because rumor had it that locals would pay top dollar to own an escape boat, one that could take them, their family, and at least some of their possessions safely to sea in case there was a complete Arab takeover of their small nation. The four sailors had found ready buyers but were having to wait as they slowly converted Israeli pounds to other currency in the flourishing black market. We were offered a 40 percent premium on any dollars we were willing to exchange, and after learning that the government ignored this practice if sums were below $500, we joined the black market.

Each of the other foreign yachtsmen we met had interesting stories to tell. A black Bermuda 40 owned by an American couple was kept moving by a bonanza charter business. Their calendar was constantly filled because of a $200-per-person air-travel tax imposed by the Israeli government to help finance the army. Charter customers were eager for a change from the tension that filled their normal lives. Besides, a shopping spree in Crete could more than pay for a charterer's holiday, since Israeli prices were then triple those of Greece and Turkey.

A small wooden Australian cutter lay, neglected-looking, bound by chains to the innermost dock in the marina. Its owner was in jail until the last day of our stay. He'd been there for six weeks after a search of his boat turned up several ounces of cocaine and a sizable amount of hashish. The Australian embassy finally arranged his release after he agreed to pay a fine of $5,000, every penny he had, then leave Israel within twelve hours. Several local sailors quickly collected some fresh food for this hapless sailor who'd made the mistake of trying to earn cruising funds by selling drugs to local people.

One of the most unusual cruising arrangements we've run into was working well for a young Finnish couple, Tapio and Eva, who cruised with their lovely year-and-a-half-old son, Mikko. Tapio and his father owned a small business near Helsinki. Together they'd built themselves a handsome, very modern thirty-eight-foot wooden racing-cruising sloop. Each family then took six months of the year to cruise, six months to run their business.

The final foreign yacht in the crowded harbor was owned by one of the more enterprising couples we've met. Jan Ebbinge had been a member of the Peace Corps in Indonesia for a few years. He'd met Carolyn Bailey, and together they'd built a handsome forty-foot trimaran, then started to collect the finest batiks and small antiques they could find among the Far East islands. They continued investing in wood prints, rice-paper paintings, and small crafts as they cruised past Thailand to Sri Lanka and India. When they reached Israel they checked with the customs office and found there were no import duties on art objects. A local couple offered their home for a show. Carolyn and Jan sold almost half of their $3,000 investment for close to $8,000 in one week, since Israelis were always looking for investments to hedge against the rampant inflation that was running at close to 100 percent a year during our visit.

We analyzed their success at trading to earn cruising funds. The keys were their knowledge of the objects they invested in and their patience. It

Carolyn Bailey on deck with some of the fine batiks she had for sale.

had taken a year to buy their goods and another six months before they found the right market.

We'd decided to take advantage of the calm, protected marina and easily available fresh-water supply to prepare *Seraffyn* for the rigors of the long, hot voyages that lay ahead. We set to work putting two coats of varnish on all of our brightwork, including the mast. We emptied each section of the boat and hosed it out to remove any salt deposits, and made a final check on stores and supplies since we knew from our discussions with Carolyn that Israel was our last chance to get high-quality canned goods. Our workload was lightened by the extremely friendly and open Israelis, who all seemed to want to take us home for dinner. Abram Aronson, the customs official, came by to take us to a real Orthodox Sabbath dinner. Then, later, he asked us to come meet his son and some of his soldier friends, who shrugged off the success of the Entebbe raid. We'd been in Israel over three weeks when we sat down for wine and some serious discussions with these young men, and they added to my impression and that of several visiting yachtsmen that arrogance and machismo are traits shared by most of today's young Israeli men. A young American girl who worked on a local kibbutz came by to join us that evening. The conversation turned heated when she brought up Erica Jong's book *Fear of Flying*, a novel about the sexual fantasies of a liberated American Jewess. "Our women don't think like that," the young men insisted. "Our women want to be wives and homemakers. They wouldn't cat around. That's for men, not women." These same men expected their wives to be able to handle a submachine gun and share the two years of compulsory active military service with never a thought of sexual or social freedom. "When that's finished I want the girl I marry to keep a kosher home and raise my children full-time,", Abram, Jr., insisted.

We had to notify the Israeli navy twenty-four hours before we set sail. They asked for a complete description of our boat and warned us not to tell the Suez officials of our visit to Tel Aviv. Sailing through the marina's shoal-encumbered entrance was much easier on a following wind, especially since we'd sailed in and out at least a dozen times on other people's dinghies during our stay. But resolving the contradictions we'd seen took months of careful thought. The contrasts of a modern Jerusalem growing around the ancient alleys of two completely separate cultures; the resentment of extremely Orthodox Jews in black ankle coats against the tanned modern sabras (native-born Israeli women) who strode proudly through the holy city in army-issue shorts; the poverty of small Arab villagers on the West Bank, unwilling and unable to accept the help of kibbutz builders who created fertile farms only a mile away in the desert; the threats against Arabs who joined the Israelis and prospered from Palestinians who sat in crowded refugee camps even though they were offered jobs and homes in the new villages—these and a thousand other glimpses led us to wonder about the future of this tiny country. We knew we would have found it difficult to live with the constant tension that Israelis accept as part of everyday life. But we felt we'd made the right choice in coming here at the cost of a pleasant cruise along the Turkish coast.

Light winds from the southwest slowed our progress as we took a long tack to the west. Late the second night after our departure, we stood in toward the Sinai Peninsula hoping to catch an offshore breeze. I heard the roar of huge diesel engines approaching and tried to locate the cause of the noise. After almost ten minutes I woke Larry. He climbed groggily on deck and listened to the powerful throb that seemed to stay at a constant distance. Low clouds hid the stars; the sea was dark and still as we beat along in a seven-knot breeze about fifteen miles offshore. Both of us began to feel nervous as the sound plagued us for almost an hour, yet no ships' lights came into view. Finally we tacked to try and get away from it.

Huge, blinding searchlights filled the air. I had a horrible feeling of being exposed and extremely vulnerable as a loud voice commanded, "Stop where you are!" An Israeli gunship came within fifty feet of *Seraffyn*. We dropped our jib and hove to. "Who are you?" the same commanding voice demanded. Larry called our boat's name and port of registry, and said we'd departed from Tel Aviv the day before. "We'll check on that, do not proceed," echoed across the undulating waves. For two hours that menacing warship kept a searchlight played on *Seraffyn*'s main sail. "Your identity is confirmed," the voice called through the night. "Proceed, but stay fifteen miles offshore." The glaring searchlight finally shut its unblinking eye. The huge diesel roared and the ship swung past us to head north.

On the morning BBC news report we learned that Arab commandos had landed a Zodiac rubber boat on the beach next to the Tel Aviv marina and placed a bomb in the lobby of the huge hotel where we'd often gone for ice cream. The explosion killed fifteen tourists and injured almost a hundred others.

CHAPTER 6

A Waiting Game

Unless other cruising sailors offered advice on good harbors and interesting food or special people, we tried not to ask too many questions about the countries we planned to visit next. That way we hoped to avoid having preconceived negative ideas about the places we sailed to. So, when we arrived in each of a dozen new lands, we'd been able to appear innocent and curious, an attitude that served us well. But it was different with the Suez Canal. We'd wanted to know everything we could before we got there.

We'd met professional divers on leave in Malta from their hair-raising jobs of combing the bottom of the canal for live ammunition and mines. They told us to take careful heed of any signs that said, "Beware of land mines." The refuse from the 1973 Yom Kippur War with Israel was only partially cleaned up; only the main channels of the canal system had been swept by mine detectors, even eight months after the canal was fully reopened. We met six cruising sailors who'd come through the canal during the previous eight months, and everyone mentioned the hassles and bureaucratic mess of dealing with the uneducated people who'd suddenly been promoted to officialdom with the reopening of the canal. *Baksheesh* was a word we came to dread, since the idea of having to bribe an official to give us permits after we'd paid the normal fees was something we couldn't quite accept. We'd heard stories about the fourth-rate pilots normally assigned to yachts, Arabs who had absolutely no idea about ships, motors, or the sea. We believed these stories of incompetent boat handling after we saw the scarred bottom of a thirty-foot sloop that had been directed into the wrong channel by one of these pilots and grounded for three days while a tug and dredge worked to free it. Add all of this to the stories of hard-to-find, hard-to-purchase supplies in the bombed-out remains of the once thriving free ports of Said and Suez, and to tell you the truth, as we reached through a maze of shipping in the approaches to Port Said, we were apprehensive. Maybe "nervous" is a better word.

The dirty gray-and-yellow hastily constructed buildings and scraggly remains of bombed-out hotels and warehouses lining the canal approaches did not reassure us. There was absolutely nothing to relieve the dreariness of the whole scene. A few palm trees struggled to survive in front of the only handsome structure on the canal, the main office for the pilots and canal controllers. A scarred car ferry ran across the canal every ten minutes just beyond the tin-roofed one-room building marked Yacht Club. Almost half of the ferry was filled with roughly built donkey carts carrying loads of ice, charcoal, and bricks. The other half of its load seemed to consist exclusively of camouflage-painted army jeeps. To add to this depressing collage, a sixty-foot wooden yacht stood in the weeds behind the dock at the yacht club, its once magnificent overhangs drooping from lack of support, black paint blistering and peeling off in sheets, tufts of cotton

The port offices at Said.

falling like hoarfrost from its gaping seams. The only other yacht at the club was an eighty-foot steel power yacht, obviously built in a Scottish yard maybe thirty years before but now suffering from rust sores and the dented scars of abuse and neglect. When we dropped our anchor into the gray water next to it, a grease-covered Englishman came on deck and called, "Put rat guards on your stern lines and make sure you are at least twenty feet from the dock. Damn rats are as big as cats. They'll jump across a gap smaller than that." So it was no wonder that as soon as Larry came back on board from rowing our stern lines ashore he said, "If this canal thing gets to be a hassle, we'll just turn around and sail across the Atlantic instead."

Our yellow quarantine flag attracted immediate attention. Ali, the Arab caretaker for the seldom used club, came down to the dock behind us. He spoke excellent English and carried a leather-bound scrapbook. "The immigration and customs official will be here within an hour. Please add your names to our scrapbook. You can keep it until another yacht arrives or until you leave." Larry scooted ashore in *Rinky*, pulling himself along our mooring lines. When he brought that scrapbook back I understood why we'd want it on board for a few days. Each of the thirty yachts that had been through the canal since it reopened was represented in the twelve-inch-by-fourteen-inch book. Boat photos, drawings, itineraries, crew lists, and best of all, comments on where to shop in Port Said or Port Suez, which agents to trust, and how much to offer as bribes. Judy Vaughn, who'd been through the canal four months previously, bound for the Seychelles on her Bowman 46 ketch, gave careful instructions on clearing your own papers for the transit, complete with a map showing where each port official's office lay and the proper order in which to approach each of the ten necessary offices. By the time our customs and immigration official arrived, we'd decided it might be wise to pay an agent $140 to clear our papers, especially since we had the added complication of needing a tow, because it was unlikely we'd be allowed to sail through the canal.

I felt sorry for the rotund, heavily uniformed man who had been selected to clear us. In gingerly fashion he got into our fifty-five-pound, six-foot-eight-inch dinghy, then looked terrified as it bobbed into the foot-and-a-half-high chop kicked up by passing ships and ferries plus a twenty-knot northerly wind. Only minutes after he climbed on board *Seraffyn* his face grew pale. I'm sure he didn't fulfill his proper duties, since he forgot even to look below for contraband. Instead he shoved six papers at Larry and said, "Sign these, I'll complete them in my office." I've never seen anyone so glad to reach shore. Unfortunately for us, his discomfort didn't leave us any time to ask about agents.

Ali took care of that for us. He placed a few telephone calls, then gave me a lesson on reading Egyptian numbers so that he wouldn't have to worry about anyone's cheating me at the marketplace. "Do not buy food from any stall that doesn't display prices. Even local people get cheated there." I carried his list of numbers with me as I took a quick run to the open market, just six blocks from the club. The limited fresh food we saw in the dusty town made me glad we'd stocked up in Greece and Israel.

Neither of us liked the shipping agent who arrived the next morning. "Sure, I can arrange your papers, only two hundred fifty dollars. A tow will be more difficult but still only six hundred dollars." That stunned us, but we remembered to bargain, so the haggling started. The agent said our offers were ridiculous. We countered, "That's the highest we can go." It took over an hour and three cups of coffee each before we realized the lowest price he'd accept to clear our papers was $140, just what Judy had suggested in the scrapbook. But his price for finding a small local fish boat to pull us through was firm at $400.

"We'll think about it and have Ali call you," Larry said. We rowed ashore and asked Ali how often yachts came through, since we felt we'd rather offer another cruising sailor some money to sweeten his kitty than pay an unscrupulous-seeming agent who'd probably give the towing captain only a few dollars of the fee. But Ali slowed us up by saying, "The last yacht was here in June. That big power yacht can't seem to get its engines started, and it's already been here for five weeks."

We spent the day going around to different shipping offices trying to arrange our own tow. Larry rowed up and down the piers asking the captains of each oil-supply boat or small ship if they would tow us. Two captains offered to lift our little ship on board with their cranes. But the slings they showed Larry couldn't have done the job without damaging our bulwarks. As we rowed away from each of those friendly ships, Larry lamented, "If only we'd built lifting eyes into *Seraffyn* like they do on the meter boats, we could have been on our way through the canal tomorrow for fifty bucks and probably had time to put a fresh coat of bottom paint on to boot." The other vessels we visited weren't headed through the canal or couldn't tow us, since they had to be in convoys that moved at nine knots.

Larry even tried to get the engines running on the steel power boat next to us. But after a depressing, sweaty afternoon on board the almost derelict ship he felt as "down" as its crew. Someone had bought the once handsome vessel with no survey, then hired an ill-assorted crew to move it from Scotland to the Seychelles for charter work. Now both main engines were down, and parts were supposedly on the way. Even as Larry tried to help, the freezer unit gave out. The next morning we were given a defrosting leg of lamb and five pounds of hamburger, since it was impossible to fix the deep freeze without parts from England. Two days later the captain woke us to ask if Larry had any suggestions for fixing a one-inch hole that had developed in the bottom just aft of the main stateroom. Their big electrical bilge pumps easily kept ahead of the water, but if the generator failed, that was the end. Fortunately we carry a quart of underwater Epoxy putty. Larry cut a plywood patch that extended well beyond the punky corroded metal, slathered putty on it, then drove small bolts through the predrilled holes to hold the one-foot-square Band-Aid in place. But even before he dove into the muddy waters of Port Said to patch that hole, it was obvious that the old power yacht would not be any part of the solution to our problem.

The old power yacht and *Seraffyn* waiting at the club.

By our third day in the opressive ninety-five-degree heat of Port Said, with the humidity standing at 85 percent and very little to do or see onshore, both of us were depressed and antsy. "Well, at least we can try and clear our own papers while we look for a tow," I suggested. "Then all we'll have to pay for is the tow. Four hundred dollars won't break us; just means we'll have to be more careful for a few months." Larry agreed. "Tomorrow we'll start on Judy's suggested route. In ten days we'll pay for a tow. We can't wait much longer. If we don't reach Sudan by September fifth or so, we'll run into head winds." Larry and I retreated into good books on the forward bunk, where the wind scoop caught the early-afternoon breeze and funneled it below.

"Sailor, sailor," a heavily accented woman's voice kept calling. I finally climbed on deck and a smartly dressed Egyptian woman of about thirty waved happily. I went ashore and Mayja introduced herself as the wife of the third canal officer. "Please come have tea with me," she asked, then led me down an alley to a tree-shaded patio surrounded by a whitewashed building and a high stone fence. "This is the officers' yacht club," she explained. A dozen children and their nursemaids played on a white-sand beach at the edge of the canal. Red-fezzed waiters in immaculate white gowns served iced tea or lemonade with date candies and honey-soaked pastries on chased-brass tables. We lounged in leather chairs in the cool shade; maybe a dozen uniformed officers and their wives surrounded us. Mayja told me she was the daughter of the former Egyptian ambassador to a major European country. She'd been born in Alexandria but grew up in Europe, with Swiss schools as her main home and Egypt as a land where she spent her summers. Mayja had married an official who lived in Cairo, and filled part of her time working as an official tour guide for highly placed European tourists. But after the Yom Kippur War her husband had been transferred to Port Said. "It's not a very nice city, and I know you'll need help finding good food. So I'd like to take you shopping with me on Thursday," she said. I was puzzled by her invitation. It was rare to be approached out of the blue as we'd been, especially by a woman and even more so in Egypt, where many women we saw on the back streets still hid their faces behind tiny veils.

On Thursday Mayja insisted that she and I take a ride around the outskirts of Port Said before we shopped. She drove south along the canal and pulled over under the sparse shade of a thorn tree about two miles out of town. "Now tell me about Israel," she insisted. "You must have been there, and I know it's a fascinating country, but our newspapers never tell us anything except bad reports of the Israelis' aggression."

At first I was reluctant even to admit having been to Israel, since we'd been warned that the canal officials would turn away any boat that had come from an Israeli port. In fact, we'd been asked to sign a paper stating that we had not been to any part of Israel before we'd been given our passport stamps. But Mayja told me, "That's only scare tactics. Egypt needs money. Israeli freighters have been going through the canal for over five months now. One of our pilot boats takes a Greek flag out to them, they cover up their port name, and that's it." So, for the next hour we had an intense conversation about what Mayja called "the outside world." Then she helped me shop, showing me the only store in town that carried cheese, a tiny basement room two blocks away from the main market. She watched me select a smart, gold-wrapped garnet as a souvenir of Port Said, and bargained for thirty pounds of potatoes and fifteen of limes. Even after I'd discussed this odd morning with Larry, I found it hard to believe that censorship kept so much information out of Egypt. But when we located a copy of *Newsweek* magazine in a hotel lobby, I became a believer. The magazine was half its usual thickness. The world-news section didn't contain one word about Israel, even though that struggling country was much in evidence in the BBC shortwave-radio world news each morning; and, finally, the page numbers in the magazine didn't relate to the index. Mayja didn't come back for the dinner we'd offered her. A few days later when we walked to the officers yacht club, which was only one long block from where *Seraffyn* lay, we were told, "Members only."

Clearing our own papers was one of the most trying experiences we've encountered. For two days we walked down hot, dusty streets and waited in steaming, cluttered offices. We'd have been furious at the long delays but learned that the young boys waiting with us were runners for ships' agents. They did the endless waiting for fifty cents a day. We did succeed, but it cost us forty-seven dollars in fees, plus five dollars for a taxi, plus sore feet, frayed tempers, and more bad impressions of our only Egyptian city. We both agreed it would have been worth hiring the agent for ninety dollars extra.

So, papers in hand, we sat and waited, took rows up the canal, shopped for a few fresh stores, drank gallons of iced lemonade, and waited, always with our ears open for a possible tow. For a week only big ships came through the canal bound south.

Larry and I have never been good at waiting. Give us a problem we can attack with our own hands, our own minds, and we're okay. We've got the patience to last through weeks of calm weather, two or three years of boat building. But let our patience be tried by outside forces and both of us are like caged animals. So, when a sixty-five-foot schooner came steaming into the yacht club ten days after we arrived, it didn't surprise me at all that Larry snapped, "Don't bug them. They'll be here for a few days. Probably just in for provisions anyway." Then he buried his nose back in the fourth book he'd read that week.

I ignored him, grabbed the Port Said Yacht Club scrapbook, and rowed over to *Vltava*, the handsome, carefully maintained schooner, with her home port at Los Angeles. A canal pilot was just leaving. At least thirty people lined the decks and I was welcomed warmly by all of them. I wasn't sure whom to talk to. In fact, I was confused by the mob of people who crowded around to look through the scrapbook and ask about *Seraffyn*. I couldn't wait. "Are you going through the canal?" I blurted at everyone, since I couldn't figure out who was skipper, crew, or charterer. Several people said, "Yes, tomorrow at seven A.M."

"Will you tow us through? We're desperate, we'll pay any reasonable fee," I said to the lady nearest me. Then I wondered if maybe I'd come on too strong when she simply said, "I don't know, I'll ask someone." I waited almost ten minutes while she seemed to wander from stem to stern talking to the other people on board. She finally came back with a slip of paper. "The captain is in this hotel. He went ashore on the boat that brought our pilot out. You'll have to talk to him." I didn't wait to say good-bye. I grabbed the paper, rushed into *Rinky Dink*, and rowed back to *Seraffyn*.

"Grab our canal papers, our passports, hurry up!" I yelled to Larry. "What's the fuss?" he grumbled from the forepeak. "Come on, we might have a tow for tomorrow morning if we hurry," I said in a low voice as I held the dinghy alongside. "No one can clear through that fast," Larry said as he put his shoes on in the cockpit. But when we reached the hotel just at 1600, we learned what a bit of money could do. Bob Firestone greeted us warmly and said, "We radio'd in last night. The pilot boat met us about three miles offshore with an agent two hours ago. Our papers are almost cleared. I'll go see him with you now, and if there's no delay, you're welcome to come along. But we must start through the canal tomorrow, because we're meeting several crew members in Port Suez in two days."

We took a taxi to the agent's office. Our papers were all in order. The agent saw no problems if, the pilot we drew was willing to take a second boat in tow and if the final clearance officer would update the one paper we'd been given that had only a forty-eight-hour limit. The second "if" was the biggest problem. The clearance office closed at 1700. It was now 1645 and that damn office was almost a mile away. Not one taxi waited anywhere along our route. We tried to run through the crowded streets, but the minutes roared past as donkey carts blocked our paths and a military convoy tied up the main street. I'd written off our one chance as Larry's watch ticked past the fateful hour. Then, five blocks from our goal, Larry had the extraordinary luck of recognizing the man we were going to see. He was strolling into a sidewalk café. I ran up to him and explained our problem, with my fingers crossed. I hoped he'd remember the pleasant discussion we'd had about small boats and dhows when we'd been to see him the last time. He did, and willingly cleared a space on the café's counter, opened his attaché case, dug through it for a special stamp, then signed our papers. We didn't accept his offer of a cup of tea. Instead we rushed back to Bob Firestone's hotel room.

The room was packed with a dozen of the people we'd seen on *Vltava*, all lined up to take a shower. Bob scared us when he said, "My agent called. You must have your passports stamped by the immigration official."

"Oh no, it's too late, the offices are all closed," both Larry and I said in defeated tones.

"Not really. My agent has arranged for an official to meet us at 1900, since all thirty-three of our passports need to be stamped too."

We carefully noted the 1900 meeting place, then spent the next hour trying to buy at least a bit of fresh meat for our voyage down the Red Sea. We had no intention of stopping in Port Suez. Not only would the paperwork for this stop have doubled our fees, but reports in the scrapbook told of the war-zone appearance of this old city plus problems with street urchins and dishonest officials and no friendly club greeter like Ali to smooth over any difficulties. So, our imminent departure meant we had only half the ice our chest could hold and maybe two or three pieces of leftover meat.

Most of the stalls in the marketplace were closed, but I remembered the cheese shop and the owner there remembered me. He got his neighbor to open his meat stall. There was only a two-pound chunk of lamb (or maybe it was goat), plus a pound of beef. But we bought those and felt lucky. Then we rushed to the immigration offices. Bob Firestone and six of his crew waited in the courtyard as the sun set. The agent was on the telephone at the guard post nearby, and in spite of his repeated dialings, foot stamping, and gesticulating, it was after 2100 when the proper official arrived to stamp all thirty-five passports. Bob told us that this rush-through by his agent plus pilot fees had brought his total bill to $800, not including the $50 baksheesh he'd been told to pay each pilot. "But when you divide that among thirty-three people, it's not much."

Our long wait was filled by the fascinating story of *Vltava* and her huge crew. Bob Firestone, a psychologist from Los Angeles, created a therapy group for patients with children just reaching their teens. This grew into a central-city commune when someone suggested, "Let's buy an apartment building. If we each sell our houses we'll be able to afford something really nice." So, a group of thirty middle-class adults bought an open-plan complex that allowed each family to have its own apartment. Communal thinking led to a shared fleet of cars. This worked, and the idea spread to include a full-time live-in chef who prepared meals for those who wanted them take-out or communal style. Insurance, food, vacations—with a pool of shoppers that included seventy-eight people, costs dropped until even high-school teachers were living like millionaires. Then someone came up with the idea of buying a yacht to give the younger people a project to work on. They located the almost finished wooden hull and deck of *Vltava* and did a good job of completing her. The young people studied rigging, boat maintenance, engine repair, navigation, and sailing. After a few local trips, a round-the-world voyage was planned. Two of the nineteen-year-old boys were appointed as full-time skippers, since they were the only ones who would guarantee they'd stay with the boat for the next two years. Various members of the group flew out to meet *Vltava* and take their holidays on board. Sometimes there were as many as thirty-three on board, sometimes only ten or twelve. Younger children spent their complete school holidays on board, while their parents went home to resume their jobs.

We were delighted to be included in the amazing warmth that seemed to flow among members of this group. During a later conversation, all of them stressed that open communication was the key. No problem is too small to bring out into the open, no thought too silly or trivial to share. Three years later, when we were building our new boat only eighty miles south of the group's headquarters, we learned that they were still going strong, still using *Vltava* for voyages to Mexico and Canada, and still communicating.

We were awake long before dawn, preparing a towline, topping off our water tanks, and detaching our stern lines. The power of green cash again amazed us when the canal pilot arrived half an hour early. *Vltava* had ten feet of draft, so we'd been assigned a full-fledged, top-rate pilot who took his job seriously. "I wish to conduct tests before we proceed," he informed us in his most officious voice. "I must know if the two boats together can maintain six and a half knots, since that is the clearance speed I've filed." He insisted on trying a speed trial run with *Seraffyn* tied alongside *Vltava*, even though both Larry and Steve Armstrong tried to convince him that this wouldn't work. *Seraffyn* tried to sheer wildly away from the bow wake thrown by *Vltava*. Before we completed the mile-long trial, the pilot agreed to try it again with a temporary towline. This time there was no problem at all. With the pilot satisfied, *Vltava*'s eager crew set to work carefully rigging a towing bridle to eliminate any chance of chafe on our lines. *Rinky Dink* was lifted off our deck to sit in splendor on the cabin of the spacious schooner. That way, not only did we have better visibility but we could also set our big sun awning as the pilot directed his mini-convoy past the ferry and into the Suez Canal at six and a half knots.

Abandoned tanks, piles of defused land mines, and scraggles of barbed wire flashed by as the last buildings of Said receded and lonely sand dunes took their place. A few palm trees marked army encampments along the

Vltava preparing to take us alongside.

canal banks. Otherwise the monotony of the long day under tow was broken only when a convoy of approximately fifty merchant ships forced us to edge over to the side of the 300-foot-wide canal. We both became bored with holding the tiller to keep *Seraffyn* riding directly behind *Vltava*. But if we let go, she'd start sheering one way or the other. Then Larry got a brilliant idea. Since there was a strong following wind blowing dead on to our stern as we were towed down the long, straight canal, he tried setting Helmer to work. The wind blew at close to twenty-five knots; we were being towed at six and a half knots. That left at least eighteen knots of apparent wind to actuate the vane, and that jumble of pipe and Dacron did it! The wind vane took complete control, so both of us could lounge under the sun cover as the desolate shores slipped past.

The Suez Canal is just under one hundred miles long. It's dug through sand dunes for over half of its length. The other half is dredged across shallow salt lakes. Fortunately there is less than eighteen inches of tidal rise and fall in the Med, none at all in the Red Sea. So, equalizing locks are unnecessary. The only real problems are keeping the drifting desert sands from filling the canal, cleaning up war debris, and avoiding the mass of sharks that follow trails of garbage thrown overboard from ships getting ready to enter the canal from the Red Sea. We saw swarms of eight- and ten-foot-long white-tipped sharks cruising along beside us.

Ismailia is an oasis town right at the midpoint of the canal. We were told to wait there for the night. Our pilot insisted that we tie alongside *Vltava* to make life easier for the guards who would be on a rowing patrol through the night. Only after we asked several times did we learn the reason for this two-man constant guard. President Sadat was in residence at his country estates, which we could see just a mile from where we lay.

We were invited for a feastlike dinner with half of *Vltava*'s crew. Prime ribs of beef, champagne, breaded eggplant slices, roast potatoes. After we'd finished, the other half of the crew, who'd eaten an hour before, came back inside and filled the huge main cabin while we talked about sailing, living together in close situations, and a dozen other topics, until someone reminded us all it was past midnight and our pilot would be back at 0700.

A tiny cool breeze filtered into our forward stateroom, caught by our wind scoop. The murmer of our guards' oars and the muted voices of a dozen of *Vltava*'s crew kept us from drifting off to sleep. We went back on deck for a while to talk with these interesting people and got a bit of a laugh when we asked about this anchor watch. "Don't have enough bunks for more than twenty of us," someone explained. "So we stand watches at sea and in port. Never any worry about things being stolen that way."

When we approached Port Suez the next day, just after noon, Larry and I were both relieved to be regaining control of our own lives. In nine years we've been under tow only four times, once for the Kiel Canal, once to get out from between some tightly packed docks so that we could leave San Diego while our well-wishers could still wave their arms, once when the port captain in Faial insisted, and, finally, when we removed *Seraffyn* 's mast to store her in Virginia. Each time it had been worrisome, since we could never be as sure of other people's gear and seamanship as we were of our own. More important than that, any skipper would naturally watch out for his own boat first in an emergency situation. So, we'd really have to think and act unbelievably fast if our towing boat sheered to avoid a collision or, worse yet, ran aground.

Vltava slowed down just outside Port Suez and her crew pulled us alongside so that we could transfer *Rinky Dink* back on board. We'd tried to pay something toward their fuel and clearance cost several times. The only thank-you gift we could think of was two copies of our first book, which we carried for times like this. When the pilot saw us pass these books across he said, "You have a gift for me too, I'm sure." Rather than cause a scene, I went below and brought up a wad of twenty one-dollar bills, while Larry set our mainsail and prepared to get under way.

As we ran clear of the canal approaches on a growing northerly breeze, Larry looked back and said. "Getting through the canal was almost as much of a hassle as I expected it to be. I feel like I've been let out of jail. You can say you told me so, but who would have guessed *Vltava* could get cleared through in one afternoon?" As we sailed past at least two hundred ships lying at anchor or preparing to join the afternoon's northbound convoy, *Vltava*'s clearance seemed less magical. Instead of pretending she was a yacht, her crew pretended she was a commercial ship. They paid big-ship fees and got big-ship service.

CHAPTER 7

~~~~~~

Sailing
through a Nightmare

O ne of the recurring stories we'd heard from voyagers who'd sailed up
the Red Sea was implausible-sounding. They'd throw up their hands
in frustration as they told us about trying to tack up the last 150 miles into
the narrow Gulf of Suez. "The ships were so close together we couldn't
sail between them," each voyager would say. Until we ran out of the Suez
Canal on a strong following breeze, we chalked up these stories as exaggerations by people who were tired after at least 700 miles of head winds. To
our surprise, the reality was very close to the stories. Even as we ran wing
and wing down the twenty-mile-wide gulf, we had to be constantly on
watch. Over 200 ships lay at anchor as far as five miles offshore. More cargo
ships came steaming up from the south at the rate of four an hour. Then,
three hours after we cleared the canal, when our following breeze had
hardened into a force-six wind, the first ship of a southbound canal convoy
came steaming past us at fifteen knots. At least fifty more followed so
closely that as we looked across the shipping lanes it seemed as if the whole
gulf were a wall-to-wall carpet of slab-sided, rushing, 300- to 800-foot-long
cargo ships. Trying to beat a course through that mess and still gain
weathering on a dark, windy night would be a sailor's version of hell.

By midnight, the second story we'd heard so frequently was confirmed.
Our following breeze had risen to a gale. The confined, shallow waters
turned the sea around us into a mess. We reefed down until we were
making five and a half knots under just our staysail. We'd met an oil
platform manager in Malta the previous winter. Kelly Wilson spent six
weeks on the rig in the Gulf of Suez, then got six weeks leave to sail his
boat. Since he was thinking of a voyage down the Red Sea, he and his rig

friends made a graph of wind speeds and directions over a one-year period. For nine months of the year, from March to December, Kelly's graph showed 60 percent of their platform anenometer readings gave northerly winds, gale force and above. Kelly choose to go across the Atlantic instead, and within twelve hours of setting off down the Red Sea, I wondered if we should have, too.

But Larry set to work doing his usual strong-wind, settle-her-down routine. First he fiddled with the wind-vane control links, damping down the trim tabs' correcting action until it held us on a very steady course in spite of the short seas and ships' wakes. Then he had me tighten in the 104-square-foot staysail to dampen our motion as *Seraffyn* lunged over one sea, slammed into the next, and rolled to recover. Instead of leaving the staysail almost fully out, I winched until it was sheeted for a beam reach. That had a surprisingly steadying effect. Then Larry got out our brand-new Tilly kerosene pressure lamp and lit it. He hung it on a bracket we'd made for our boom gallows, and now it served as an extraordinarily bright stern lamp. Finally I brewed up a pot of hot chocolate, because in spite of its being late August, the damp air and strong wind were chilling. Our three-hour night watches went quickly as we watched the parade of ships passing up and down the gulf. Even though I hate standing watches when I have to be out on deck every minute, thinking about how much worse this night would have been if we'd been headed the other way kept me almost happy.

The Tilly lamp did a great job for us that first night. It never worked as well again and within two weeks it started giving us so many problems that we finally tossed it overboard. But I felt it had paid its way in the Gulf of Suez.

By midafternoon we'd cleared the gulf. The land to the west pulled away until it was only a darker smudge in the distant haze. Dead ahead a large ship seemed to be approaching at a very slow pace. Only when we were within a mile of the ship did we realize it was perched on a reef. Its paint was still bright, its flags flying but tattered until only one stripe of the Liberian ensign still showed. Not a soul was on board. The ship had obviously run hard aground in recent weeks. I think its eerie appearance, rocking gently to the eight-foot swells, made us decide to duck into an anchorage indicated by half an anchor on our chart just north of the Queesam lighthouse and behind South Queesam Island, to wait for the wind to die down a bit.

Our chart seemed reasonably accurate as we sailed behind the first of the low sand islands. We sailed into the first shallow sandy area shown by the Admiralty chart. We'd have liked to sail on another mile to where the anchorage looked better, but the sun was just kissing the horizon, and one rule we remembered about coral-reef sailing is "Don't go anywhere without the sun to show you what lies underwater." So, we settled in behind the deserted-looking island. Between us and the shore a coral reef spread its brown and yellow hues just a few feet below the clear water and stretched for almost half a mile. Then it shelved off to where we'd found a sandy patch with eighteen feet of water. So, we set our anchor and paid out 150 feet of chain even though we were almost a mile from shore.

This was the first time in over five years that we'd anchored near coral reefs, and that's why Larry got out his mask and fins, then dove overboard to check the holding ground. He wasn't too happy when he climbed back on board. "There are lots of coral heads down there, not much sand. I hooked our anchor behind a coral head just in case the wind gets up any more. But hope we don't drag, because the water shelves off to sixty feet only twenty yards past our anchor," he said as we both rinsed off in fresh water. Then we climbed below as the wind started to increase until it was blowing a gale.

Seraffyn lay comfortably in the two-foot chop that grew in the mile-long fetch between us and the sandy island to windward. We'd just completed dinner, cleaned up the dishes, and climbed into our sleeping bag when we heard a voice call through the night. "*Capitan, capitan!*" It was almost completely dark; only a faint glow of sunset showed on the horizon. We'd seen no other boats around, no buildings or signs of life onshore. That voice seemed like a bad spirit, but it couldn't be ignored.

Since I was on the outside of the bunk, I climbed into the main cabin, wrapped a towel around my bare body, then climbed the first step of our companionway ladder. I was just in time to feel a dinghy laden with four white-robed Arabs crash into *Seraffyn*'s side. Two of the men held submachine guns high over their heads away from the spray thrown by their bucking, eight-foot-long plastic dinghy. "*Capitan, capitan, passaport, passaport,*" one of them called when he saw me.

Larry was climbing out of the forepeak and rummaging around for his shorts and a sweatshirt. "What do we do?" I whispered.

"I'm sure as hell not going to give them our passports," he muttered through his sweatshirt. "I'll go out and hold them away from *Seraffyn*'s side. You make up a crew's list, make it look real official. Maybe that will satisfy them."

I quickly put on some clothes, then got out three sheets of typing paper and printed our names and details from our passports, and put a flourishing signature across all three copies of our made-up crew's list. Then I put a stick-on, return-address label in the corner, and to impress our very unofficial-looking visitors, I pasted half a dozen Italian and Maltese postage stamps on the top copy. I carried this out into the whipping wind along with our passports. There was just enough light between the last rays of sunset and our anchor light for me to show the four Arabs our passports, then point to the identical names and numbers on the paper. From the way they looked at those faked-up crew's lists, we could tell none of them knew how to read English. But the leader was satisfied. He folded the papers carefully and tucked them away inside his billowing robe. "Cigarette, cigarette," he asked in a pleading voice. We indicated we had none, and Larry started saying, *"Salome, salome,"* which we'd learned as Arabic for "good-bye." We both sighed with relief as four hands let go of our bulwarks and the two men without bulky guns started paddling furiously toward the mile-distant shore. Our relief quickly turned to concern. Those poor men in their bobbing, jumping, square-fronted plastic boat couldn't make a bit of headway against a wind that was now blowing over forty knots. If they didn't get some help they'd be blown onto the reefs four miles to leeward or out into the Red Sea. Larry hesitated only a second. He grabbed the mainsheet, which was hanging on the boom gallows, coiled it carefully, and tossed. One Arab grabbed that line as if it were a blessing from Allah. He almost lost his four-foot-long paddle in the process. But somehow he managed to secure our mainsheet around the bow eye on his dinghy, and there we were, darkness all around us, a rising gale, and a dinghy full of gun-toting Egyptians tethered behind us.

For a few minutes everything seemed under control. I just had time to get a jacket out. Then the Arabs pulled alongside *Seraffyn.* "Motor, motor," the headman said, pointing at *Seraffyn*'s stern and indicating with hand signals that he wanted us to tow him closer to shore. I got out our big flashlight to show him there was no propeller under *Seraffyn*'s stern, no outboard motor for our dinghy. The true situation began to dawn on those four men, who we'd now concluded were army guards camped somewhere on the sandy island with orders to check each boat that came in to anchor. The headman showed us the water collecting in his overloaded dinghy, and I got a bread pan to work as a bailer for the frightened quartet. They again trailed aft, bailing all the time.

It was only minutes later that a fish boat came steaming slowly around the end of the island. Her crew got ready to let out an anchor, maybe a quarter mile past us. Larry started signaling at them with our quarter mile flashlight, and then one of our unwanted guests frightened the hell out of us. He aimed his submachine gun and let off a blast of bullets right at that fish boat. Long tongues of flame split the night as bullets flew from that heavy gun to just clear the running lights of the only possible rescue boat. Motors revved up; the fish boat's skipper turned off its lights and chugged back out to sea. I sure didn't blame them. Up until that moment the Arabs had been just a nuisance. But after that round of gunfire we were scared. Only the fear that they'd turn their guns on us kept Larry from casting them off to get blown down the Red Sea.

For maybe ten minutes the wind held steady at forty knots. The Arabs took turns bailing as two-foot swells tried to invade their tiny boat. Then a sudden gust of wind heralded a nasty night. I couldn't stand worrying about those four men anymore. "Bring them on board," I told Larry. "I'll take care of their submachine guns."

As the first two men gratefully began climbing on board, they laid their guns on deck, then scrambled over the lifelines. I picked up each gun, talking in what I hoped was a reassuring voice and pointing below at the dry quarter berths. The men seemed more than pleased to have their weapons out of the salt spray that was now blowing across our decks as *Seraffyn* plunged and bucked into the growing chop, shoved by force-ten winds. The four men seemed relieved to be on a safer platform. They huddled behind our cabin and tried lighting cigarettes. I went below to brew some tea, since Larry reminded me that this was the month of Ramadan, the religious time when Muslims are not allowed to eat or drink from sunup to sundown. Our guests were extremely grateful for the mugs of tea and plate of buttered bread I handed them. Larry rigged our canvas companionway cover to give us some privacy and keep at least a bit of the ashes from their constant chain of cigarettes from blowing into our cabin. We were both almost laughing about the situation. We had their weapons; we were now in charge.

Then nature took over. The wind grew quickly until it screeched through our rigging. *Seraffyn* bucked violently and our anchor chain transmitted a grumbling, clanging crash that resounded through our tiny cabin.

"Anchor's dragging," Larry yelled as he jumped for the companionway. The Arabs had heard the noise too, and our agitation destroyed any confidence they were gaining in the situation.

We were more than a bit worried. The wind was above force ten. Reefs surrounded our anchorage and the water below us shelved quickly, so that any dragging would put our gear in deep water. Larry was tugging out our thirty-five pound folding fisherman anchor. "Get a bearing on the lighthouse and see if we're dragging," he yelled over the howling wind. I climbed past the four worried men huddling away from the flying spray in our cockpit. The flashing light four miles away on our beam confirmed that so far we weren't dragging seriously. One of the Arabs seemed to understand our plan as soon as I began unlashing the dinghy. He tried to help us put it overboard, then, as soon as Larry got his wet-weather gear on and climbed into the jumping, bucking dinghy, he helped me hand the anchor over the lifelines to Larry. We secured a 200-foot-long mooring line to *Rinky Dink* so that Larry would never be loose of the boat in the howling darkness. Our anchor light glowed over an unkind scene. Charging whitecaps shoved the dinghy's bow three feet into the air; Larry's oars hit air as often as they hit water. Before he got even with the end of our bowsprit he'd been blown forty feet away from our beam. The dinghy was half full of water and Larry was close to exhaustion. I reeled him in. The Arabs helped get the anchor, Larry, and the dinghy safely back on board, chattering away in tones that sounded like reassurance. "I'll let this storm anchor down at our forefoot," Larry said as soon as everything was back on board. "If we leave the line loosely around the cathead and secure the bitter end, it will start paying out if we drag. That should give us a second chance."

I got him below and warmed up with a cup of hot buttered rum as soon as I could. Our anchor chain was quiet; *Seraffyn* lay head to the howling wind, changing her position only when a gust hit from a slightly different direction. My newest bearing showed that the lighthouse hadn't moved. But still we were concerned. "If we have to, we'll just slip the anchor rodes and reach back and forth toward the lighthouse," Larry said. "There's four miles of clear water; it's only six hours until daylight."

"Sure," I said sarcastically, "and what do we do with those Arabs? They'll vomit all over the place if we put them down here; they'll be in the way up there!"

"Hey, hey," Larry said, "calm down, Little One. Everything's okay right now. If the wind doesn't get any stronger we're fine. I'm just planning for the worst." He took me in his arms and held me against the bucking motion. "Climb into the bunk and we'll try to get some rest."

"What about those men?" I asked.

"They're wearing heavy robes, so they won't freeze," Larry answered. "They'll have to take care of themselves for a little while. We need as much rest as we can get just in case things do get worse."

I lay in the bunk listening to Larry's fitful sleep. The wind did seem to be dying; the anchor chain was quiet. I climbed out to check on our Arabs. When I slid the companionway hatch, they all jumped up, startled. "Okay, okay," I said in a soothing voice. Then all four lay back down into the cockpit like sardines. They were dry and relatively comfortable, the anchor light was still on, that beautiful lighthouse flash was in the exact same position, and the wind was above force eight still but seemed less frightening, so I finally dozed off.

At daylight Larry got up, then came back to the bunk and whispered, "Wind's down; we don't seem to have moved. Those four guys are dead to the world." We too fell into an exhausted sleep.

We were as eager to have our guests leave as they were to leave. By 1000, the wind was down to twenty-five knots; whitecaps bubbled on top of foot-and-a-half wind chop. But the shore did look a long way off, even in the daylight. Their dinghy looked even more frightening now that we could really see it. Less than one foot of freeboard, no seats, no oarlocks, really just a square, oversized washtub. So Larry tied our 200-foot warping line to their stern seat and pantomimed, "See if you can row against the wind. If not we'll reel you in." Meanwhile I got out every plastic bag we had and wrapped their submachine guns to protect them against the saltwater. During the night Larry had told me, "Since the Egyptian soldiers threw their guns down during the retreat from Israel's Yom Kippur War, any soldier who looses his weapon is liable to be shot."

The four men got into their tiny boat and paddled like mad. They gained on the wind and soon grew confident. As one untied our line and tossed it overboard, they all yelled the Arabic words for "thank you, good luck, good wishes." We waited as they paddled across the reef. Long before they reached the shore, the men jumped into waist-high water and pulled their frail boat the last quarter mile. I wasn't surprised when two of them dropped down and kissed the sandy beach.

It was only after we'd watched our four guests reach shore that we both

The line in the foreground leads to the weary men in their overloaded dinghy.

turned and really took note of a sight to bring horror to the heart of anyone who has ever owned a bare teak deck. Our guests had left gobs of crude oil all over. Their shoes, their dinghy, their painter had all been covered with thick black glop. A hundred splotches of oil marred the teak, the white-painted bulwarks, our mainsheet. *Seraffyn*'s side, where their dinghy had smashed against her, was a three-foot-long smear of crude. Even a towel I'd left out to dry was full of the stuff. It took two hours and almost three gallons of kerosene plus every rag we had on board to restore our home to a cleaner state, but only time would get the black stains out of our deck. By then the wind was down to force six and we felt like having a good wash ourselves.

We dove over and swam along our anchor chain. To our mutual amazement, our anchor hadn't moved at all. But the three-foot-high coral head that had been just behind our anchor now lay split and toppled, torn from its roots by our chain. That explained the horrendous noise we'd heard the night before.

"I need a good night's sleep," Larry said when he came up for air. "Let's set another anchor. Besides, I want to try something new." So, rather than get the dinghy overboard, he took a fender and tied it as a float to our twelve-pound Danforth anchor. He then swam just below the foot-and-a-half-high wind chop, his snorkel tracing a straight, accurate course to windward as he pulled our 200-foot warping line. I paid the line out from the foredeck and secured it after he dove down and set the small anchor. Then he tied the fender around his waist and pulled himself back along the new anchor line. We tied three fenders to our thirty-five-pound fisherman with its thirty feet of chain and 300-foot-long, five-eighths-inch nylon rode. I paid the rode out as he pulled himself and the floating anchor along the first line. When he untied the fenders, that anchor fell into position 150 feet ahead of *Seraffyn*. Larry pulled up the twelve pounder and I reeled him back in. "That worked easily," he said when he was back on board. "I think I could have done that last night if I'd thought of it." I agreed that it would have been worth a try, since he'd never once been detached from the boat during the whole maneuver and he hadn't had to fight the windage our dinghy presented. Larry is a strong swimmer and completely unafraid of the water. So, it might have worked.

A few hours later I was glad we had two anchors out. The wind rose until it was blowing at least as fiercely as it had been the night before. But with no uninvited Egyptian soldiers, no submachine guns on board, and two anchors set, we got a very good night's sleep.

When the wind dropped off to ten knots three days later and the barometer showed a four-millibar rise, we lifted both of our anchors and sorted out the gear. Then we set a course to wind twenty miles through the reefs bordering Egypt's southeast coast. I think both of us felt less apprehensive about the rest of the voyage down the Red Sea. We'd survived the Gulf of Suez, an occupation by the Egyptian army, and winds as strong as any we'd felt during our stay in the Med. Now we were ready to handle the 1,150 miles that separated us from the Indian Ocean and real open water.

CHAPTER 8

A Voyager's Nightmare Continues

The reefs along the Sudanese and Egyptian coasts are one of the main attractions in the Red Sea. These fantastic coral formations are filled with an unparalleled variety of sea life, yet are virtually untouched and unexplored. The natives almost never dive on these reefs, since fishing by hook and line is far simpler. Foreigners rarely visit, because there are no resorts on this desolate shoreline. We'd heard of a few tours being organized out of Port Sudan, but these were limited, since the best reefs, such as the Sanganeb, lay thirty miles beyond the nearest hotel, and the only available skin-diving boats in 1977 were a few local launches. Although we were aware of the need to reach the south end of the Red Sea before the middle of September, when the monsoons would change our following breezes into head winds, Larry did want to try some reef diving.

But after only five hours of sailing in the Red Sea's inner passage, we changed our minds. The first beacon we had to find to lead us into the safe channel between these steep-to reefs popped into view right on time. We changed course, eased sheets, and almost immediately got worried. According to the chart we had spread on the cockpit sole, we should have seen no islands at all for the next fifteen miles. But dozens of sandy mounds lay all around us. Larry kept a careful watch as I dug through our British pilot book. A little caution note at the end of the chapter on Egypt's shore solved the puzzle. "During the intense heat of summer, evaporation can cause the water level in the Red Sea to drop as much as 8 to 12 feet." It is amazing how confusing it becomes when you have to work with a chart that takes no account of tidal rise and fall, where shoals become islands and underwater reefs become mounds of exposed rocks.

Then, as we searched for the next beacon, which should have been dead ahead, we found it well off to port, even though we'd sailed only two miles since changing course at the last beacon. Our compass was accurate—we'd swung it only a month before—and no metal or flashlights were lying within three feet of it. We sheeted the sails in, reached past the metal stake with its fifteen-inch-wide, targetlike marker perched on top, and noticed the bow wave climbing one side of the stake, trailing wavelets that indicated almost two knots of current setting toward the west. We adjusted our course to take this set into account, but at the next beacon, four miles farther to the south, we were out again. This time the current was running to the southwest at one knot. "The hell with skin diving, I want to be out in the open," Larry said after that discovery. I couldn't have agreed more. No fish or photographs were worth the risk of stranding our boat on a reef. Not only were we far from the nearest villages and off the normal shipping routes, but these reefs were steep too, so even if we'd tried to pull ourselves off, we'd have been unable to set ground tackle in depths that often ran 100 fathoms only thirty feet from the edge of the now four-foot-deep reefs. So, we reached for the first safe opening through the reef and shoal areas. For the rest of the trip we stuck to the relative safety of the open waters in the middle of the Red Sea, where we found almost no current at all until we reached the straits of Bab El Mandab. We've since learned that currents run most strongly near and through the reefs during the hot summer months. Several voyagers made enjoyable day-hopping passages through this area by short tacking north behind the reefs during midwinter. They sailed only when the sun was high enough to show water color changes, and anchored inside the reefs at night. These people told us that although the beacons maintained by the Sudanese seemed to be very accurate, those maintained by the Egyptians were less dependable. Their skin-diving stories still make me envious.

By midafternoon we'd cleared the reefs, set our lapper and main wing and wing to a fresh northerly breeze, and relaxed as we made five knots through the water. The sailing for the next 1,100 miles was outwardly uneventful, wind constantly from the north or northwest averaging ten to twenty knots with only a few hours of calm. The only sail changes we made were occasional gybes or a shift from main and lapper wing and wing to lapper wing and wing, with our big nylon drifter lead to the end of the vanged-out boom. But the terrific heat made every move, every decision a difficult feat. Days averaged 110 degrees, nights 90 to 95 degrees, and the humidity was exceptionally high. Even though we rigged our small awning so that we had some shade to sit in while we kept track of the ships that were always in view, our tempers were more than a bit frayed. We were carrying thirty gallons of water in jugs on deck to supplement the thirty-five gallons we had in stainless-steel tanks below, but still we had to be extra careful since we were both drinking almost a gallon a day besides the soft drinks we had in bottles. So, despite constant wash-downs in saltwater, the only time we felt comfortable was in the late evening when we both sponged down with half a gallon of fresh water. At night we struggled to sleep. We rigged our wind scoop on the forehatch to funnel a breeze into the forward bunk, and finally through sheer exhaustion found we could get enough sleep to keep going.

Added to the heat was the problem of getting accurate sights. Books like the *Pilot, Ocean Passages for the World,* and *Bowditch's Practical Navigator* and other voyagers had warned us that the tremendous heat rising from the surrounding deserts plus blowing sand made daytime sights unreliable. We confirmed this problem of refraction by taking a round of sights while we were right next to the Brothers lighthouse, 300 miles down the Red Sea. The sights showed us twenty miles east of our true position. Only by taking a round of star sights just at daybreak or catching Polaris by the light of the half moon that shone briefly just around midnight could we get an accurate fix.

Then, five days out, when I opened our locker to get something to make up an acceptable dinner (since we'd run out of fresh meat and ice), I found that every single can had swollen and now had the bulging ends that usually indicate botulism. I was near tears until Larry used careful logic. "Can't be anything but heat expansion. It would be impossible for every can to go bad at the exact same time. They don't have the same things inside, they weren't bought at the same time." When I checked the water temperature and found it was over ninety degrees, I went along with this logic. We used the canned food with no ill effects, and sure enough, three weeks later in the Indian Ocean where the water temperature dropped to seventy-eight degrees, all the cans resumed their normal shape almost simultaneously.

As we passed the latitude of Port Sudan, a sandstorm added to our discomfort. The wind didn't change at all, ten knots from the northwest. But a red cloud surrounded us, visibility dropped to about half a mile, and for two hours fine salmon-colored dust filtered onto us, piling in little mounds against the cabin back, behind the stanchions and winches. We closed the boat tightly and removed the ventilators and capped them. But when the blue sky and relentless sun returned, we opened the boat up to find a film of sand covering the bunks, counters, floor, and every book.

Two days later we had a bit of refreshing excitement. For years we'd dragged a fishing line with absolutely no luck at all. Then, in Rhodos, fourteen-year-old Simon Irvine had asked Larry to show him how to splice so that he could help his father rerig their thirty-one-foot Australian ketch. In return, Simon gave us a lure and fishing rig he said were guaranteed to catch fish in the Red Sea. We'd had the three-prong hook with its lead-weighted skirt of pink plastic out on a hundred-pound test monofilament line for two days. It was attached to a shock-cord-activated alarm. Just as I was serving cocktails that evening, I said, "Let's reel in the fishline so it doesn't foul the taffrail log spinner." I hadn't said the last word when that can full of nuts and bolts started jumping and clanging like mad.

Larry almost knocked me over as he grabbed for that fishline and started pulling it in hand over hand. "We've got a fish!" he yelled. "Slow her down, head her into the wind, get a drop board in, get me something to kill it with, it's a big one!" His commands came faster than I could sort them out. Since I could imagine the chaos caused by a huge fish flopping down the companionway into our quarter berths, I got a drop board in place first. Then I rushed forward and dropped the lapper. Our speed slowed from five and a half knots to a more sedate three as I lashed the sail roughly against the bowsprit. Then I ran back to look at that beautiful fighting fish, two and a half feet of flashing silver, wrestling only five feet from our stern. "Grab a bucket of saltwater and slosh the cockpit down or the blood and guts will never come out. Get me a winch handle so I can kill it," Larry shouted as he struggled to swing the twenty-pound kingfish on board. I was as excited as a kid on Halloween, but when Larry took the first whack at that jumping, living fish, I ran and hid on the foredeck, covering my ears to shut out the sounds of the slaughter.

I took a real ribbing for that, especially since I eagerly ran to get our fish-filleting knife, cutting board, and a plate to hold those pure white steaks. That was the first fresh meat we'd had in seven days! I may not be much of a hunter, but I am an eager eater.

By dark we had five pounds of fish sautéing gently in olive oil, garlic, and lemon juice. The cockpit was clear of most of the blood, guts, and scales. We toasted Simon and his fine lure with a glass of Israeli wine. Our stereo played a medley of Roger Whittaker songs; the stern light cast a warm glow over the cockpit. *Seraffyn* ran comfortably along at four knots, her blue-and-white-striped drifter outlined against the bright stars and a waning moon. The fish escapade had broken our heat-induced funk, and

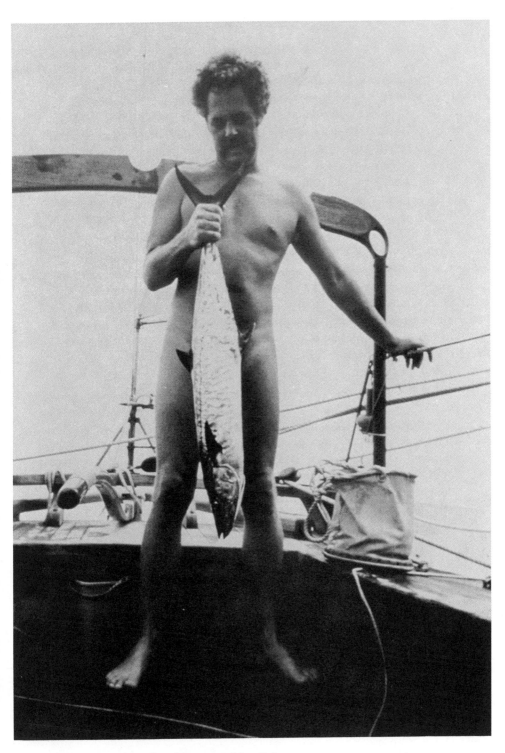

Simon's lure caught this great kingfish.

we enjoyed lying together in the relative cool of the breeze-fanned, cushion-covered cockpit until our ship's bell rang 2300 and reminded us of the need to start watches for the night.

Although there are military zones where entry is restricted along the Egyptian and Arabian shores of the Red Sea, cruising sailors found they could safely anchor almost everywhere else they wanted. Israel and the Sudan warmly welcomed sailors who stopped, and crews of the offshore oil rigs were eager for visitors who could tie to their mooring buoys on calm days. But once you sail south of Sudan, the whole situation changes. In 1977, Eritrea and Ethiopia were at war. North Yemen was in revolt. Djibouti, a French colony up until a week before we set off down the Red Sea, was now in the throes of a painful French withdrawal, and street-to-street fighting was tearing up the outskirts of the port city.

So, added to the tension caused by sailing in the extreme heat, difficult navigation, and increasingly heavy shipping was the fear of venturing away from the fifteen-mile-wide clear stretch of water into the maze of islands at the lower end of the Red Sea. Then, to make things worse, less than 300 miles from the Straits of Bab El Mandeb, in the most restricted area of the Red Sea, we had a day that tried Larry's stamina and patience to the utmost.

At first light, when he went to check our night's run, the taffrail log wasn't spinning. Larry pulled in the fifty-foot trailing line and found that some kind of fish had bitten off the bronze spinner. We'd dragged that same spinner for over eight years. But we had two spares, so he set another. Two hours later, that one was gone too, and there were teeth marks on the lead weight two feet in front of the spinner. So, when I first opened my eyes that morning, Larry was busily rummaging through our tool locker for parts to make a stainless-steel leader for the last spinner we owned.

I started to turn over in the forward bunk, where I had been sleeping under the wind-scoop breeze. That slight move set off a shooting pain from my left foot right into my groin. It was so intense that I screamed. Larry dropped everything and came running through the boat. By then I was crying from the sharp pain that spread throughout my leg. "What's wrong, is it a charley horse?" Larry asked as he looked on helplessly. I couldn't tell him. I had no idea what it was. The pain was like nothing I'd ever experienced before. In fact, I broke my leg two years later, and the pain I had that morning in the Red Sea was far worse! Larry tried to hold me and figure out what was wrong. He got me a codeine pill from our medical kit and a glass of apricot nectar. But then he had to leave and go on deck, as we were approaching the Farasan Islands, a military area owned by the Saudis and strictly off limits. "Do you want me to stop a ship and ask for help?" he asked when he came down the next time. "Two just passed us. There are more on the horizon."

"Not yet," I said as I struggled to lie absolutely still so that the pain didn't have a reason to increase. Larry tried messaging my leg, but that didn't help. "If you really need it, we can stop the next ship and ask if they have a doctor on board. But it's pretty unlikely they will. I don't think they have to carry a doctor if they have fewer than twelve passengers, and all of the ships I've seen so far are freighters or tankers."

Under the influence of the codeine, the pain was subsiding until only my lower leg felt as if it were crushed under a pile of stone. "If we can't get a doctor, it's not worth stopping anyone. We've got everything they carry, in our own medical kit," I said, trying to be logical. "Besides, they'd just want me to go on board their ship. I'm not going to leave you alone to sail *Seraffyn*. I just won't do that."

"That's my kid," Larry chuckled. "But if you really need help they could radio for advice. On the other hand, if you can hold in there, we'll be out into the Gulf of Aden in a few days. Probably reach help just a day later than a ship could get you there."

All during that hot, dreary day Larry had to stay on deck checking our course, avoiding ships. But in between he'd rush below for a few minutes to check on me, urge me to try moving, bring me a glass of juice or some cheese. But night was coming and Larry had already been on deck since 0500. There was no place we could safely anchor until we reached the Zubair Islands, 130 miles farther south. "Don't worry about me," Larry said soothingly when he brought me his dinner specialty, peanut butter and jam on Saltine crackers. But I was worried, and by midnight, since I'd been able to sleep under the influence of the maximum dose of codeine our medical guide recommended, I insisted he carry me into the cockpit so that he could rest. Larry padded a corner with our sleeping bags, propped me up with our bunk pillows, then lay down on the cockpit sole right next to me and was almost instantly asleep.

Every ten minutes or so I'd give a hard pull on the tiller to bring *Seraffyn* far enough off course so that I could see the part of the horizon our cabin blocked from view. Ships came within 100 yards of us, and several shone spotlights over our tiny rushing boat as they passed. I signaled back with our big torch, and almost every one flicked their lights in return. Larry managed to get some sleep, though I had to wake him four times during the next four hours to gybe, then take down the pole as the wind shifted forward. Thank God for that steering vane, because even pulling the tiller sent pains coursing down my leg.

Somehow Larry was able to carry on with less than four hours of sleep, and when he rounded *Seraffyn* up a quarter mile off Zubair Island and set the anchor in twenty feet of water, he still had energy enough to dive over for a swim and the usual anchor check. He urged me to try it too, then helped me get overboard without bumping my still throbbing leg. It did feel wonderful, and the massaging effect of the warm water helped subdue the pain a bit more. We splurged and used a full gallon of fresh water for a rinse-off. Then I tried standing up for the first time in thirty-five hours. My left leg would not support my weight. It took a week for the pain to leave completely and three weeks for the leg to regain normal strength. An English doctor we contacted in Aden told us the cause was simple: salt deficiency. The huge amount of fresh water I'd been consuming, the sweating, and my natural tendency to avoid salty foods had starved my body of the salt it needed. Larry didn't suffer, because he pours salt on his food. One teaspoon of salt swilled down with some water once a day or two salt tablets would have prevented the whole problem.

I must admit this incident did give us a few minutes' pause. What if it had been something more serious? What if we'd needed medical aid immediately? Then, as we looked over the sailing we'd done and thought of the hundreds of voyagers we'd met, we came to the conclusion that being at sea is hundreds of times safer than being onshore. We could recall only one or two situations where injuries or sudden illness caused voyaging sailors more than temporary extra discomfort or danger because there was no immediate medical assistance other than that which could be provided by a crew member trained in first aid and equipped with a good medical chest (such as the one recommended in *Being Your Own Wilderness Doctor*, by Dr. E. Russell Kodet and Bradford Angier, published by Stackpole Books, Harrisburg, Pa.). We did hear of a few instances where dangerous burns or fractures occurred on racing boats in full-out gale conditions. But a well-outfitted cruising boat properly sailed with vangs, careful galley arrangements, and some prudence is a very safe place to be. Besides, there comes a time when you must take some carefully calculated risks in order to have an interesting life. A cruising sailor at sea, like the climber on an isolated peak or the diver on an offshore reef, must seek the training to take care of himself and his partners.

We stayed at anchor for the night but left as soon as we woke, because strange-looking clouds covered the sky and our barometer started to drop. We were worried that we'd lose the last of our northerly winds before we cleared the narrow southern mouth of the Red Sea. So, with both of us feeling rested, we set off into the hottest, most humid day we'd had so far.

At 1800 we picked up the light on Hamish Island, three hours before we should have. A southerly current was shoving us to freedom. The wind held, our current held, our fishing luck held. By evening, twelve days after leaving Queesam Island, we sailed past Perim Island with two knots of current, fifteen knots of following wind, and a five-pound kingfish hooked on our fishing line. I steamed its fillets on a bed of onions, then topped it with Bolognese sauce. Larry dug out a bottle of champagne we'd saved for just this moment, and I unearthed a can of Danish Brie. As we sped into the open waters of the Gulf of Aden, Larry helped me stand for a toast to the Red Sea and our release from the place that could be any voyager's nightmare.

CHAPTER 9

Aden

The dark glow of highly polished mahogany floors added to the cool comfort of the air-conditioned room. Lace curtains swayed to the hum of three blowers. Outside the second-story window, ships and bumboats seemed bleached out and wilted by the glaring desert sun. A white-robed servant slid quietly into the huge room and left a tray of iced lemonade and small hors d'oeuvres on the low table between Audrey and me. We'd spent most of the morning talking, moving quickly past the introductions, "where have you been"s, and "have you met"s, until now, two hours later, our conversation was deep into the personal problems of colonial life and every ex-patriot Englishman's desire to retire home, back to a quiet cottage somewhere in a green, insect-free land inhabited by English-speaking people.

Charles Watts came through the ten-foot-tall mahogany doorway just then, his only concession to the 105-degree heat outside, a broadcloth suit instead of a more formal wool one. "I've sent Larry for a cool shower before lunch. Imagine him working down in our machine shop right alongside the workmen. I'm sure we could have had someone here do the job, but Larry insisted. Quite clever with his hands, isn't he?"

When Larry arrived, we sat down at a polished table where a four-course lunch was carefully served on Worcester china. I had a hard time reconciling this scene with the reality of the deteriorating port of Aden.

It was just one day since we'd sailed into the protected waters behind the extinct volcano that forms the backdrop to one of the ugliest cities I've ever seen. Not one tree grew within sight of the waterfront. Gray-and-yellow concrete buildings seemed to be moulting; billboards advertising Coca-Cola seemed to be moulting; even the customs and immigration boat that came out almost immediately seemed to be shedding its skin of paint. The anchorage around us held two dozen foreign ships, three wearing the Soviet flag, the rest mainly oriental tramps from Hong Kong, Singapore, and Indonesia. I was surprised when we went ashore to find almost none of the ships' crews were taking advantage of a chance to stretch their legs and have some shore leave. Within two hours I understood the reason. There was absolutely nothing for the average crewman on shore. Shops carried a dull assortment of Arabic comic books, old suntan lotion, and pencils. The daytime heat seared the few lemonade stands; goats were the only things that moved on the streets, though I did see some heavily veiled women peering after us from inside their tiny, dark, concrete houses. The marketplace was almost deserted except for one man selling rice from fifty-pound bags and another selling bundles of weeds, which we later learned were a mild narcotic chewed by local people to ward off hunger. The only hotel in town had a faded-looking bar and restaurant on the top floor, where an acceptable lunch cost us twenty dollars. But we couldn't complain, since the air conditioning alone seemed worth the price. After dragging our lunch out for three hours, we could think of no more excuses to avoid thinking about the new sailing situation we'd been forced into by our decision to sail on toward Canada by way of the Far East.

Now we had to accept having our lives, our decisions, controlled by the seasons. No longer could we come into a port, sit back, and wait to see what developed. No longer could we wander from deserted anchorage to quiet village to city yacht club unaffected by any schedule other than a once-yearly haul-out that could happen any time it seemed convenient. Now we had to get moving if we wanted any chance of catching the last of the southwest monsoon for our 2,200-mile voyage to Sri Lanka. We had to sail hard if we wanted time to haul *Seraffyn* in Galle at the only shipyard we'd heard about that had a ways car between Rhodos and Singapore, yet still head across the Bay of Bengal before the typhoon season, in December and January. It was September 12 now. To cut our chances of meeting a typhoon, we had to sail 3,600 miles in two and a half months and haul the boat too. The vast differences between cruising as we'd done for the past nine years and voyaging as we'd now decided to do came home to us with a hammerlike blow as we sat at that restaurant table in Aden and forced ourselves to set a definite departure date only hours after we'd arrived. The departure date was Thursday morning, ready or not. "That gives us three days," Larry said. "You find any fresh stores you can, I'll find some way to fill our butane tank, and if I'm lucky, maybe there's a machine shop where I can have a couple of extra spinners made for our taffrail log." So, instead of trying to get to know Aden or meet local people, Larry headed off toward a BP sign he'd seen up the harbor, and I located the only ship's chandler in town.

I was absolutely amazed at the assortment of food I was offered by the agent. He took me into a warehouse full of English canned goods but couldn't sell me even one onion. He showed me cases of duty-free Scotch, sherry, and wine at a third their normal price but said he had no potatoes at all to offer. "Eggs?" he answered in a surprised voice. "Haven't seen any eggs here for almost four months. Not since the government ran out of foreign-exchange reserves. But I've got some excellent peanut butter from Sweden. We've still got a credit with them."

"What about the big ships? Where do they get onions, potatoes, fresh vegetables?" I asked.

"They are all angry at me too," the sweating chandler said. "But I still can't get them potatoes."

I headed back to *Seraffyn* after ordering some liquor, canned stores, frozen meat, one hundred pounds of ice, plus half a dozen five-pound watermelons. Then I decided to be bold and set off in *Rinky Dink* in the relative cool of late afternoon to approach each of the nearest cargo ships. At the first one, a Singaporean freighter, I was welcomed on board and taken to the captain's quarters. He called to his cook, who said, "I've got five pounds of onions left and only twenty eggs, but I can spare some cabbage." After thirty minutes I left with three cabbages plus an invitation to return to use the crew's washing machine and join an end-of-Ramadan party in two days. The Soviet ship I approached next seemed deserted. Finally a watchman came to the boarding ladder and waved me away. The British-owned Blue Funnel Line ship lying closest to *Seraffyn* gave a warmer welcome. "We'll be under way in an hour, but I'll get the purser for you," the second officer said. The purser shook his head at my request. "There are no fresh vegetables, no eggs to be had between Sri Lanka and Suez," he told me. "It's the same every summer. No way to store them in these depressed countries, no way to grow them in the heat. How long will you be at sea?" When I told him we estimated twenty to thirty days, he personally went into his cold-storage room and counted through a pitifully small barrel of onions. Then he got a sack and put twenty precious onions into it. "That's all I can spare. Sorry." He refused the money I offered and apologized for the lack of eggs in even his normally well-stocked freezers. "Chickens don't lay in the heat of summer, either," he said as he escorted me to the boarding ladder, where *Rinky Dink* was getting in the way of the pilot boat.

Larry had had far more luck than I. He'd gone directly to the British Petroleum compound and asked to see the manager. Instead of taking him to see the manager of the butane filling station, the Yemenite gate man escorted Larry to the office of the English manager of all British Petroleum operations in South Yemen. Charles Watts had been more than pleased by Larry's arrival. The advent of a militaristic, socialistic regime in South Yemen had caused a virtual collapse of the economy. This, coupled with the six-year-long closure of the Suez Canal, had convinced most shipping firms to send their vessels elsewhere for fuel. So, the once thriving BP refinery and refueling facilities were now operating at less than one-fourth capacity. The contingent of British employees was down to about thirty men and their wives. Two other yachts had stopped in Aden for a few days, since the French withdrawal from Djibouti had caused a warlike atmosphere there. But Larry was the first visiting foreigner to make his way to Charles's office in over a year. He came away with full assurances that our butane tank would be refilled even if a special adapter had to be custombuilt, an offer of the use of a very complete machine shop, plus an invitation to bring me over to have coffee with Charles's wife the next morning.

Our lunch with Audrey and Charles was an introduction to an important aspect of the Far East. In each country we later visited we met English advisors, foreign-service people, plantation managers, and their families. These "ex-pats," as they were called, lived in sometimes lonely splendor, isolated from the local people by the vast differences in their wealth, education, and customs. Although British colonial rule had supposedly disappeared years before, local people had not taken over the complex operations of oil refineries, iron mines, and tea and rubber plantations. English investors demanded English supervisors to oversee the use of their funds. So, in almost every port we visited, we met Englishmen eager for new faces, frustrated by their attempts at leading an English-style existence in the heat and humidity of the tropics, eager to return to the place they called home even after thirty or forty years in the Far East, yet worried that they wouldn't be able to maintain their present standard of living once they moved into England's inflation-ridden economy.

Audrey gave me Somerset Maugham's collected short stories about ex-pats living in the Far East. "He describes it all in there. The only thing that's changed is now we don't have the moral support of feeling we have a God-given right to be in charge."

Our third day in Aden, Audrey insisted on taking us for a tour of the area. There was little to see. The once spectacular English gardens were falling into ruins, since the main water pump that had drawn water from underground reservoirs 3,000 feet below the rocky landscape failed. Roads were in disrepair, and only a few people seemed to be moving even in the center of the volcano-shaded town. When we returned to join Charles for dinner, there was another guest, Nigel Davenport, the captain of BP's largest tugboat. "Ever since Audrey called, I've been asking around for eggs. If you stay until Saturday, one of the men up-country has two dozen he can spare. We'll all make a party if you come by, get out some of the good records, dance, barbecue . . ." There was a sad note of eagerness in this invitation, and at any other time in our lives we'd have changed our plans and probably been rewarded with a great round of parties and new friends. But our work list was cleaned up, and the invisible hand that pushes "voyagers" on their way was firmly at our backs. We invited our hosts and Nigel for cocktails on board *Seraffyn,* then spent our fourth and last day in South Yemen on board the Singaporean freighter *Brani Island.*

This tired old 8,000-ton steamship was a true tramp. One month *Brani Island* picked up coal from China to sell in Malaysia; the next, tea in Indonesia for transshipment at Singapore; then, construction equipment from Denmark to deliver to Saudi Arabia. Half the year it seemed to lie in Singapore's backwaters waiting, rusting, waiting. Now Saudi Arabia had purchased 8,000 tons of rice to give to the people of South Yemen as a gift and bribe so that the narrow entrance to the vital Red Sea would stay safe for navigation. South Yemen gladly accepted the gift but not only had no ships to send for the grain but also no warehouses to store the rice in, so the Saudis hired *Brani Island* to move it. Now the old ship was being used as a free storage shed and had been sitting in Aden for six weeks, her crew restless to get home, her captain four weeks beyond his retirement date. "If it weren't for the gunboats we'd just lift our anchors and leave. But these crazy people would shoot us out of the water and say we were stealing their rice. So here we sit, food supplies being depleted, crew unhappy, company losing five thousand dollars a day." We were having drinks in the captain's air-conditioned quarters when a crewman came running to say the ship's washing machine was acting up with our clothes in it. We hurried along the hot metal decks and saw a steady stream of soapy water flowing out from under the laundry-room door. The whole crew of *Brani Island* seemed to be jammed inside the tiny laundry, yelling advice to the chief engineer, who lay on the floor behind the misbehaving appliance. Their ribald comments and obvious joy at this break in their daily routine stressed, as nothing else could, the boredom of being stuck in a port like Aden.

When we began to hoist *Seraffyn*'s sails the next day, Audrey and Charles came out on the BP launch. "I've managed a small gift for you," Audrey said, handing me ten eggs in a padded basket. "Must you leave today? We could plan such a good party by Saturday."

But again we said we must be on our way. Our minds were set on the passage that lay ahead. The typhoon season loomed like a small, dark cloud on the horizon. As we cleared the first point, Nigel appeared at the helm of BP's tug. We heard his shouted orders, and four turbaned Yemenites directed a beautiful fanlike flow of water from the huge fire-fighting nozzles on *Habab II*'s upper deck. Long, mournful horn blasts cried farewell as the tug paraded majestically beside us. A light southerly wind kept *Seraffyn* moving away from the tragic remains of the once fabled steamship port at Aden.

Our sendoff from Aden.

CHAPTER 10

The Arabian Sea

Four years later, when we were in California remembering the passage we'd made between South Yemen and Sri Lanka, the first thing that came to mind was calms. "I've never felt so becalmed in my whole life," Larry commented. "It did seem as if that voyage took forever," I added. "Remember when I just up and quit?" But then we started looking through our tattered logbook. The days of calm faded away until we realized, during that 2,260-mile, thirty-six-day-long passage we were completely becalmed for only five days—days when our noon-to-noon runs showed gains only because a favorable current carried us toward our goal. I wrote down the daily noon-to-noon runs from that frustrating voyage, and the inconsistency is what struck us most, 106 miles one day, two the next, a week of ninety-mile days, then five of less than twenty. Instead of being able to settle into some sort of daily routine with watches regulated by meals and the chimes on our ship's bell, five frustrating weeks of our lives were dominated by constant sail changes, course changes, and wind shifts.

We had very little idea of what to expect as we set off to cross the Arabian Sea late in September. We later learned we were only the sixth yacht to head east from the Red Sea in almost ten years. Most cruising boats came the other way during the winter months; a few sailed south to the Seychelles later in the fall. But we could get no sailing suggestions from people who'd made the same passage we were setting out on now. We'd studied the pilot charts and sailing directions carefully. They showed medium to light winds at the end of the southwest monsoon. Gale percentages across this whole area were low in autumn, ranging from three possible days near Socotra to only one day per month near the Maldives. Well north of our planned course, each pilot chart showed a dotted line marked

ITCZ. We searched the notes and found "Intertropical Convergence Zone, the boundary between the high-pressure area of the two monsoons. Winds in this zone tend to be light and variable, especially as the northeast monsoon moves south in late October."

So, we reached innocently out of Aden, half expecting gale-force winds near Socotra but fair reaching breezes for the rest of a pleasant passage across the Arabian Sea.

We settled easily into our seagoing routine, Larry busy securing things on deck, I busy securing stores and equipment below. We'd sailed more than 42,000 miles with our CQR anchor hooked onto our bobstay ready to let go with a flick of the windless clutch. I especially liked this arrangement, since it meant neither of us had to lift the heavy anchor onto the deck. We kept our sail-handling area uncluttered this way, so that when it was time to set or reef a jib, there was one object fewer to stub toes on or catch the sail. But each time we set off on a more than one-day voyage, Larry would go forward and shove the anchor farther up the bobstay wire, so that its flukes were above *Seraffyn*'s normal bow wave. Then he'd secure a gasket around the anchor chain and the cathead on the windlass. The only way the anchor could get loose then was in the unlikely event that we broke off the bowsprit.

Soon I heard Larry getting our dinghy ready for sea. We carried the six-foot-eight-inch glass pram upside down on our cabin top. Its three-eighths-inch nylon painter was long enough to lash the dinghy to its chocks. To let it loose we'd have to take only one-half hitch off a cleat right next to the companionway. Now Larry was storing the oars, dinghy sail, rudder, daggerboard, and emergency kit inside the dinghy. This was our lifeboat. Foam sealed in each seat would keep it afloat even if it filled with water. A Dacron spray dodger folded into the emergency kit would give us shade. The fourteen-foot mast which was stored against the shrouds in a quick-release holder would support the radar reflector we kept in the dinghy. Although we both dreaded the thought of losing *Seraffyn* for any reason, we'd carefully considered the question of life rafts versus hard dinghies. In Malta we'd watched three people test their one-year-old life-raft cannisters only to find that the CO_2 containers didn't work or the life rafts didn't hold air. Then we'd heard the terrible story of a couple whose boat sank fifty miles north of Mallorca, Spain. Those two unfortunate people drifted helplessly in a life raft for twelve days within sight of the land while fish boats passed only a mile off, yet they couldn't propel themselves toward help or attract the attention of potential rescuers over the four-foot wind waves. We couldn't picture sitting passively waiting and praying for rescue. We wanted to be able to sail actively toward help. We also worried about putting our trust in some packer in his secure shoreside job, some manufacturer who never went to sea. The possibility that too little talcum powder inside that sealed cannister could cost us our lives seemed a risk we weren't willing to take.

As I listened to Larry finish lashing our emergency supplies inside our tender-cum-lifeboat, I was struck again by the difference between the emphasis put on emergency equipment by people who were just planning to set off cruising and by those who are actually out there. Before you set off, life rafts, EPIRB's, radios, man-overboard poles, medical kits seem to dominate your thoughts. Then you make a passage or two, and those items become just one more detail on a checklist that includes spare cotter pins, extra paperback books, candy bars and treats, tomatoes and onions. I don't think it's a matter of complacency; it's more the realization of what a small part of voyaging store-bought emergency equipment represents. Most sea stories are about sails that split, shrouds that should have been replaced, water tanks that leaked. If we felt that sinking was more than a one-in-ten-thousand chance, I doubt that most of us would be out there crossing oceans. So, almost as soon as Larry came below and announced, "Dinghy's all packed. Got any coffee left?" we both forgot about emergency equipment and got involved with the more immediate problem of planning our passage route.

A seven- to twelve-mile-a-day fair current lay only 300 miles ahead of us if we sailed through the passage between Socotra and the islands off Somalia. This route would also cut about one hundred miles off our voyage. The current was almost 600 miles away if we went north of Socotra. On the other hand, the sailing directions warned about unfriendly natives in this area, and Somalia was at war with Ethiopia. So we chose to head well north, clearing Socotra by at least fifty miles.

By our fifth day out we were glad we had. A southeasterly gale filled in and we could just lay our planned course with a triple-reefed main and staysail. If we'd decided to go south of Socotra, we'd have been forced to tack south against the current with an unhospitable shore only forty miles away from us.

The day-long gale shoved us out into the Indian Ocean, then left us completely and utterly becalmed. I've never seen the ocean fall so flat. In the heat of midafternoon we both climbed off the bowsprit to have a swim. I quickly tired of paddling around the bobstay trying to keep my hair from

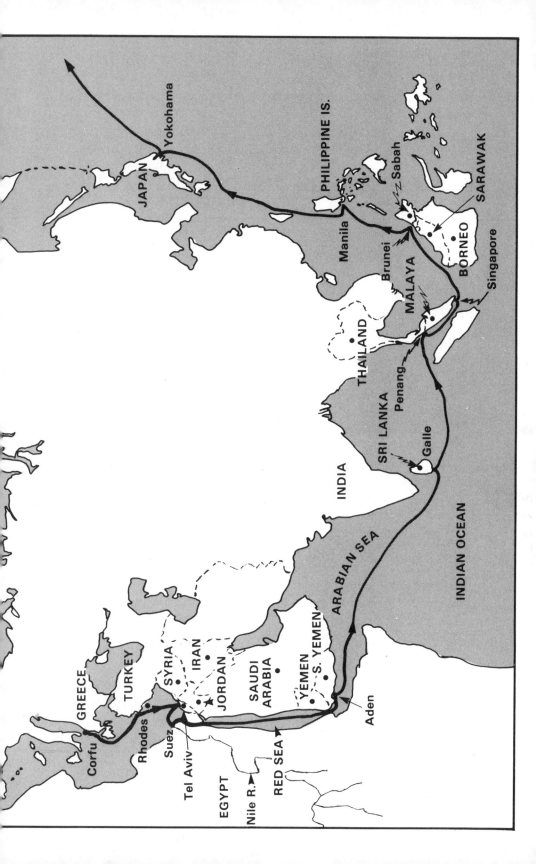

getting wet and salty, so I climbed back on board. Larry asked for our Nikonos underwater camera. I got it for him and he swam off a couple hundred yards to take a photo of *Seraffyn* sitting on the flat sea, her blue-and-white-striped nylon drifter barely moving. Then he handed me the camera and asked for his fins, mask, and a scrub brush. I lay on the cockpit cushion in the shelter of our small sun awning, my chin on the taffrail. The barnacles dislodged from *Seraffyn*'s bottom by Larry's scrubbing drifted slowly deeper and deeper in the crystal-clear water and turned from white to gray, then became specks a hundred feet below us as the blue of thousands of feet of water darkened into black. A slowly moving shadow caught my attention but for a few seconds I lazily ignored it. Then it registered in a terrifying flash. "Larry, Larry!" I called, trying not to panic. His snorkel came up close to me and I screamed at him, "Shark! Get out of the water, quick!" He'd already seen it and was swimming firmly but slowly toward the chain plates, trying not to make any splashes. He was just like a seal when he reached the handhold offered by those bronze straps —up and over the rail in seconds. The two of us stood on the stern mesmerized by the slow, undulating movement of that twenty-five-foot shark swimming in circles below us, investigating the barnacles which were still slowly drifting downward.

We'd been at sea eighteen days. For almost three weeks we'd worked to get the best speed we could from *Seraffyn,* adjusting the jib, setting the drifter wing and wing opposite the genoa whenever there was a following breeze, putting up our four-ounce 135 percent genoa and staysail for head winds. We'd changed sails so often that I'd started keeping a daily tally. Sometimes the number approached twenty-five even though we have an inventory of only six sails. I was down below, writing in our log, chuckling over the growing statistics, content as we skimmed along at three and a half knots. At that rate we'd beat our daily average of seventy-one miles noon to noon. On previous passages we'd come to expect 100 miles a day, but this one was definitely special. I heard a ping, not a loud ping, just the sound a tennis ball would make if it was lightly tossed against a barrel. Then Larry called, "Need your help, Lin." So I climbed on deck. Our drifter was gone. At first it looked as if it had disappeared. There was just a big, empty space out at the end of our bowsprit opposite the genoa on its pole. Then I saw the nylon 350-foot sail lying in the water alongside us, held by its sheet and the tack. "Halyard broke," Larry said, as we set to work hauling the soggy mass on board. "I should have relead the halyard when we gybed last time. Instead I let it lie across the head stay. Just chaffed through."

As soon as we got the sail on board, we set up the bosun's chair on the main halyard. The genoa kept us moving steadily across the low ocean swell, so it was easy to work on deck. Larry attached a safety line around his waist, then around the mast. He got another safety line ready to use when he got above the spreaders so that he'd be able to keep the first line secured as he tied the second one in place. Then he took part of the strain as I winched him up the mast. I secured the halyard around two separate cleats, just in case. Since the motion aloft wasn't too bad, he sewed a leather chafing guard on the headstay after he rerove the halyard.

When I let him down the mast thirty minutes later he said, "Guess we ruined our record." We'd worked hard to be able to say that in all of our voyaging we'd never had a gear failure. Several times we'd changed or replaced gear we didn't trust. In a few cases we'd inspected the rig and found worn shackles that could have let go during the next voyage. But this was the first time we'd been forced to make an at-sea repair. I think a large part of the credit goes to *Seraffyn*'s designer, Lyle Hess, who drew a boat that was easy on its gear. His engineering had helped us rig *Seraffyn* so that the strains were well spread. We'd also chosen to use the simplest gear possible, to eliminate gear failures. No roller furling, no wire reel winches, just simple, easy-to-inspect pawled winches, blocks, and tackles, solid cleats, and hand-spliced rigging wire.

I think it was after we'd finished fixing that halyard that we first noticed "the tail." We didn't see the whole fish during the four and a half days it spent under our boat. Its tail flickered just under the transom, the body hidden from our view and the hot sun by the shadows. We'd been dragging a fish line since we left Aden and never had a nibble. Our fresh meat was long gone, our diet down to canned and dried food, half an onion a day, an occasional watermelon, and a carefully rationed cabbage or cucumber salad plus fresh bread twice a week. So, catching that tail, which obviously belonged to ten or twenty pounds of tasty meat, became an obsession.

By that evening it became obvious that we'd sailed right into the ITCZ, the Indian Ocean's answer to the doldrums. Or, to be more accurate, the ITCZ had decided to move south over us a month earlier than normal. Our following breeze died out to nothing. Fantastic jumbles of cumulus cloud stood absolutely still all around the horizon, while the setting sun used them as props for a light-and-color show. The last of the southwesterly swell died away until the sea was flat, only occasionally disturbed by two- or three-inch ripples which could have been the fading wakes of the ships that passed 100 miles north of our course. For the first time during our passage, the heat made itself felt even after sunset, so we pulled our quarter-berth cushions out into the cockpit and lay together watching the stars creep past the edges of each cloud.

Sometime after midnight Larry woke up, and I felt him carefully pull his arm out from under my head. He checked the kerosene running lamps, shone the flashlight beam on our absolutely limp drifter, then looked over the taffrail to check our log. "Hasn't moved," he whispered when he saw I was awake. "That damn fish is still there. Tomorrow I'm going to catch him." Larry came back and lay down with me under the light cotton sheet. "Seems silly to keep a watch. Haven't seen a ship in two weeks. Shipping lanes are nowhere near us. Any breeze will wake us," he said and we slept through the night together.

Larry spent hours trying to lure that tail out from under *Seraffyn*'s stern. He cast our shiniest spinner. The fish dashed off so fast we couldn't really see it, looked the lure over, then dove. Five minutes later it was back under the boat. We dangled bits of canned bacon on a hook; no interest at all. Larry got out his spear gun and tried shooting from a prone position on the boomkin, but his shadow coaxed the three-foot-long fish closer to *Seraffyn*'s keel, so any shot would have gone right into our hull. I must admit I was almost in tears from laughing at Larry's antics. A cat's-paw of wind darkened the water behind us. "Larry, forget that damn fish. We've got wind," I called.

We rushed around setting the drifter, the mainsail. The mini-squall caught us with a fifteen-knot kick. *Seraffyn* burst ahead at five knots. Our visiting fish streaked after a flying fish sent off by our bow wave. The wind started backing; we sheeted the sails in for a beam reach. Still the wind crept forward. "Drop the drifter," Larry said. "I'll put up the genoa." We hauled the genoa up. I sheeted it in; Larry bagged the drifter. The wind disappeared completely, and all around us the ripples on the water flattened out. Fifteen minutes after I'd seen that first cat's-paw, we were again absolutely becalmed. The tail was back in position under our stern, and the horizon was still decorated with majestic jumbles of cumulus cloud standing absolutely still.

Every two or three hours another mini-squall tantalized us. Every time, it was the same routine. Rush to set sails, sheet them in as the breeze clocked. Watch that damn tail streak off after a flying fish, feel *Seraffyn* die in the water as our wind laughed and quit. This went on for five days. We slept in the cockpit just in case a breeze sprang up at night. We tried to trap that damn fish, and I began to worry about water. We'd left Aden with forty-five gallons of slightly brackish water on board, the only water we could find. That was about two gallons per hundred miles, more than sufficient for a normal passage when we considered that Larry and I got along well on a gallon and a half a day including a wipe-down with one quart every evening. But now we had only eighteen gallons left and a thousand miles to go; and our last daily runs had been seventeen miles, thirteen miles, sixteen miles, with over half due to current. I decided we'd better ration down to one quart per person per day plus a quart of soft drinks, juices, and beer. We dug out two plastic jugs and set the day's limit on the stove.

The more difficult sailing situations become, the harder Larry works. Now he began to anticipate each mini-squall long before it reached us. "Even if we only move an extra two miles, we could reach another wind system a day sooner," he told me as he pumped on the rudder to keep *Seraffyn*'s bow up to a beam reach.

My reaction to the same situation was anger. After two days of chasing around after those fickle winds, I just quit, went below, and started sewing, writing, answering letters, and pouting. "Come on, Lin," Larry said, at first trying to coax me into a better mood. "Just think of the poor square-rig sailors. Everytime there was a situation like this they had to reposition every yard on the ship. They couldn't move the ship to meet the wind just by pumping on the tiller. They had to lower the launches and tow the ship into position. And they did it, because their captains had to keep those ships moving!" But I stayed below, plowing through paperback books, trying to invent new menus, baking cookies despite the heat. Only at night. did I come out of my sulk to lie with Larry and listen to our stereo or talk about the plot for a novel that might be fun to write when we were landlocked somewhere, some day.

I'm surprised and grateful now at Larry's quiet acceptance of my sulky attitude. Apart from once saying, "If you'd come out of that cabin and do something to help us get sailing, we might find a new wind," he just let me be. And I did come out only to use the rail, check and see if that damned fish tail was still there, then go below again.

I can't remember if either of us mentioned wishing we had an engine during those frustrating days. I don't think it ever crossed our minds. If it had, something we learned when we reached Sri Lanka would have canceled the thought completely. Don Windsor, who greets visiting cruising sailors in Galle, kept a scrapbook and record of each arrival and their passage times. The other five yachts that made this same voyage during the ten-year period his records covered had also chosen September or October because of the wind patterns in the Red Sea. Each one had an engine. None beat our time of thirty-six days. One took fifty-eight days; another fifty-three; the fastest, forty-six. Don recalled how each of them arrived with maybe a gallon of fuel left. "There just aren't many sailboats that carry enough fuel for 2,300 miles," Larry concluded. "So they probably powered on days when they were moving only two knots. Then they ran out of fuel and didn't have the light-air sails to keep them moving when the winds got even lighter." Because we planned to sail *Seraffyn*, we'd had her designed with a maximum rig. We had extra-light wind sails and learned to use them. I often wonder if we'd have done the same if we'd installed an inboard engine. Or would we have become lazy and expected to power through light wind patches only to be trapped when the calms filled in and lasted longer than our fuel supply?

In retrospect we see that all six of us sailors who signed Don's book made a basic error in our voyage plan. Since there is little firsthand information available from voyagers down the Red Sea and eastward across the Indian Ocean, we all used the pilot charts and chose to have almost guaranteed fair winds down the last half of the Red Sea, then avoid the high gale percentages shown near Socotra during August. I know I personally was spooked by the threat of ten days of gale-force winds per month. But a southwesterly gale would have been easier to ride out than these calms, especially since those percentages were only for a very limited sea area. If we'd come through the Suez Canal a month earlier we might have had some head winds in the southern Red Sea, but we'd have found much better conditions as we made the long passage across to Sri Lanka.

After three days I got tired of my blue funk, walked into the cockpit after breakfast, and announced, "I'm back. I'll take the next four hours." Larry looked up from where he was watching that tail flickering under our stern. His smile was fleeting but delightful. "I've got to try one last thing," he said. "Since you're back, I'm going to put on my snorkel and climb overboard quietly and try to sneak up on that fish. You keep a watch for sharks. Okay?"

We tiptoed around the deck, trying not to transmit our plan to the enemy cruising just four feet below us. Larry slid quietly over the bow as *Seraffyn* lay absolutely still in the water. I handed him his spear gun cocked

Some Arabian Sea visitors.

and ready to fire, then tiptoed aft to report in a whisper, "Tail's still there!" Larry swam slowly toward our stern. That curious fish swam right at Larry until they were eye to eye, only inches apart. I tried to hold back a scream as I saw the complete, beautiful, silver, gold, and royal blue body of a twenty-pound mahimahi for the first time. Larry had to back paddle to get enough distance between himself and the fish to raise his spear gun and fire. He didn't try any fancy shots. He aimed dead center at that swimming fillet and nailed him, grabbed the two-and-a-half-foot-long spear, and passed it with the impaled, struggling fish to me. "Hold him, Lin," he called. "He won't hurt you; just don't let go."

"Don't leave me alone with him!" I shrieked.

Larry was on board in seconds. He stalked back to where the flapping fish and I stood on the side deck and took two whacks with the bronze winch handle. The mahimahi lay still in our scuppers. At first I felt regret at killing such a beautiful creature. Larry had a mist of tears in his eyes as the brilliant stripes of the magnificent fish faded from royal blue to silver, then dead gray. But that lasted only minutes. I rushed for the fish knife, steel, and cutting board. Larry set to work carving off four large fillets. We put every other chunk of meat into ten glass peanut-butter jars and filled them with vinegar, olive oil, and spices for a fine seviche that we enjoyed for over a month. I remember the rest of that day as a feast of fresh sautéed mahimahi, baked potatoes, canned butter, white wine, close companionship, and shared dreams. Yet each time a mini-squall came up we both jumped to catch it.

For the first time in five days we set watches. I drew the twelve to three and did catch one puff of wind that gave us an extra mile. Maybe it was the overly replete feeling, maybe the mystique of the Orient, maybe the spirit of the fish that had been our tormenter and our dinner, but a strange, persistent set of thoughts kept filling my mind. I finally wrote in our log book:

October 9th, 0100
1. There will be a definite change in the weather within 19 hours.
2. We will reach Galle just after midday on October 21st.
3. Our mail package will contain one letter that surprises and disturbs us but doesn't directly affect us.

I didn't show the log to Larry. He rarely reads it unless he is looking for information like the date of the last time we painted the bottom or varnished the mast. In fact, our log is really more a personal journal than a ship's record, since we pencil course changes, barometer readings, and other important information right onto our chart.

At noon I got out our two quart bottles and refilled them from the diminishing supply in our last water tank. Larry seemed delighted with his noon sight, which showed that our extra work had gained us twenty-three miles instead of the usual sixteen.

The once-every-two-hours mini-squalls continued through most of the day, but at 1600 one actually moved a cloud with it. I couldn't believe my eyes as drops of rain started to fall on deck. I ran for our big bucket to catch the stream that fell from our tiny cockpit awning, while Larry sheeted the sails to grab another couple of miles toward Sri Lanka. The bucket filled completely; then my big stew pot filled up too. In ten minutes the squall left with the wind, but we had four beautiful gallons of fresh, sweet water. Like kids we splurged and put only half of the water in our tanks, then used the other half to finish the rinse-off that the squall had started. I sudsed my long hair in Larry's rinse water, then scrubbed all over and ran the luxurious gallon of fresh water over my head, down my clean body, and into the big wash basin we used as a catcher, time and again.

Then, wonder of wonders, just as we cleared away dinner and lit the oil lamps, a real wind filled in from the north. We rushed to set sail, prepared for another round of sheeting in and then losing the breeze. But the wind didn't quit. *Seraffyn* roared across the empty sea, her wake glowing green with phosphorescence. The taffrail log began humming at five and a half knots. "It feels like we're flying low, not sailing," I said as I cuddled against Larry's side until another rain squall set us to work filling our water tanks. I wanted to show Larry the predictions I'd written in the logbook, but then I worried that the wind would feel I'd cheated and leave us. Later, when we were still making day's runs of seventy to eighty miles, I mentioned my midnight scribblings to him, but he said, "Show me when we get there."

Twelve days later when we anchored in Galle harbor at 1400 on October 21, I got out the logbook and had him read it. Larry was shocked. "I was sure we'd be in last night. But the current and those fickle winds, just couldn't beat against them," he said. I'd been glad the current kept us from entering Galle after dark, since our daytime entry showed that several important buoys had been shifted from the charted position. But I was also a bit concerned about the accuracy of those predictions, especially four days later, when we got our mail package.

We were both reading eagerly through a stack of fifty letters when Larry said, "This is it! The one you said would be here." I listened as he read aloud; one of our favorite sailing friends, a person who was known for his careful seamanship and his love of the old wooden boat he cruised on, had decided to run on toward Fiji rather than heave to in a force-seven wind with poor visibility and rain squalls, even though he'd had no sights for four days. He'd picked up one beacon on his radio direction finder but couldn't find a cross bearing. He'd run onto a reef and lost the boat and everything he owned except for his hard dinghy, which survived the rough ride across the coral and carried him and his crew to the safety of a small sand island inside the reef. When the squall cleared, he found he was only a quarter mile from the lighthouse he'd gotten his radio bearing on. A current had sent him twenty miles off over four days of running.

Yes, the letter was surprising and disturbing. It reminded us of the countless decisions you make at sea that could change your whole life. The letter didn't directly affect us, but both of us found it hard to shrug off the accuracy of those three predictions—especially as they became reinforced by events that followed us through the mystical Far East.

CHAPTER 11

Green and Friendly

I doubt we'll ever again encounter a contrast as shocking as the one we found when we sailed out of the Middle East and finally reached the Orient. Color was the first thing that hit us. Where Egypt and Aden had presented a facade of grays and faded browns, Sri Lanka glared almost garishly from under a cloak of green and oranges, reds and yellows. Palms crowded the skies, flowering trees dropped fragrant blossoms along the roadside, houses sported deep blue paint, and bright white trim. Even the clothes of the poorest people glowed with color.

The sounds were different, too—alive, vibrant. Parrots squawked and called through the trees, chased by chattering monkeys and apes, which were as common here as squirrels along the roadsides of Virginia. Fishermen chanted as they hauled their nets up onto the beach. Radios played soft sitar music that sounded sweet to our ears after the wail of Arabic dirges.

Then there was the casual attitude of the few officials we had to deal with. Instead of arms and military trappings, they wore haphazard uniforms and relaxed expressions. We never saw a gun, only billy sticks, a legacy of Sri Lanka's long English domination. We'd arrived on a Friday, when the pilot book indicated that customs and immigration offices were closed. When we rowed ashore and walked to the customs post shown on our chart, the two men who were drinking soda from bottles offered us a sip, then used their lilting English to explain, "You are not supposed to come ashore today. But you probably want something, so walk to that third house and ask for Don Windsor. As long as you return within two hours and don't go anywhere else, we'll pretend you followed the rules."

Don Windsor himself was a part of the contrast we felt. "Welcome,

Don and Prima Windsor, the yachtsmen's hosts.

welcome," he called with a huge grin and outspread arms. "You must be L. and L. Pardey, captains of the *Seraffyn*. Your mail is safe in Sri Lanka. My home is open to you!"

We'd read about Don Windsor in the Port Said Yacht Club scrapbook. Cruising sailors who'd stopped in Galle all said, "Use Don's address for mail." Three or four had wondered in print what Don was up to with his hospitality and apparently free assistance. One had felt that Don didn't steer him right on the purchase of some gemstones. The uninformed sailor had expected to make a lot of money buying in Sri Lanka, selling in Europe. But he'd found he only got his money back from the eventual sale of the gems he knew so little about. From the first, I liked and trusted this dark-skinned, smiling man in his vivid African shirts, cotton sarong, and bare feet. I could understand his scam. He just loved the interruption of foreign visitors in this very quiet, out-of-the-way harbor. His life was easy, as he was the son of a wealthy merchant family. Twenty servants waited on his needs; his gem-finishing factory ran smoothly, with or without his help. So, Don's hobby was entertaining the crews of the twenty or so yachts that sailed into Galle each year. If he did make a bit of money from the deals he arranged for yachtsmen, I didn't care, because every time he offered to purchase or arrange something for us, we ended up paying less than we would have on our own.

Don had known our name because visitors were rare at this time of the year. Our mail package was waiting at the customs house in Colombo, according to the sheet Don handed us. "In two days I will put you on the train to the capital," Don said. "But right now you must want some fresh food, since you have just come from the sea. The shops are closed, but Prima will find something for you!" He whispered to one of the servants who always seemed to be nearby, and minutes later an elegant, dark-eyed woman glided out onto the veranda in a silver-edged, glowing pink silk sari. Prima seemed the shy opposite of her husband as she listened to his list of suggested ingredients for the dinner we would eat on board *Seraffyn* that night. But as I came to know Prima, I found that her shyness was only the expected deference of a Sri Lankan wife in public. We later spent an afternoon giggling and gossiping in the back of the rambling Windsor house while Prima showed off her favorite saris and taught me how to wrap myself in seven yards of gauzy fabric held only by one simple pin at the shoulder.

We left Don's house carrying a double rattan basket laden with fresh eggs, tomatoes, green peppers, sausage, and tiny ripe bananas as Don called, "Don't worry, you can pay me in a day or two or three, it doesn't matter!"

Rain started to pelt down as we rowed toward *Seraffyn*. That's why we ignored the rule we'd learned years ago in Central and South America. Instead of taking the food out before we boarded and leaving Prima's basket in the dinghy, we rushed below with the whole lot and pulled the companionway cover closed behind us. We were laughing and chattering about Don, the rain, and the casual officials, as Larry lit the oil lamps and I pulled the fresh, fragrant food out of the purselike carrying basket. Poor Larry almost hit the cabin top when I let out a shriek. "Spider, it's huge, kill it, kill it!" I screamed. The three-inch-wide hairy monster had run out of the basket, across my hand, over the counter, and across the quarter-berth cushion, then disappeared behind the ceiling. Cushions, bunk boards, cans, packages of noodles came flying at me as Larry rushed in pursuit. "Get me something to kill it with!" Larry shouted. I reached into the utensil box and handed him a wooden salad-mixing spoon, then tried to stand clear. The squish that huge spider made when Larry trapped it almost turned my stomach. When he finished wiping its gooey remains off the planking and two cans of juice with paper towels, Larry said, "Welcome back to the tropics."

The sari-draped health official who arrived the next day with six other customs and immigration officers said it too. "Your typhoid and smallpox shots are up-to-date, but you must have a cholera shot if you wish to visit any other country when you leave here." So, when the voluminous but simple paperwork was finished we got out two of the disposable sterile hypodermic syringes we carried in our medical kit and found her office. She used our syringes and charged us only two dollars for the injections. It's well worth carrying a dozen of these inexpensive syringes as you travel. We've seen Mexican doctors administer shots to three different people without changing or cleaning their needle. Here in Galle, the health official owned only three syringes and needles. Hepatitis is only one of the possible diseases that can be transferred by a contaminated syringe.

When we rode the rickety old steam-driven train for the two-hour trek into Colombo to claim our mail pack the next day, the overgrown jungles and carefully laid-out tea and banana plantations were a feast to our eyes. Dark-skinned, slender women bathed half-nude in streams two hundred feet from the train tracks; thirty children ignored their books and turned to watch us from their thatch-roofed, open-sided schoolroom. Then we burst free of the junglelike vegetation and out into the bright sunlight of a clear white-sand beach that ran for miles. The indigo of the Indian Ocean washed lazily at the sand; dugout canoes lay awkwardly on the beach, their double outriggers looking like spider legs.

The congested, noisy train station at Colombo was almost enough to turn us back on our tracks. But the first mail package in three months bribed us into facing the swarming foot traffic, honking taxis, begging children, heat, and confusion. In the stuffy customs house we soon learned that no foreign packages can be sent beyond these carefully barricaded desks without proper clearance. We could have hired an agent in Galle to save us the trip in; it would have cost only about five dollars. But, in our case, it was fortunate we didn't. The customs officials wanted to charge us two dollars duty on each magazine in our package, five dollars for each box of developed slides. The total bill would have been close to fifty dollars. As we read the regulations the official pointed out in his huge book, it looked as if we were going to have to pay, since he couldn't release just a part of the package. But then we proved we were foreign journalists by finding a check from one of the English magazines we wrote for. That put a different complexion on the whole matter. Now, these magazines and slides were tools of our trade, not items to be sneaked into Sri Lanka and sold for a profit. The customs official in charge of local morals checked each picture in each magazine, then each of the 144 slides, and bundled everything together, then handed it over.

If you visit Sri Lanka, we'd suggest having letters packaged separate from any other items. They will clear customs without being stopped. But from our experience and others we've heard of since, it would be difficult to try and receive any parts or equipment there.

We spent the afternoon visiting the shops of Colombo. I was disappointed to find almost no canned food at all. Peanut butter, rubberlike canned processed cheese—that was it. Larry had more luck in the back-street bazaars, where he found wicks and chimneys for our oil lamps, new fishing lures, and braided line for our taffrail log.

The last train to Galle headed slowly south just at dark. A tropical deluge spattered on us through the broken windowpanes. A washed-out crossing kept us waiting three hours. But the protective net that Don Windsor spread over his sailing friends covered us when we arrived, cold and tired, four hours late, in Galle. Don's driver was waiting for us and drove us through the pouring-rain right to the edge of the harbor, where our upside-down dinghy was sitting waiting on the pier.

The warm hospitality, the easygoing officials, the very low prices we found in Sri Lanka made us almost change our plans. We'd met the owner of the 300-year-old New Oriental Hotel when we ate dinner in the building that had once been the barracks for the Dutch East Indies company. Nesta Brohier urged us, "Stay, I'll take you touring. My friends up-country would love to have guests. There's so much excitement in the air, now we've gotten rid of the Socialist government and Sri Lanka can start rebuilding." This lovely woman, who was a quarter Sri Lankan, three-quarters English, tried all of her wiles to get us to linger. She invited us to watch the fakirs and fire dancers exorcise an evil spirit from her hotel lobby; she planned afternoon rides into the nearby hills, where the son of one of the largest tea-growing families mournfully showed us the damage done by neglect to the country's main export crop when an ill-informed, idealistic Socialist government nationalized all of the tea plantations. "Four years later they ask me to come back and fix everything up. They say the land is mine again. But what about the rare hybrid tea plants my father and I worked to nurture for over fifty years? Those were the backbone of our prime tea crops. They are all dead now, and I can't undo that overnight."

Don Windsor tried to slow down our rush to reprovision, then move on. He organized a picnic and packed us into his old VW van along with four children, two servants, Prima, and a huge food hamper, then drove along the coast to one of the most perfect, palm-edged, reef-fringed beaches I've ever seen. "Stay and sail inside the reefs. Then take a trip up into the mountains near Candi. That's the most wonderful part of our country. I've got relatives there who will help you explore the old temples, the wonderful gardens. They grow strawberries in Candi, the best in the world."

And we were tempted. We got out the trusty *Ocean Passages,* reread the weather section of the Indian Ocean sailing directions. "If we don't leave in two weeks, we'll have to stay around for five months," Larry said. "Then we'd have to wait almost a whole year before we can sail across to Canada."

I listed the things we could do for the next year: explore the reefs and bays along Sri Lanka's east coast, get a cruising permit for Indonesia and sail to Sumatra, Bali, Timor. "We could even change our minds and go to Australia instead of home." But the word "home" held the key to the voyager's syndrome that had us in its grip. Home: friends and family we hadn't seen in nine years, the place where everything would seem familiar and we could relax and forget about local customs and language problems. "Wouldn't it be nice to be able to communicate with everyone we met just for a little while?" Larry asked. In the back of our minds lurked the dream of turning the drawings that lay folded under our quarter-berth cushion into the dream ship we wanted to build some day, to try out the ideas we'd come up with during our cruising on *Seraffyn*, our visits to dozens of yacht-building yards in European countries. So, after an evening of hesitation we shoved our cruising instincts to the back of our minds and set to work making Sri Lanka what it really was, a pit stop on our way to Canada. We had fourteen days to go over our work list, buy what fresh stores we could find, and still try to enjoy the delights of Galle.

That's when we became even more convinced that whatever we changed on the boat we'd build someday, we'd never give up the simplicity we had on *Seraffyn*. Our work list after two long voyages included only:

Scrub and antifoul the bottom—extremely important;
Paint bulwarks and bowsprit—not too important;
Regold leaf name on transom—cosmetic only;
Repair radio receiver—would be nice;
Find or make new burner stems for oil lamps—not too important.

Don Windsor introduced us to a diminutive radio repairman in a five-foot-by-five-foot cluttered cubbyhole in the main marketplace. Hundreds of old radios dangled from every spot on his walls; wires, tubes, transistors littered his workbench, where the only tools we could see were pliers, screwdrivers, and a tiny voltmeter. "I can fix any radio. I make my own spare parts," the repairman said in a shy voice, swaying his head back and forth in the Sri Lankan nod that meant yes. We didn't have as much faith as he did. We'd been told in Malta that the salt-air corrosion in our Zenith transoceanic radio was like a malignant cancer. During twelve years and maybe 60,000 miles of life on *Seraffyn* and on each boat we delivered, that radio had gone through hell. It had accidentally been half submerged in saltwater, tossed across a boat. If the corrosion on its outer casing was any indication of its internal state, it's a wonder it worked as long as it had. We had two almost new quartz watches with exceptionally constant rates that we used for navigation time, so we didn't absolutely need that radio. But we did miss our BBC news broadcast, VOA classical, and country music schedule; we even missed the outrageously extravagant propaganda broadcast by Radio Moscow. So, we were thrilled when our trusty old radio came back working perfectly. "I had to rewind the speaker and

At the main market
in Galle.

rewire the antennae," the repairman explained modestly. "Is five dollars too much for that?" We later learned that this very delicate job was usually attempted only in well-equipped, sophisticated electronics plants. But the repairman told us, "In Sri Lanka there is a 200 percent duty on radios and parts. So I have to be able to fix anything."

When we had *Seraffyn* safely hauled at the fishing co-op shipyard, the poverty of the average people in Sri Lanka came home to us even more strongly. Unemployment was running at close to 60 percent in most parts of the country, so we were able to hire a hardworking family man for two dollars a day to help scrub the bottom, sand, and run errands while Larry checked the through-hull fittings, put new nylon bushings on the gudgeons and pintles, then did the final paint work with supplies we carried on board. Meanwhile I carefully sanded the carved-in lettering on *Seraffyn*'s transom, primed, then laid in the gold leaf. When we were finished I offered our hired hand two used cotton shirts that were a bit small for Larry. He became almost ecstatic. He offered to work the rest of the week for free, especially if we'd let him take the cotton rags we tossed away after cleaning our paintbrushes. When we insisted on paying for all of his work, we found we'd earned a daily supply of yellow drinking coconuts, fresh pineapples, and the beautiful but tasteless local star fruits.

There were two other cruising yachts lying in Galle while we were there. Both had arrived well before us. One, a forty-year-old cutter, was being restored by her owner. The thirty-five-foot classic wooden boat had been purchased in Singapore and was headed eventually for the Med. We became friends with Eric Hansen, one of her crew, and his bimonthly letters kept us abreast of *Joya*'s progress. At first the letters told of crew problems, a favorable passage across the Arabian Sea, then official hassles in Aden. Eric's last letter came from his home in San Francisco and told of the abrupt end of *Joya*'s sailing life, five months after we left Sri Lanka. "We got blasted into the Red Sea on a southerly gale. Most of the crew turned seasick. The skipper and I got too tired to carry on, so we went in to anchor at a deserted island just fifteen miles away from the main port of North Yemen. Unfortunately we chose the wrong spot, too many coral heads and not enough dragging room. The anchor dragged; we couldn't row it back out with the rubber dinghy. So *Joya* ended up a loss on the beach. That's when the problems started. We couldn't get any ships to stop. We could see dozens passing each day. We even dismantled the solar-powered lighthouse on the tip of the island and used that to signal. Some ships returned our signals, but no one stopped. Finally, two weeks later, a dhow from Ethiopia got blown off course. It was loaded with goats, and the skipper stopped at our island to feed them. We bribed him into taking us to North Yemen. Turned out we were wrecked on a militarily sensitive island. Even though people on shore had seen our signals, they were afraid to come out to see what was happening."

The other yacht, *Crusader,* a twelve-year-old Canadian-built inland racer, seemed an odd choice for offshore cruising. Her lightly built hull was already leaking near the garboards just above her fin keel. Her huge mahogany doghouse, with two-foot-high, three-foot-long glass windows on three sides, was weakly constructed. If it was washed off in a seaway there would be a nine-foot-by-twenty-foot gap exposed to the seas. Her new owner, Don Sorte, a retired deep-sea, hard-hat diver who we later learned was known for his devil-may-care attitude, shrugged off the fears of his pay-your-own-way pick-up crew. "Sure, the spreaders are rotten," he said. "But I can get that fixed when I check the keel bolts back in Singapore. Never any strong winds between here and there. Besides, I carry enough fuel to power all the way to Thailand. And I'm in touch with the ham net twice a day if something does happen." Judy Vaughn, who'd left her husband in the Seychelles to sail onward with *Crusader,* commented, "Don is pretty casual about sailing and navigation. Doesn't take sights until a day or so before he makes his landfall." We both sensed her concern and I suggested that Larry talk to Don.

Fortunately, a chance comment when we met Don Sorte at the dinghy landing led to an afternoon of going over the *Ocean Passages for the World*'s suggested sailing route in *Crusader*'s spacious main cabin. "The book's suggestion that we swing south to about three degrees north latitude before we cross the Bay of Bengal makes sense. Almost no typhoon tracks that low at any time of the year," Larry said. Don agreed with that at the time. But we both remember feeling a bit uncomfortable when *Crusader* powered out of Galle two days ahead of us with Don, Judy, and a crew of four twenty- to twenty-three-year-old wanderers who'd each paid $200 for a chance to sail from Sri Lanka to Thailand.

When we set sail, our canned-stores lockers had little more in them than the day we'd sailed in. But the settee lockers were crammed with eggs, melons, onions, and limes. The ice box held ten pounds of assorted fresh meat and fish. Better yet, Don Windsor and Nesta Brohier had traded with us, and our paperback-book collection glowed with new titles.

Seraffyn slid clear of Galle with a perfectly smooth bottom, shining new topside paint, and her name and calling port glowing gold across the transom. A report of no disturbances from the radio tower at Colombo's airport, plus a high barometer and steady north wind, made us feel sure we'd caught the beginning of the northeast monsoon season for a comfortable dash across the infamous Bay of Bengal.

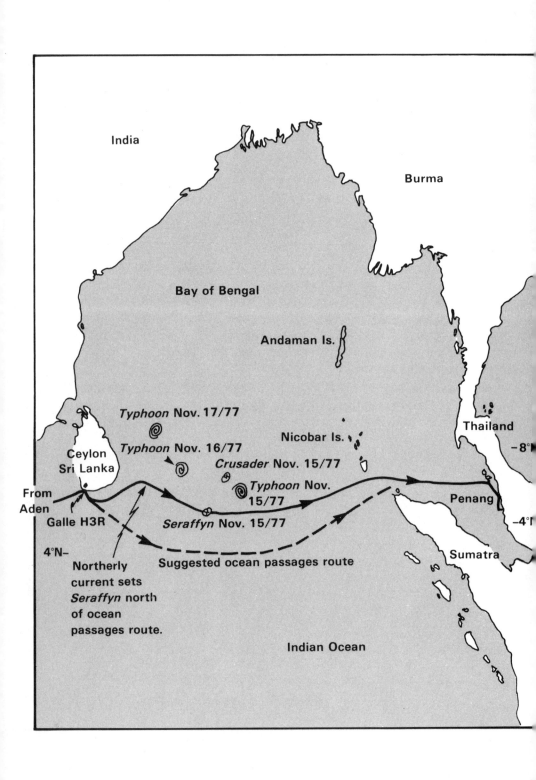

India

Burma

Bay of Bengal

Andaman Is.

Typhoon Nov. 17/77

Typhoon Nov. 16/77

Nicobar Is.

Thailand

Ceylon
Sri Lanka

Crusader Nov. 15/77

–8°

From
Aden

Typhoon Nov. 15/77

Penang

Galle H3R

Seraffyn Nov. 15/77

–4°

4°N–

Suggested ocean passages route

Sumatra

Northerly
current sets
Seraffyn north
of ocean
passages route.

Indian Ocean

CHAPTER 12

~~~~~~

Typhoon

"Wonder if the shipping routes shown on our pilot chart are wrong," I asked Larry our fourth night out of Galle, Sri Lanka. "I was thinking the same thing," he answered. "I saw three ships on my last watch. How many did you count?"

I'd seen the lights of four freighters on the horizon to the north of us as we reached along on an easterly course.

We'd headed southeast for the first three days of this voyage; our goal, three degrees north latitude, the normal lower limit of the typhoon zone. When our log reading and DR track showed we'd reached this point, we changed course to head directly east for six hundred miles before working northeast into the Andaman Sea. We'd had cloudy skies for two days, so when our first sight this fourth morning out made no sense, we waited anxiously for our noon sight, while we both went over Larry's navigation figures trying to find some mistake in the arithmetic. The noon sight seemed so out of whack that we wanted to ignore it. "We couldn't possibly be a hundred ten miles north of our course" was Larry's grumbled comment as he rechecked his figures and read the sextant again. Then I reminded him of the ships we'd seen. They should have been at least a hundred miles north of us. "If some sort of current was setting us north . . ."

"Can't be a two-and-a-half-knot current," Larry stated. "Pilot charts show a southeasterly current coming out of the Bay of Bengal at this time of the year!"

But our first afternoon sight made sense only if we accepted our noon sight. That started us worrying. "If something has caused a current that strong, it must be a pretty big disturbance," Larry said. "Let's get headed south again." We tightened in our sheets until we were sailing on a close reach forty-five degrees away from our rhumb-line course. Within a few hours the last ship dropped below the horizon astern of us. Then we got the second sign.

A long, slow swell began to interrupt the steady pattern of the seas that came rolling toward us. Along with the normal wind waves, this rolling surge added an awkward motion to our five-knot charge into the sea. I got out our stopwatch and counted the seconds between each crest of these obviously different swells. Four swells passed each minute instead of the more normal eight or ten. Their unusually slow spacing began to add to our certainty. There was a big weather disturbance somewhere ahead of us! Then the barometer needle moved more than one millibar from the spot it seemed to have settled in over the past three weeks. Each hour it dropped another notch, moving slowly from 1008 to 1007 and down to 1000. Each drop was accompanied by another hint at the winds that lay somewhere ahead and slightly to the east of us. Fine mare's tails began to lace the sky above us, radiating from the east, causing the sun to glow yellow and milky. Then the humidity began to increase until we shed all of our clothes to try and be comfortable even during the night. The second day after we'd discovered the strange north-moving current, our winds began to get squally.

Two of our working sails, the main and lapper, were now over three years old. We'd had to patch a few holes already. The lower panels of the mainsail were pretty tender from the burning ultraviolet rays of the sun. In Sri Lanka we'd sent letters off to sailmakers in England and Hong Kong, asking for price quotes on new sails. Our plan was to have them built and shipped to us in Singapore for our April departure up the China Sea. So, when our lapper developed a split eleven feet long just at the reef points, we weren't too shocked. But as Larry set to work taking a long line of herringbone stitches while I helped hold the fabric in place, this sail failure added to my apprehensions. We sat wedged against the dinghy on the cabin top, working on that sail for three hours as the ominous swell grew ever more apparent. *Typhoon.* The word loomed ever larger in my mind. I tried talking out my fears, but after two days of gradually increasing signs, of reading every word we could find in our limited shipboard library about tropical disturbances and the best way to handle them, there just wasn't anything left to say. "The boat's as ready as she'll ever be. From the information we have now, we're on the right tack. If we keep trying to get south and east, it's the best we can do," Larry said, as we finished patching the aging sail. "I've got the sea anchor where I can get at it easily. You've got bread and fruit ready in case you can't cook up anything else. It might pay to make some soup up after dinner, just to have something extra. Other than that, it's just wait and see. Might already be past us."

By the time the lapper was patched, our wind had steadied at twenty knots from the east-northeast, so we stowed the sail below and continued romping on with our staysail and single reefed main as dark settled in.

Then the mare's tails thickened into rolls of gray cumulus. I'd seen clouds like these one time before. They'd crept over us as we lay at anchor in the Chesapeake Bay and got whipped by Hurricane Agnes. So, I anxiously tapped the barometer while Larry trimmed and lit the oil lamps. The needle steadied at 999 millibars. Not very low, when I considered the barometer readings we'd had in the Chesapeake. That time we'd had pressures as low as 987.

"You've got to stop worrying this storm in," Larry said through a mouthful of fish cakes. "Best thing you can do is get some sleep. If you're well rested, you'll be far better off if something does hit us." So I climbed into the bunk and, in spite of the stuffy heat in the closed-up cabin, did fall asleep. When Larry shook me awake three hours later the motion was a bit rougher. "I've put in another reef. Squalls and lightning to the north of us," Larry said, as he had a small shot of rum. "Everything seems fine, winds up, maybe thirty knots. Barometer hasn't moved. Maybe we'll miss the worst of it."

I climbed out from between the cotton sheets and took a look around on deck. Even the occasional light spray that hit my bare body felt warm in the sultry, wind-pushed air. Thunder rumbled in the distance; lightning hidden by the clouds lit the sky ahead and north of us like flashbulbs behind a shaded window.

I went below and pulled out our tattered copy of Bowditch and again read, "The passage of a tropical cyclone at sea is an experience not soon to be forgotten." An hour later, that sentence came rushing through my wind-whipped mind.

I'd watched the squall line creep closer, its majestic clouds outlined by lightning, its movement orchestrated by thunder. Nothing else seemed to change. The swell ran at the same ten- or twelve-foot height; the wind waves crashed just forward of our beam. *Seraffyn* drove through the seas at five knots; her motion, if not steady, was at least predictable. Then a separate jarring crash of lightning illuminated my whole world in eerie gray and white. I could see the creeping foot of a granddaddy squall only

300 yards to windward, pouring rain forming a ruffled skirt over its froth-white toes. I charged below and grabbed my wet-weather jacket, then climbed out into the cockpit as fast as I could. I barely had that plastic-coated parka on when the first gust hit. *Seraffyn* staggered until her cabin side kissed the rushing waves. I slid to the leeward side of the cockpit, threw loose the staysail sheet, and let the sail flog. *Seraffyn* steadied, and I crawled forward to drop the staysail before it ripped itself to bits. Driving rain hit at me; spray flew across the foredeck. I didn't need a light: flashes of lightning were almost continuous now. When I bent to lash the staysail down to the bowsprit and windlass, wind-driven rain and spray stung at my bare rear end like buckshot. Tears or saltwater filled my eyes—I'll never know which—and I kept thinking, "I should go get Larry . . . I can't leave this sail until it's lashed down . . . Should call him at least . . . I'd better slow *Seraffyn* down some more . . ." But I just kept working, remembering the times I'd helped Larry settle the boat into a hove-to position. I put two extra lashings under the bowsprit and around the staysail just to be sure it would stay put. I crawled aft and started hauling in the mainsheet. That's when Larry came into the cockpit decked out in foul-weather gear. "Did you unclutch the wind vane?" he yelled directly into my ear. I shook my head no, and he began doing the things I usually did while I remembered each detail of the jobs Larry handled when we lay *Seraffyn* hove to to face the howling wind. I grabbed one of the cockpit flotation cushions and lashed it to the taffrail knee where it would act as a shock absorber for the tiller. Then I lashed the tiller firmly twenty degrees to leeward against the cushion. *Seraffyn* heeled but soon stopped moving forward. I climbed up the rain-slicked deck to look at the wake she was making on her windward side. A smoothed-out patch of water began to form, disturbed by her long keel. Now we were making no headway at all, just drifting slowly, dead downwind, the bow pointed about fifty degrees off the wind. Waves broke forward off the bow and astern of us, but when they hit that protective slick, they seemed to crumble, then turned to powerless foam. So, I checked over the deck as Larry unlashed, then removed the wind vane's Dacron cover.

It's amazing how much calmer everything seemed with the boat settled down, the halyards tied off, the vibration of that six-square-foot vane quieted down. *Seraffyn* seemed to ride like a duck over the building seas. Lashing rain smashed the wave crests so that they were too flat to break, but nothing muffled the sound of the constant thunder.

When Larry came close and yelled, "I'll take one last look around. You get below before you catch pneumonia," I gladly climbed into the comparative quiet of the cabin. As soon as Larry came in, he shed his dripping foul-weather gear and began toweling down my legs and back. That's when he noticed the red dots all over my thighs and bottom. He collapsed into roars of laughter, then dug out a mirror so I could see the bruises the driving spray had left. We needed that break in the tension. Neither of us wanted to say the word *typhoon*. But when I was wrapped up in a blanket and slowly warming in the bunk, Larry drew a rough sketch of the typical typhoon wind pattern and reasoned, "We're definitely on the safe semicircle. The winds and our drift will shove us away from the center. Nothing more we can do but hope our mainsail holds. If it doesn't, I'll get the sea anchor out."

For the next eight hours the wind shrieked and howled through our rigging. Seas grumbled and washed along our leeward deck each time a swell passed under us. The lightning and thunder would have kept us awake if the increasingly rough motion hadn't been enough. How hard did it blow? Far over gale force was all we could guess. How high were the seas? Not as big as we'd seen them in the north Atlantic, when we lay hove-to for three days with full storm warnings in all sea areas. But the wind and sea were irregular, puffing, changing direction, unstable. Through it all *Seraffyn* rode lightly, her tightly sheeted double-reefed main trying to drive her up into the wind, her lashed-down tiller working to keep her there. She made almost no headway, giving easily to each sea that crested against her bow. We rarely heard anything more than heavy spray hit the deck. Her drift seemed to be about three-quarters of a knot dead downwind. I remember saying at some time during that long night, "The reality is easier to take than the two days of anticipation."

Larry agreed, but later, while we lay in the quarter berths opposite each other, bracing to the lurch-and-lunge motion, he suddenly thought out loud, "What about *Crusader*? If Don didn't take any sights, that current would have set him way north and he'd never have known it. That could have put him on the wrong side of this typhoon." I considered this for a while, remembering *Crusader*'s leaking hull, her large windows and rotten spreaders. Then I dismissed it all. "They left two days ahead of us. *Crusader* powers at six knots. Probably almost in Thailand by this time."

Daylight slowly crept into the closed boat; occasional patches of blue sky passed the salt-stained port lights. Our double-faced compass showed that the wind had shifted more to the west; our barometer was up two millibars. But now the seas seemed worse, more confused. Larry got on his wet gear, took out two drop boards, and climbed into the cockpit for a look around. The oil lamps were miraculously still burning, giving us even more faith in their rebuilt burners. *Seraffyn* seemed to be forereaching just a bit, maybe because the wind was gusty now and a bit lighter. She was definitely moving out of the slick her keel made, so Larry yanked on the mainsheet to try and get it in even flatter. That did it. Our tired old sail split. I heard it go and felt the boat's motion change. Now she rolled between each lunge. "Get ready," Larry called down the companionway, "I'm bringing the mainsail down below. Get me a screwdriver." I struggled into the tool locker, with lack of sleep, the rough motion, and a new set of worries putting me on the edge of seasickness.

Larry brought in good news with the unruly mass of shredded-looking sail. "Sea's going down fast. Still blowing close to a gale, but there's a line of blue sky ahead. I think we can lie ahull safely. Let's get this sail fixed."

I was fine as we worked together drying the torn part of the sail with towels, then piecing the two halves together. I held the edges of the eleven-foot tear roughly in place while Larry took huge herringbone stiches with waxed Dacron thread. In the worst places we used duct tape to hold the sail temporarily together. I prayed we were matching the two halves somewhat closely, because we could spread only three feet at a time in the sail-filled cabin. Then Larry did it. He opened the one-quart can of contact cement and started gluing a three-inch-wide strip of Dacron over our stitching. One whiff and I was out the companionway and in the lee scuppers; the hell with foul-weather gear. I lay in the fresh air watching Larry work and mentally awarding him a hero badge as he gooped that smelly glue over the patch, patiently waited for it to dry, then lined the now self-stick strip over the stitches. But I had my consolation as I watched the sun creep over us and the seas slowly start to take on a more normal pattern.

When the patch was finished Larry came out on deck and watched the jumbled twelve-foot seas that rocked *Seraffyn* unevenly about. "Let's try sailing, might steady us out," he suggested. "We can't set the main until that glue has a couple of hours to go off. But we can ease onto a reach with just the staysail."

It's surprising how that 104-square-foot sail steadied us out, not only physically but mentally as well. Now that we were sailing again, the fear of the unknown represented by that word *typhoon* was behind us. Yet that unnamed storm came back to haunt us time after time as we sailed eastward.

Two days later, as we beat tack on tack against twenty knots of wind with our two roughly patched sails holding together and setting nicely even if they did look ugly, we sat back and listened to our favorite BBC news broadcast. "Unseasonable typhoon whips across Bay of Bengal, disrupting shipping with 100 mph winds, killing at least 200,000 people in southeast India. Tides rise ten feet above normal." It was hard to believe that was our storm. By this time the winds and seas had diminished in our minds until I concluded, "Good, strong gale." "We were on the very edge, didn't get much of the real wind," Larry agreed. But some very sad events that occurred two months later proved us both wrong. We'd been less than eighty miles from the center of that typhoon in an area where satellite weather photos indicated sustained winds of eighty knots.

Once we'd cleared the typhoon area of the Bay of Bengal, once we'd decided that our gooey yellow sail patches were going to hold up in the head winds we were having, I expected the last 500 miles of our passage to be uneventful. But the tropics held another secret to torment us. I noticed some insect bites on my ankle one morning when I climbed out of the bunk. They itched like hell. Couldn't be mosquitoes; we had no cockroaches on board; we couldn't see any flying insects. Later that morning Larry was sitting on the settee reading when he slapped at his hip. "Look at this bug," he said. I put down my mixing spoon and examined it. "Looks just like a weevil," I said. Then it hit me. "Oh my God, get off the settee," I ordered Larry. Sure enough, inside the locker was a crawling colony of the little black monsters. They'd bored perfectly round one-sixteenth-inch holes through my Tupperware flour-storage tubs, eaten into noodle and spaghetti packages, attacked the biscuits. I'd expected a few weevils when we'd had to buy flour from fifty-pound sacks in Sri Lanka. In fact, we'd joked, saying they'd add a bit of protein to our diet. But this was more than a joke. As I set to work cleaning each locker, spraying the corners with mosquito killer, then sifting all twenty-eight pounds of flour, Larry urged me onward. He watched me struggling to keep my balance against the heeled, pitching boat; he laughed at my frustration as a particularly large sea unbalanced another stack I'd taken out of the lockers and tried to balance against the side of the stove. "I may do the harder work during storms," he said, "but times like this are when you do your bit."

I did get him to patch my perforated flour tub with contact cement out in the cockpit as far downwind of me as he could get. Then, five days later, when we spotted the Langkawi Islands just coming over the horizon, I emptied the last twelve pounds of flour overboard. Newly hatched weevils wiggled on the cream-colored flour as it slowly sank into the black evening water.

Seraffyn skimmed lightly through the smooth waters of the Andaman Sea, our heavy winds a day behind us, our typhoon a distant memory. I spent every spare minute on my last night watches answering the letters we'd received in Sri Lanka. This is a favorite task that I usually finish during our first ten days at sea. But this eighteen-day passage had been far from normal. We'd never been able to fall into a seagoing pattern. Events kept us busy every single day. I was glad we were sailing into a quiet, almost deserted island group instead of into the hustle and bustle of a city as we usually did at the end of a long voyage.

CHAPTER 13

~~~~~~~

An Oriental Pause

The Langkawi Islands turned out to be a perfect introduction to the Far East. We skimmed between the deserted, jungle-covered outer islands on a clear, sunny morning. Strange animals called across the water; tropical birds flashed their brilliant colors along the growth-tangled shores. The deep green of the ocean depths gave way to turquoise as the islands closed behind us and passage making quickly became a distant memory. Even though we had almost twenty-five miles to sail before we reached one of the three villages shown on our detailed chart, we didn't really care whether or not the wind held. All we had to do now was ease over near the shore that lay only half a mile away on either side of us, drop our anchor, and share the night, unmarred by watches for the first time in nineteen days.

It was dusk when we anchored south of the biggest settlement in the island group. We had no desire to rush ashore. Instead, we relaxed in the soft, warm evening air and listened to the few voices that seemed to whisper to us from the thirty wooden buildings nestled under the coconut palms onshore. A fisherman answered our hellos as he rowed past in a fifteen-foot canoe. No one else seemed to care that we'd arrived. The euphoria that sets in after a difficult passage seemed heightened by this almost fairyland peace. The knowledge that the monsoon seasons, which now controlled our lives, dictated a four-month pause before we could sail north through the South China Sea added to our peace of mind. We had 120 days to enjoy and only 450 miles to sail in order to be in place for the next leg of our homeward dash. Typhoons wouldn't threaten us; no pirates, reefs, or revolutions lay waiting along our path to Singapore. I'll never forget that evening of complete relaxation, that prelude to two

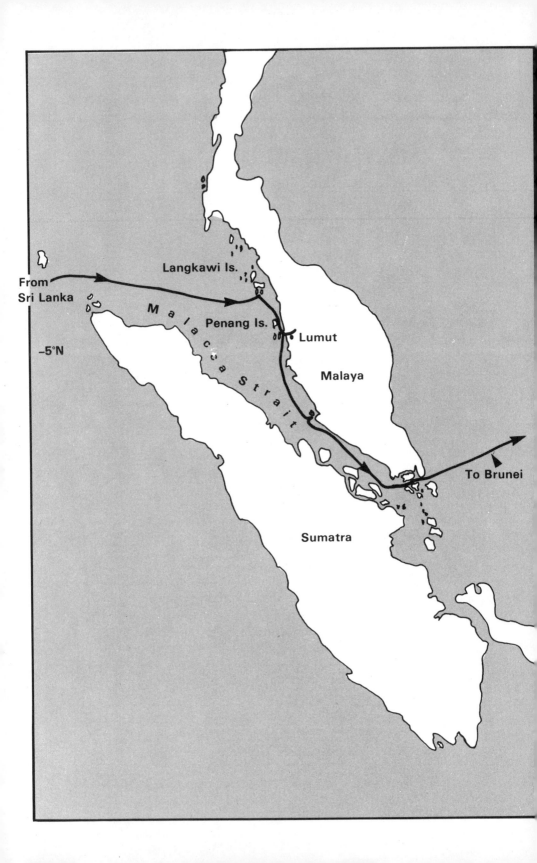

beautiful weeks of the kind of peace every person dreams of but so few seem to find.

We walked along the wooden sidewalks of the village the next morning, our heads swiveling to take in each strange new sight and smell. It was hard to be serious about locating a customs and immigration official, when no one in the village seemed very concerned. We asked the Chinese man behind the counter in the first shop, "Is there a harbormaster here?" He shrugged his shoulders and answered in an almost Oxfordian English, "I've never heard of one, try the bank." The lovely dark-skinned Malaysian bank teller ran for the manager, who said, "Try the post office." We changed a few traveler's checks and walked down the street to the tiny hotel, where the post office nestled in a corner of the foyer. It was closed. But the dark-skinned East Indian hotel manager dug out a battered-looking phone book for all of Malaysia, a book only half an inch thick. He seemed to get very excited, grabbed his telephone, and burst into a flood of words in some local dialect. After an almost interminable time he hung up, shaking his head seriously. "Come with me," he said and led us to the edge of the dirt road in front of his two-story-high, thirty-foot-wide hotel. Almost before we knew what was happening, we were inside a battered taxi with instructions to pay the driver the equivalent of nine dollars when he brought us back to town.

We both felt a bit as if we'd been fleeced, as the rickety car dashed over the rutted main road, then turned away from the water and headed into the hills. But our momentary annoyance turned to amazement as the ride across the beautiful island grew longer and longer. For an hour and a half, small farms with thatch-roofed, open-sided homes broke the expanse of jungle into comfortable, understandable chunks. Ocean vistas flashed past as we wound along the hillsides. We met only one other car as we bumped over the partially paved road. Occasional pairs of oxen pulled basketlike carts onto the shoulder to let us pass. Then we finally saw it; two small buildings stood in lonely splendor at the head of a beautiful, sand-edged bay. A huge Malaysian flag flew from a tall pole on the beach. A uniformed man finally strolled out to quiet our driver's insistent honking. "Oh yes, I'm glad you dropped by," the smooth-faced immigration, health, and customs official said when he saw us in the backseat. "Do come in for a glass of lemonade."

As we filled out two simple forms, the relaxed official explained, "Nobody comes to Langkawi from the east. But trading boats from Thailand anchor here. To keep them honest, this entry post is in the best bay. Oh yes, I did have four yachts come by last year. Nice people."

Our taxi driver spoke very little English, but he did understand our desire to find a restaurant when we finally got back to the village. The café he suggested seemed strange to us that day. But during the next four months we grew used to seeing a fire inside a fifty-five-gallon drum on the sidewalk in front of each Indian café. A flat sheet of metal lay across the drum to serve as a griddle. The restaurant owner kneaded and stretched balls of rising dough, coated them with oil, kneaded them again, then quick fried the dough into flaky, twisted rolls, between taking trips to the back-room kitchen for tiny bowls of shrimp, chicken, or fish curry and tall, ice-filled glasses of lemonade.

Late in the afternoon we strolled through the tiny, cluttered provisions shops. There seemed to be no recognizable organization to these all-in-one emporiums. In the first shop we visited, the same shelf held margarine, lard, canned butter, all-purpose motor grease, and canned sardines. A young boy sat at the back working over a wicker basket full of squirming, two-pound crabs. He dextrously tied each of their claws closed with pink plastic ribbon and ended up with a bow across the crabs' back, which he used to hang the gift-wrapped crustaceans on a clothesline for our selection. A lady sat on the front porch measuring out kilos of onions with one hand while she held her nursing baby in the other. A large cut-glass bowl full of water sat on a fifty-pound sack of rice, fresh bean sprouts floated on the surface, and a red hibiscus blossom decorated the center.

Our choice of provisions was limited to the simple needs and budgets of island people who depend on fishing and small farms for their income. But after nineteen days at sea, a dinner of creamed clam chowder, steamed crab on a bed of spinach, and sautéed prawns seemed like a gourmet feast.

The only hotel in town was deserted except for the manager and a helper. But they willingly let us use their rickety washer and dryer. They also assured us that the twenty-two letters we posted there would go out on the ferry in two days and speed to their destination by air once they reached the mainland.

We set sail three days later to see if the tales we'd heard about a magic freshwater lake only fifty yards from the sea were truth or only sea stories embellished by cruising sailors tired from a passage across the Indian Ocean. Twenty miles from the village, on a deserted, jungle-covered rocky island at the far edge of the quiet Langkawi archipelago, we found a bit of enchantment.

Legend says that a jealous fisherman took his beautiful wife away from

her home village and built a shelter on this deserted island. Only then did
he feel free to spend days out at sea fishing, since there would be no other
man to tempt his wife. The lonely woman pined away in her tiny home
next to the freshwater lake that had formed in an extinct volcano crater,
until one day she caught and tamed a mongoose. Her fisherman husband
returned from the sea and became violently angry when he saw the tender-
ness his wife lavished on this small black animal. He flew into a tantrum,
grabbed the mongoose from his wife's arms, and threw it into the deep, still
lake. A lone crocodile rose to the surface and slowly ate the animal that had
been like a child to the imprisoned woman. She turned to her cruel husband and screamed, "I can't bear the solitude!" Then she leaped into the
blood-streaked water, where the crocodile killed her with one snap of his
terrible jaw. The fisherman, who had lost his beautiful wife not to another
man but to a creature who was completely indifferent to her beauty, cursed
the crocodile and condemned the ugly creature to a life so long and lonely
that its skin would fade to white. Now the huge white crocodile is said to
lie in wait in the depths of the bottomless lake while the spirit of the lonely
wife sits on the one sandy beach of the island, waiting and watching for
another mongoose to tame.

We lay anchored 300 feet off the tiny beach for over a week. In the late
afternoon we'd row ashore and tie our dinghy painter to the overhanging
limb of a jungle tree. Then we'd climb the thirty-foot-high ridge that
separated the sweet water from the sea. We bathed in a small pool cut off
from the rest of the lake by a line of just submerged rocks. The spreading
limbs of the oppressively close jungle trees shaded us from the tropical sun.
No birds seemed to call; only cricketlike creatures broke the silence with
their quiet questions. No fish, reptile, or animal ruffled the surface of the
lake.

Then, one afternoon as we headed toward shore, I noticed something
moving on the sand. I whispered to Larry and pointed. He stopped his
rowing and we both watched in quiet awe as a mongoose walked to the
water's edge, reared up on its hind legs, and stared out across the water at
our dinghy. The round black head seemed to sway back and forth as if to
say, "No, she's not the one I loved, he's not the one I hated." Then the
richly coated animal fell back onto four feet, lowered its head, and slowly
climbed back into the jungle.

Now the anchorage which had seemed a haven of peace to us as we
refreshed *Seraffyn*'s varnish, worked on our writing, and enjoyed quiet
nights together seemed sad and lonely. We did go ashore and have our

baths that evening. But without one word, Larry decided to watch the mirrorlike surface of the lake while I bathed. Then I watched for him.

As we climbed back down the moss-encrusted rocks we saw a bright yellow ketch tacking slowly into the bay on the last of the evening's breeze. They anchored almost half a mile away from *Seraffyn*, but we seemed to both want and need company to break the spell that mongoose had thrown over us. Lynne and Claude Arnould saw us rowing toward them and called the usual greetings. "Come on board, where you coming from?" Then as soon as we had secured the dinghy painter, Lynne asked, "Did you go near the lake? It's dangerous, you know. I heard that a white crocodile lives there." But rum cocktails, cheese, and a rush of information trading that happens whenever sailors headed in opposite directions meet quickly drowned any memories of our strange afternoon.

Lynne and Claude were planning to stop only for the night. They were bound for Sri Lanka and eventually France after six months of cruising and outfitting their still unfinished steel thirty-six-footer. They'd built the hull, deck, and rig in Australia; the interior was an underway project. We looked over their charts of Malaysia, noting anchorages they'd especially liked, writing down places to buy stores or haul out if need be. We were getting ready to leave before complete dark cut us off from *Seraffyn* when Claude said, "I am having trouble with my ham radio, but before it started getting so much interference I heard someone ask about you on the South Pacific net. Some one said, "Have you sighted the Pardeys or *Seraffyn?*'"

"Probably Don Sorte," Larry answered. "I told him we might decide to go to Phuket in Thailand. That's where he was headed." This bit of conversation quickly slid into memory as we said our good-nights.

We were pleased to see *Joya*'s brilliant hull still in place against the jungle green on the far side of the bay when we got up the next morning. "Guess they've decided to accept our dinner invite," Larry said, as we got out the blue paint and brushes to put a fresh coating on our bulwark rail.

The evening on *Seraffyn* was the reverse of the one before. Now it was Claude who traced anchorages off our charts, Lynne who picked our brains for stores ideas. As they shared the last bottle of Greek wine we had on board, Claude said, "I'd really like to buy that book you showed me, but I saw it cost you twelve dollars and we don't have anything but hundred-dollar traveler's checks."

"Don't worry, take it," Larry answered. But Claude insisted on finding some medium of trade. "Whiskey," he said. "I've got some duty-frees somewhere in the bilge. Do you drink whiskey?" "Sure," I answered.

The next morning, when the early-morning light turned our forward cabin into a glow of rosy wood tones, I climbed out on deck and saw only a solid green wall where *Joya* had been. Then as I turned to go below and start the coffee, I noticed a small pile of goods resting just inside our bulwarks. Two bottles of Scotch whiskey, three beautiful tomatoes, and two dollars and fifty cents in assorted Malasian, Singaporean, and U.S. change rested on top of a note. "0400, hope this is a fair trade. Hope you enjoy Penang as much as we did."

Yes, it had been more than a fair trade, and the pleasure we'd had in the company of two other wanderers set us free of the need for any further solitude. As the coffee started to perk, Larry unfurled the main, then cranked in the anchor chain. I brought our coffee and toast into the cockpit as the outermost rocks of the Langkawi archipelago slipped aft of our beam. On the edge of the western horizon I saw a bright dot that could have been the tip of *Joya*'s sails headed toward Sri Lanka. Or maybe it was just a whitecap on the huge expanse of sea that stretched toward another world we'd known.

CHAPTER 14

Oriental Justice

After two weeks on the island of Penang we felt as if we'd had a sneak preview of the whole Orient. From the moment we settled into the small-boat anchorage just off the main city of George Town at 0300, our senses were continually assailed with new sights, new sounds, new smells, and new ideas. Even at this late hour, a seemingly endless parade of sampans glided by. Tiny Chinese women sculled past us in wooden dories, offering rides ashore for the equivalent of twenty-five cents each. Ninety- and one-hundred-foot-long junks worked quietly past on the light breeze and ebbing tide, their bat-winged sails blocking out the stars, kerosene lights twinkling from open-sided shelters on their sterns.

In the morning, when the wakes of high-powered launches and a three-knot tide started *Seraffyn* bucking and rocking like a dinghy, we decided to go ashore and find out if this really was a shopper's paradise. I'm sure glad we weren't forced to be in a hurry. The sights that lay waiting for us made every shore excursion an adventure.

We tied our dinghy among a dozen sampans at the pontoon dock that floated almost half a mile from the shore at the end of a wooden village perched on pilings and stilts. As we walked along the slatted sidewalks and listened to the water lapping just ten feet below the tiny homes that leaned against each other, we were shocked to think of hundreds of Chinese people spending their whole lives in ten-foot-by-twelve-foot rooms with no apparent privacy, no dry land beneath them. But as we became used to this pathway to the city, we began to see the exquisite cleanliness of each home, the carefully dressed children scampering about the narrow side-walks, the friendly, wizened faces of the old folks who lounged on benches in the sun. Occasional glimpses inside open doors showed carefully stacked sleeping mats, delicate wall hangings, tiny cooking platforms with charcoal stoves smoking next to windows that reached almost to the floor. At each intersection, miniature religious places were set aside, with gaily decorated five-foot-tall candles burning on red-and-gold altars. It took us almost ten minutes to reach the main street, which lay just fifty feet inshore from this suspended village of 2,000 people. As soon as we began walking along the pavement we understood why these Chinese Malaysians had chosen to build their homes over the sea. Cooling breezes meandered between each home and up through the slatted floors, fanned by the restless tide. Here on the roads of town, the black asphalt and solid buildings reflected and magnified the heat of the relentless sun until shade, air conditioning, and yet another cool drink were all we could think of.

East Indians seemed to dominate the street life. They recklessly pulled trishaws laden with whole families and heaps of groceries through narrow, crowded streets. These three-wheel bicycles with their double-wide passenger seats became our main means of transportation. It took us a short time to get over the seeming unfairness of asking a man who probably weighed little over 100 pounds to haul all 270 pounds of us plus another fifty pounds of groceries for only two dollars a day. We felt bad watching our driver work and sweat in the hot sun, protected only by a straw hat, after he'd carefully arranged a perambulator-type cover over us. But the first driver we chose had obviously worked for foreigners before. "Not to worry, not to worry. I make good money. More than factory workers. I wait for you each morning onshore and show you every place you need to go." He was as good as his word. That first day, he helped us find our three-pound package of mail. He pulled us back to the dock that formed the edge of the anchorage where *Seraffyn,* lay and waited while we took a sampan out for our cameras and the typewriter that needed repairing. When we came back ashore, he took us aside and suggested we pay the guard on the dock twenty-five cents. "Then he will love your little boat and watch it all the time. Then you can go for a tour and return safe late at night." At that time we laughed at this little con game. But during the next few months we grew to respect if not understand the oriental system of justice.

Penang did have everything. Our trishaw peddler found us a modern-looking typewriter-repair shop at the English end of town just opposite a splendid green cricket field surrounded by colonial-style mansions. Then he pulled us into a maze of narrow, cluttered streets where Malaysian fruit vendors crowded the walkways and Chinese women hand-painted greeting cards in the doors of minuscule shops. An ancient Chinese gentleman found a beer bottle to give us a sample of the kerosene he sold from a battered fifty-five-gallon drum stashed under dozens of oil-lamp burners and wicks. (We'd learned the hard way that it pays to test burn any kerosene before we fill up our main tank.)

Then we asked our guide-chauffeur for a restaurant. He didn't hesitate. "Your boat is from Canada, so you will want to go to the Australian restaurant." We didn't understand his logic, but after a dinner of fine Australian-grown sirloin steaks, baked potatoes, oysters on the half shell, and our first Australian wine, we did appreciate his suggestion. The air-conditioned, dimly lit room was a haven after the heat and confusing babel of voices that had surrounded us all day. Our delicate-boned Balinese waitress explained that this was almost a clubhouse for the Australian air-force officers who worked at the Butterfield base, just ten miles from Penang. Then she listed the favorite restaurants for the English residents, the American businessmen, the New Zealanders on cheap holiday tours. It was from her that we first learned that every city in the Far East sports special cafés or restaurants, which become meeting places for each nationality. Here you can buy beer imported from your homeland, read familiar, week-old newspapers, hear the accents you knew, and sometimes, in bigger cities such as Singapore or Kuala Lumpur, even get meals cooked the way they were at the café down the street back home.

We decided to walk home that evening. The bright lights and snips of music on the main street of George Town reminded us that cities could be special too. We looked over the wares offered by each vendor and bought pirated cassette tapes for fifty cents each from stands set up against closed shop fronts. The tapes turned out to be quite good, but my favorite souvenir is a tiny card I bought for Larry at a corner stationery stand. It shows a drawing of the Schulz cartoon dog Snoopy skipping through a patch of flowers, a basket full of roses on one arm, whistled notes of music over his head, and a complex caption all in Chinese characters. We never did find out what the caption really meant. But that night I handed it to Larry and made up my own translation, "Isn't it great being alive with time to smell the flowers." That same card hangs next to my desk as I type this and remember those special days.

One thing I learned only by accident is that the posted prices I saw in each shop in George Town did not mean I could forget about bargaining. Since we'd been unable really to fill our stores lockers since we left Rhodos, five months before, they were almost empty now. Penang's shops held a wondrous display of canned and packaged foods from Australia, the United States, and England. After looking over the stocks of several shops, I took our trishaw driver to the one I'd chosen, went inside, and began pointing, "Ten of those, twelve of those." The clerks rushed around filling cartons with my order while the shopowner shoved the beads of his abacus up and down their bamboo rods. I ordered more than my peddler could load onto his trishaw. So he said, "I will take you to your boat first and come back for everything else. But did they give you the discount?"

"What discount?" I asked.

"You have spent more than fifty dollars, so you should have a discount." The tiny barefooted man stomped into the grocer's shop and started an argument that flowed too fast for me to comprehend. Then the abacus worker's fingers flew, the cash register rang, and my driver bowed, then turned to me. "You must let me get the right prices for you." He handed me a twenty-five-dollar refund from my hundred ten dollars worth of shopping.

We'd heard from several sources that the officials at Singapore had discovered a way to irritate foreign cruising yachtsmen and also earn close to a hundred dollars in extra fees. They simply required a deratification certificate for each entry from any Far East port. If you did not have this certificate dated within six months of your arrival, you were put into the quarantine anchorage and inspected, detected, and fined. Since we have heard of no other port in the world that asked for a deratification certificate from yachtsmen, we weren't surprised that this had caused a bit of an uproar in the cruising fleet. In my Pollyanna way, I tried to justify their rules, saying, "They just want to avoid spreading disease on their small island." But when we applied for a deratification certificate at the port captain's office in Penang, I became convinced that this whole process was a scam. We paid the equivalent of twelve dollars. An inspector came out to *Seraffyn* and drank a cup of coffee, then asked, "Did you notice any sick-looking rats on board during the past month?" Larry laughed and answered, "Only my wife during the typhoon." The official signed an elaborate-looking form, stamped it, and signaled to the customs launch that lay waiting a few hundred yards away. Larry and I stood there trying to look serious as he handed us the form and announced, "I've given your ship a clean bill of health."

The days disappeared as we lay in the small-boat anchorage in George Town. If we weren't ashore shopping, we were off on rented bicycles to tour with some Australian people we'd met. Other afternoons we rowed over and had tea on one of the rough old junks that lay anchored only 200 yards away from us. These hardwood, bargelike sailing ships carried charcoal from tiny villages in Thailand and Indonesia to sell in Penang. Given the abundance of hardwood and low wages in Indonesia, a load of charcoal sold at the right time could earn a junk owner enough to buy a diesel engine. So, we learned to judge the profitability of each junk by the condition of its bat-wing sails. If the cotton fabric was carefully mended, times were rough. If they were tattered and full of holes, engine-buying time was near.

It was amazing to watch family life go smoothly along on these heavily laden junks. A brazier stood next to the sheltered steering station. Clotheslines were strung between the thick hardwood spars. Children played on top of the canvas-covered cargo. But what shocked me was that the six-inch-diameter, ten-foot-long, carefully charred logs that would be broken up to fuel the cook stoves of Penang were still warm to the touch. Our host, a man of Chinese descent whose home port was Bangkok, explained in halting English, "Sometimes we get fire. That is very bad, especially in strong wind. Those Indonesians try to cheat. They load not finished charcoal." The skipper-owner of this junk had invited his wife's brother to live and work on board with him, his wife, and four children so that they could inspect each piece of charcoal that was loaded. But I could imagine how it would be possible to sneak one or two overly hot logs onto the eighty-foot-long, fourteen-foot-high stack that weighed fifty tons or more.

There was only one problem with the fascinating crossroads at George Town. We couldn't force ourselves to set aside even four hours in the day to work on the book project we'd promised to finish for our publisher within the next three months. So we got out our chart a week after we'd arrived and searched for the perfect place to write a book. "It should be near a village so that we can get daily provisions," I said. "Yes, but near a main road leading to a city in case we need to buy anything special or want a night on the town," Larry added.

A tiny village just twelve miles south of George Town looked like a place to check out. Its anchorage lay protected by a sweep in the coastline on two sides. Barely submerged sandbars protected its other sides. This was one of the anchorages for the George Town pilot boats.

While I rode off behind our trishaw chauffeur for the last time to pick up our rebuilt typewriter, Larry walked across town to say good-bye to Peter and Patsy, the two Australian tourists we'd shared our bicycle expeditions with. "I'll ask them if they'd enjoy sailing with us for the day. Then they can take a bus back here this evening," Larry said. So, two hours later we lifted our anchor and reached through the fleet of junks, lighters, and sampans with a very festive group on board which had expanded to include two Canadians on a three-month walking tour of the Orient.

It took us most of the day to reach our chosen anchorage. We'd stopped for a swim and lunch halfway down the island. We'd tacked in to inspect a tiny resort that lay on a half-acre island along our way. We'd talked and laughed, sung songs, and discussed the state of the world all afternoon. When we finally set our hook just astern of a pilot boat and not far from a police launch, I was ready for a quiet evening on board with just the two of us. But when Larry came back from ferrying the last of our guests onto the beach in front of the tree-lined village he said, "Patsy found the local café and says there's an hour wait until the next bus. She wants us to come ashore for a farewell beer. I said we'd meet them in ten minutes."

I didn't really want to go. With hindsight I could say I was reluctant to leave *Seraffyn* alone in a strange anchorage until we checked with locals on the safety of the area. But in reality I just wasn't very interested after the long day of partying in the hot sun. I wanted to clean the boat up, do the dishes, and get to bed early. I think Larry felt the same way, but we didn't want to be spoilsports. So I went below and grabbed my wallet but left my purse on the quarter berth while Larry lit the oil lamp and hung it on the staysail stay as an anchor light.

One beer led to two, the first bus came and went, so all of us ordered a dinner of nasi goreng, a spicy mix of fried rice, vegetables, and meat tidbits. We couldn't quite see *Seraffyn* from the open-sided café, but the pilot boat was just visible and it lay quietly on the smooth water that seemed to reflect every star.

We were feeling quite mellow when we finally said good-bye two hours later and started walking along the beach path that led to the spot where we'd secured *Rinky Dink*. Even in the dark we could see that the dinghy was full of sand. "Some damn kids have been playing with it," Larry said as he sponged the seats off. "We should have rowed it right over to the café." I don't think we were too concerned at that moment, because we began recalling other times when playful children had chosen *Rinky* as their toy. Once in Mexico we'd come back from the market and caught young boys jumping off a ten-foot-high dock into the dinghy, trying to see if they could land without capsizing. Another time we'd come back from a walk and found the dinghy propped up as a sun umbrella for two dozing youngsters. So, we'd almost forgotten the whole matter when we reached

Seraffyn sitting quietly a quarter mile off the beach. Then I took off my shoes and climbed on deck. Sand! There had been no sand on her decks before we left! Now it was everywhere. Larry reached inside the companionway for a flashlight, and then I sat down and began to cry when I saw that the whole interior of *Seraffyn* looked as if it had been ransacked.

Larry climbed below and almost immediately said, "Our cameras, they're gone." He picked up my purse, which had been tossed on the floor. "Your wallet, it's missing, but they left the traveler's checks." That made me laugh a bit through my tears. "No, I've got my wallet, thank God. There's four hundred dollars in it. Sure lucky we bought traveler's checks in Penang instead of carrying two thousand dollars more cash on board."

Fortunately for us, Larry didn't get as hysterical as I felt right at that moment. Here we were, all alone in a foreign country, anchored off a tiny, innocent-looking village, away for only two hours, and for the first time in our lives we'd been robbed. My home and privacy had been invaded; hundreds of transparencies had been tossed on the floorboards; sandy footprints covered the decks. "Let's get out of here right now. I want to get away from here," I decided out loud.

But Larry was more determined than I was. "I'm going to get the police. You wait here. Don't touch anything. There might be fingerprints."

"Sure," I said scornfully, "and Dick Tracy's just around the corner. How do you expect to find the police tonight? You don't even know where the main street of this place is. They won't care even if you find them. We were dumb enough to leave the boat unlocked. We got what we deserved." Larry turned and took my shoulders in his hands. "Stop it, I'm going to get the police. They are going to find our cameras. We are not leaving here until they do." Then he took a flashlight, climbed into *Rinky,* and rowed toward the police launch astern of us where a light glowed from the cabin. I saw a man come out on deck. Then he and Larry both rowed toward shore on *Rinky Dink.*

The wait seemed to drag on as I poured myself a drink of sherry, lit the cabin lamps, and sat torn between my urge to clean up the cabin and leave things as they were on the off chance that the police did care. Just when I'd decided to sweep the deck clear of sand, the pilot launch pulled alongside with Larry calling, "Get some fenders."

That started an invasion that would have been comical at any other time. Two very diligent Malaysian officials tried to squeeze into the narrow forward companionway to see where our slide boxes had been opened and dumped. "What are these?" one asked as he held up the small woven pouches that had held a beautiful antique silver waist chain and four silver and tourmaline hairpins we'd bought in Sri Lanka. That's when Larry and I began to wonder what else was missing. Two other policemen sat in the cockpit asking Larry endless questions and filling out forms. I got our passports and ship's papers, heated coffee, and tried to stand clear in the two-foot-by-six-foot floor space of our main cabin while the interior police dusted the slide boxes and linen locker with black powder, looking for fingerprints. When they climbed into the cockpit, I got to look for any other missing items. All we found gone besides the jewelry and cameras were a stack of my T-shirts, Larry's ten-year-old sports jacket, and my leather jacket from England. After two hours, the last policeman left, saying, "We want tourists to visit our village. We cannot have robbers here." Then we were finally able to clean up the mess and pick up the miraculously undamaged transparencies.

I can't say I felt any happier when morning came. A restless night's sleep made me even more sure we'd never see anything of ours again. Larry rowed ashore in the late afternoon and told the police, "We cannot leave without those cameras. We need them for our work. We can't afford a thousand dollars to replace them." He tried to cheer me up by saying, "We're lucky because we can stay and wait and haunt the police. Most tourists who are robbed have to catch a plane, so the police give up."

"Did the police encourage you at all?" I asked.

"They said they had some leads, that's all," he answered.

That evening as I cooked dinner I had a strange vision. I looked out of the porthole over the sink and saw the Tupperware box we used to hold our two Nikkormat cameras and three lenses sitting against the bulwark. I blinked my eyes and the picture disappeared. But just to show Larry I was trying to be optimistic I said, "We are going to get our cameras back." I felt a bit silly as I described the sight I'd just seen, and Larry teased me, saying, "Wishful thinking."

The night was warm and breezeless. The forward bunk felt hot and close, so we set our quarter-berth cushions in the cockpit. *Rinky Dink* kept bumping into *Seraffyn*'s stern, driven by back eddies of a two-knot tide that wound through our anchorage. Larry got up and eased out her painter until she quieted down and trailed thirty feet astern.

At 0100 that mischievous dinghy slammed into *Seraffyn*'s side, right next to the chain plates. "Tide must be changing," Larry said, as he sat up to look at the dinghy. He jumped clear of the sheets and grabbed a flashlight. "Look at this!" he shouted as he reached down into the dinghy and lifted out a gunnysack. He put his hand inside the sack and pulled out our box of cameras. Then, without thinking or hesitating, he set them down right where I'd pictured them earlier that evening. "You were right, Lin, you really knew," he murmured as he reached in and found my suede jacket. Once again we spent a restless night, slightly disturbed by my premonition, thrilled to have our cameras back, and unconcerned for the rest. The jewelry was of little importance, just souvenirs; the half dozen T-shirts were old and easily replaced; Larry's jacket had been close to the antique stage and we decided he now had an excuse to have a new corduroy one made to order when we reached Singapore.

When we went into the police station the next day we were amazed at the officials' complete lack of surprise. "It's simple," the youngest officer said. "We applied the squeeze. We put the headman of the village in jail and told everyone he'd stay there until your things were returned. Your small things were probably sold before the culprit heard the news."

A month later, when the roll of film that had been in one of the cameras came back from the developers, we had a good laugh. The thief obviously had played with the camera and accidentally shot off half a dozen photos of the inside of his thatched house. They were fuzzy, underexposed pictures, and if we hadn't settled into our own private yacht club on the most perfect river in Malaysia, we might have taken them to the Georgetown police. But by then far more interesting matters had filled our days and our minds.

CHAPTER 15

~~~~~~

A Malaysian Haven

We knew that the Dindings River would be our writing haven as soon as we eased our sheets and began reaching toward the village of Lumut. A banana plantation and rest home seemed to hold back the jungle on the north side of the one-and-a-half-mile-wide river. The neatly laid out village tamed its south side. A dozen fish boats and sampans lay anchored just off the main square; fish vendors and ice-cream sellers lazed under a huge banyan tree in front of the yellow clapboard building that had to be the post office.

Our detailed chart showed a shipyard and yacht club about a half mile past the village, so we sailed through the town anchorage and past the fleet of work boats moored near the ramshackle buildings of the shipyard, and both of us chuckled with delight when we saw the building so grandly described in our pilot book as the "Royal Perak Yacht Club." Heavy jungle growth seemed to crowd in on an old, tin-roofed structure whose wooden side panels were hoisted open like wings. We could see right through the clubhouse. Three big fans revolved slowly over half a dozen tables. One yacht lay tied to a mooring in front of the quiet club. The man standing in the cockpit was the only living soul we could see. As we reached slowly past the tidy white ketch he called, "Welcome to Lumut. If you are looking for a bit of paradise, you've found it!"

"Sure hope we have," Larry called as we set our anchor a hundred yards from the small, sandy beach that served as the dinghy-launching ramp for this old-fashioned yacht club. Within a week we agreed with Peter. In spite of the heat, the three-times-a-week squally, torrential rains, and occasional rushes of mosquitoes, Lumut was a virtual paradise.

Peter Thuell rowed over from his boat and explained, "I'm the manager of a tin mine at Ipoh. That's about fifty miles inland from here. Been a member of this club for twenty years. But tomorrow I retire and in two weeks I'm sailing off for the Mediterranean and then home to England." That evening as we got to know each other better over a dinner at a great Chinese café down the street from the club, Peter said, "My wife is having a Christmas party tomorrow night. Why don't you come up to the city with me? You can stay at our house and I'll bring you back the next day with my crew." We told him about the robbery in Penang and Larry added, "Until we know a place, we're not going to take any chances."

"I'll introduce you to the head river pirate. Then you won't have any problems," Peter said.

We were still reluctant to leave the boat unattended for two days, but the next morning Peter led us through the tangled path across the yacht-club grounds, across a little swamp, and into the shipyard we'd seen as we'd sailed in. Three Chinese families called the shipyard their home. A vegetable plot lay neatly tended between stacks of drying mahogany boards. Two dozen chickens made their nests inside the hulls of several rotting sampans.

Peter Thuell setting off for England on his all-teak ketch *Labi Labi*.

A mean-looking pig scavenged under the pilings of the shipyard, his chain dragging through mud, clams, and scraps of wood. The main entrance to the buildings sheltering the ways car and workshops was also the owner's home. We sat in wicker chairs next to his desk while a shy, slippered lady poured lemonade into old-fashioned ice-cream-sundae glasses. The head river pirate plus Chinese shipyard owner was obviously an old friend of Peter's. He smiled, shook our hands, and told us, "For five dollar Malay, I protect your boat. But tonight number-one son sleep on boat. I not have time to tell river people before then. Lock boat, son sleep outside. After, no lock, no problem. Maybe lock if foreign boat come to anchor." And that's what we found. For two dollars U.S. per month we carried complete theft insurance.

Peter's tour was a great way to meet the business people of Ipoh—people of English, American, and Chinese descent. They almost immediately invited us to be their guests and friends. But we'd have met most of the same people even without Peter's invitation, because the Perak Yacht Club was "the" place to get away to on weekends.

From Monday to Friday the club was deserted except for an old Chinese couple who worked as caretakers and lived in a small tin-roofed house out back. They cooked meals on request, washed, dried, and ironed laundry for five cents a pound, and sold fresh eggs for a penny per dozen less than the shops in town. But weekends were different. On Saturday morning we'd swim ashore at 0900. While we showered, Seaman, the caretaker, would set out a full English-style breakfast of scrambled eggs, sausage, toast, and marmalade, and as we were drinking our third cups of coffee and tea, the Ipoh sailors would arrive.

Rosalind Foo was one of our favorites, a tiny, gracious Chinese lady who was the owner of one of the largest Malaysian banks. We soon began joining her at her beautiful orchid-filled home in the city whenever we needed to shop for things we couldn't find in the village. Ah, a young Chinese industrial designer, was vice-commodore of the club. He loved dinghy sailing and talked us into joining the club for eight dollars per year so that we could use the club dinghies and race against him. They were only two of the gracious members who arrived early each weekend to start the day's activities.

By eleven o'clock the shipyard owner's third son came over to rig and launch the three Lazer dinghies owned by the club. Then we began the first of the day's round of races. In the early morning, when the wind blew at only ten or twelve knots, one person sailed on each Lazer, and it soon

Seaman and his wife.

became apparent that lightweight Ah was club champion. But by one P.M. the northeast monsoon wind filled in to its normal twenty-two to twenty-five knots, and everyone doubled up. Then Larry and I had a definite advantage, since we outweighed Ah and Irene, the local girl he usually sailed with, by sixty pounds.

After two months of weekend dinghy racing, about thirty of our new friends had a race-off and party, since we were planning to set sail for Singapore the next day. When we were having a final farewell drink, Ah teased me, "Why didn't you feel afraid about capsizing your dinghy so often on the far side of the river?" I laughed at the thought of a dozen unplanned capsizes. The first day I'd ever sailed a planing dinghy was at the Perak Yacht Club. I'd set off across the river on a fifteen-knot breeze and been thrilled by the flying sensation. But a gust caught me a mile out and over I went. Unfortunately the strap on my bikini top caught in the mainsheet block and I lost it. It took me almost ten minutes of searching, then some very careful maneuvering, to get that top back on before I righted the dinghy. When I reached back toward the club, Ah had been getting ready to launch the club motorboat to come after me. After that,

If Somerset Maugham had chosen to write about a yacht club in Malaya, this could have been his model.

my capsizes became less frequent. But as I explained to Ah, who cared if you held a gust a bit too long and went over, the water was warm, the Lazer easy to right?

"But weren't you afraid of the crocodiles?" Ah asked.

I thought he was joking until we said good-bye to the head river pirate. When I asked him about crocodiles he shook his head. "Not to worry, no see this year. But far side of river, I no walk there."

When dusk came each Sunday the last race of the day came to an end, the boat boy quietly took over, and the Lazers seemed to disappear. Then the people from Ipoh packed kids, pets, and wet clothes into their cars to drive off toward the highlands. We'd wave good-bye, then settle into the wicker basket chairs in the suddenly quiet clubhouse and feast on one of Seaman's Chinese specialties under the whirring fans. For the rest of the week it was as if we owned the club. Mornings we'd write, on board *Seraffyn*. Afternoons we'd come ashore to shower, shop, or spread any maintenance projects that were too big for our decks out on the club's lawn. Just as we'd noticed during our previous nine years of cruising, having to work along the way offered us a completely different view of the people around us. The whole village learned about our project almost immediately because Larry asked Irene Khor, the young girl who crewed for Ah, if she knew someone who could type our final manuscript. Irene was finishing her first semester of typing lessons and decided to earn some money for a new school uniform. So for twenty cents a finished page, I was relieved of a chore I hate and we had an insider's introduction to a Chinese family. The other people in the village soon began asking about our progress each time we came into their shops. The postmaster would send a message via the shipyard if any mail from our publisher arrived. Even the fishermen were careful not to come close to *Seraffyn* in the morning. But after two P.M. they'd often motor by, wave, and ask how things were going. For some reason all of the villagers seemed more comfortable about us once they knew we also had to work for a living.

Although our first few days near Lumut were a perfect foil to the ocean voyaging that lay both behind and ahead of us, a simple note that appeared at the yacht club brought the open ocean back into our lives with a frightful jolt. We were having a nightcap with Peter Thuell when Seaman pinned up the piece of paper. "Anyone knowing the whereabouts of the yacht *Seraffyn* please report to the port captain of Penang." All we could think of was that we'd accidentally forgotten to pay some fee, or maybe our stolen jewelry had been recovered. The next morning we both walked

Irene: typist, guide, and excellent Laser sailor.

down to see the Lumut port captain in his side room at the post office. The wide-faced Malaysian reluctantly took his feet off his cluttered desk when we came in. He dug out a copy of the note we'd seen and lazily dialed the telephone. We watched in amazement as his eyes grew wider and wider, the longer he listened to the voice on the far end of the line. He set the receiver back in its cradle, stood up, and adjusted his uniform shirt. He coughed, stuttered, then started. "Don't you know . . . I mean, you must realize . . ." Larry and I both began to lean forward in our chairs. "You are missing," the flustered man finally blurted out. "You've been missing for over six weeks!"

"What?" we chorused.

"You were reported lost in that typhoon. You went missing. Another Canadian yacht went missing. There was a search. The port captain in Penang was in charge."

"But we were anchored in front of his office for ten days," Larry said. "We registered at his office and got a deratification certificate there too!"

The sweating man wasn't listening. "You must wait right here. Don't go beyond the square until I call for you." We could get no more information at all from the port captain, so we went out under the banyan tree, bought a slice of chilled pineapple from a vendor, and tried to figure out what was happening. "Do you suppose Don Sorte reported us missing when we didn't go to Phuket?" Larry asked.

"No, I'm sure he wouldn't have done that," I said. "We told him we might go there if we had southerly winds, but we had northerlies. Besides, didn't the port captain say another Canadian yacht is reported missing too? *Crusader* is Canadian-registered. Could be her. I can't imagine any other yachts would have been out in that typhoon." For an hour we sat and tried to unravel the threads of this bureaucratic mix-up. Then a young boy came over and told us to hurry, the telephone was waiting. Larry spoke for almost twenty minutes. When he finished he looked drained. "It was *Crusader*. They're gone, missing, all six people. That was the Canadian embassy in Kuala Lumpur. Did you know our parents were notified four weeks ago that we were lost at sea?" Larry paused and I said, "Sure glad we sent them letters from the Langkawi Islands. They couldn't have worried for too long." Larry shook his head. "Those letters didn't arrive. My parents were in touch with the embassy just two days ago. But the embassy promised to telephone direct to Canada today. I can't believe it all."

Over the next week the story gradually began to sort itself out. About once a day a youngster would find us at the club and ask us to hurry to the port captain's office for a telephone call from the embassy, the Penang port captains, and, saddest of all, from the parents of some of the young people who'd paid to sail on *Crusader* from Sri Lanka to Thailand.

It seems Sorte reported very strong head winds when *Crusader* was four days out of Sri Lanka powering toward the Nicobar Islands. Twice each day Don Sorte reported on the ham radio to contacts in both Sri Lanka and Bangkok. On the fifth day he called his contact in Bangkok and said, "Wind and sea very rough, too rough to sail, am powering towards Thailand." The next day he radio'd, "Too rough to continue. Having trouble figuring our position, taking on water, going to turn and run."

His message was far from clear, but it seemed he estimated wind speeds of seventy knots and above during those three days. For a day and a half he ran before the wind, dragging warps and old tires. On the last morning, the same morning we'd split *Seraffyn*'s mainsail in half while we lay hove to, the Bangkok radio contact heard a jumbled report from *Crusader* giving a position and asking for standby radio contact. Her reported last position put her northeast of us by only 110 miles. From our calculations and the weather-satellite photos we later saw, *Crusader*'s last radio contact came while she was right in the center of the typhoon, while we lay hove to on the southern side. When Sorte decided to stop powering and turned to run, he'd run right into the full force of the storm. The Bangkok radio operator contacted the Canadian embassy and when they found there were several other people from England, Australia, and the United States on board *Crusader*, they arranged an air search through the Australian air force at Buttersworth, in Malaysia. Pilots were in the air for fifty-two hours and covered over 100,000 square miles of ocean but spotted only one bit of wreckage, some pieces of yellow line and blue scrap wood. We didn't find out that the Sri Lankan officials had accidentally listed us as part of *Crusader*'s crew until we got a surprise visitor from Australia.

Bob MacDonald had called to talk to us via the port captain's office three days after this affair began in Lumut. "Can you prove my son Glen was on board *Crusader* when she left Sri Lanka?" he demanded. Larry described the young Australian, repeated the address Glen had written in our guest log, and said, "Yes, we called good-bye as they powered out the breakwater."

Three days after this conversation there was a farewell banquet for Peter Thuell at a local restaurant. It must have been after midnight when we all got ready to leave. We were standing outside on the walkway teasing

Peter about the voyage that lay ahead when a tall, dark-haired man burst into our crowd. "Are you Larry and Lin Pardey?" he asked. "I've just flown from Australia. I've been on buses and in taxis all night. I hoped it was you. I didn't think there could be any other foreigners in a village this small. I must talk to you right away. I won't believe Glen is dead. I know he isn't."

Bob MacDonald had been part of the search efforts from the beginning. He stayed with us for a day and showed us the met charts he'd received, the reports from the Australian air-force search, transcripts of radio reports. We got out our passage chart and log, then compared notes. Bob left to begin a search that included visits to Thailand, Sri Lanka, Sumatra, and Singapore—with no results. But even now, four years later, he refuses to accept the idea that his son drowned during that hurricane.

When Bob left, we called our folks just to be sure they'd stopped worrying. It was the day after Christmas. "I found you were safe Christmas Eve," my mother said. "We got a letter you'd sent from Langkawi. Why didn't you buy airmail stamps? That letter took six weeks to arrive."

That solved another part of the mystery. But to this day we wonder why two port captains in ports seldom visited by foreign yachts never connected us with the search that was supposed to cover the whole Far East. Search messages were obviously circulated, because at every port we visited after we left Lumut and until we reached Brunei, we were informed we were listed as missing.

Larry and I spent most of our evenings during the next few weeks discussing *Crusader*'s disappearance. The facts we knew for sure were that *Crusader* had been taking on fifty gallons of water a day even while she lay at anchor in Sri Lanka. This was because of a leak caused two years before by a grounding on a reef near Bali. Don Sorte had tried to repair the damage with internal hull strapping going along the frames to the keel. He said he would have hauled the boat and done a more complete repair the last time he was in Singapore, but, "This new ham set cost me nearly two thousand dollars, so I was short on cash." Larry had inspected *Crusader*'s lower spreaders and found rot at the inner ends. Sorte planned to repair those and the keel leak when he laid up in Singapore after his visit to Thailand. So, we knew the boat was vulnerable, especially since Sorte radio'd that he was powering directly into the seas generated by winds he estimated at seventy knots. Since *Crusader* had a very heavy fin keel and flat, spoonlike forward sections, the pounding she must have been taking could have strained the defective hull-to-keel connection even more. Sorte reported having trouble getting a fix during the storm. If, as he mentioned in Sri Lanka, he rarely took sights until he was approaching his landfall, he would not have known about the unusual current that was setting into the Bay of Bengal at close to sixty miles a day. That would have accounted for his final position 110 miles north of us and 180 miles north of the rhumb-line course we'd all wanted to stick to.

There were several lessons to be learned from this tragedy. First, the crew who answered the ads for a ride to Thailand were taking a big risk by assuming that the boat was seaworthy and the skipper was competent. Only two out of the five crew on board had ever sailed before. Two others had joined the boat only two hours before it left. Had they known the boat was taking on water even in port, they might have changed their minds. Second, if Sorte had kept an accurate daily fix and followed the course set out by the *Ocean Passages for the World*, he would probably have missed the typhoon completely. Third, *Crusader*'s position forty-eight hours before he sent the Mayday was on the dangerous semicircle of that typhoon. If Sorte had chosen to heave to or lie to a sea anchor instead of running, he might not have sailed into the path of the storm, where two ships reported winds in excess of 100 miles per hour. (See Chapter Twelve for diagram.) But the most important thing we learned from all of this was never to assume the weather will be cooperative. No matter what the averages shown on the pilot charts suggest, storms can happen on any ocean at any time of the year.

CHAPTER 16

Ship's Business

This two-month stay on Malaysia's Dindings River was good for all three of us. Our orderly life gave Larry and me more time to explore onshore, to get to know the people around us. We also were able to set aside time each week to work on our list of maintenance jobs so that *Seraffyn* would be in top condition for the long ocean passages that lay ahead. Since we were staying still for once, our mail, our friends, and our new sails finally caught up with us.

We sent our 330 pounds of five-sixteenths-inch BBB chain up to Ipoh to get it galvanized. This was the third time in its eleven-year life that the chain required work. We'd bought hot-dipped galvanized chain before we left California. When we'd reached Florida two years later, there had been spots of rust showing on the last fifty feet at both ends of the chain, since we'd end-for-ended it once a year to spread the wear. A galvanizer in Miami had hot dipped the chain for us at a cost of fifty dollars. Then, in Malta, four a half years later, rust developed on several of the end links. We cut them off and had new, larger end links welded on and spray galvanized. Then we'd taken the whole length of chain to the Maltese government shipyard and watched as they tested the chain to its maximum safe working load. Now, two years later, there were spots of rust showing along most of the length of the chain. None of the links looked pitted or old, just slightly brown and mottled. If we got the chain galvanized before the rusting was any worse, it would probably last another ten years. Since this was our real insurance—this slightly heavier than recommended chain that had held us through gales and hurricanes—and since new chain would cost us two or three months' cruising funds, we felt it was worth a bit of hassle to get it to the city while we had time. It turned out that getting it

Larry marking our regalvanized chain.

galvanized was no more hassle than moving to the only mooring the club owned, off-loading the chain into the dinghy, then dragging it across the club's tiny beach into a truck owned by one of the Ipoh members. Getting it home was more interesting.

When the chain was ready, we took two days off, rode the bus up to Ipoh, and spent the first day shopping with Rosalind Foo. Larry paid the galvanizer fifty-six dollars and went to hire a taxi. The taxi drivers' unofficial union is very strong in Malaysia. Larry had to take the first in line even though it was a rundown-looking, fifteen-year-old Mercedes that seemed unable to carry the two of us and our groceries, let alone our 330 pounds of chain. Two hours later Larry came to pick me up. He got out of the chain-laden taxi and almost panicked. All of that weight in the trunk of the rusted old car was pulling it apart. A three-quarter-inch gap had opened between the rear window and the trunk. But the driver didn't seem the least bit worried. "We move chain," he said calmly. So he and Larry transferred the chain from the trunk to the floor of the backseat. The gap closed and we headed down the rough road to Lumut.

Since no one else wanted to use the only mooring at the club, it seemed unnecessary to wet our bright, new-looking chain. So, we continued to lie tied to the buoy which Peter Thuell had assured us was linked to a three-eighths-inch chain that led to a half-inch chain, then down to a 400-pound block of concrete secured to two lengths of railroad track. The water was too murky to allow us to inspect the mooring. But we slept assured, since Peter's thirty-five-foot ketch had sat out at least a hundred squalls over the past year on this mooring and the local shipyard had inspected it three months before. For six weeks we lay comfortably through monsoon winds, through fifty-knot squalls.

Then, one night, the bright stars lured us into sleeping in the cockpit. We'd had a lovely evening celebrating the end of a good working week. At ten o'clock the next morning we were going to take Irene Khor, our typist and guide to all things Chinese, out for a sail. I was really looking forward to this, since we'd grown to love the giggles of this sixteen-year-old schoolgirl, and now we'd get to meet her older brother and sister, who had just returned from school in Singapore.

Larry woke first, as the heat of the morning sun began to beat against our sheet-covered bodies. He stretched and yawned, and I began to wake. Then Larry suddenly lay very still, head on his pillow, eyes riveted on mine. "Lin, there's something wrong," he whispered. I could feel it too. The boat was swaying oddly, not moving, really. It felt more like an exaggerated vibration. There were no strange sounds, almost no breeze. We both seemed to register the same thought simultaneously, *no sounds*, no birds squawking from the tree in the yacht-club parking lot, no chickens crowing from the cook's garden. Larry slowly lifted his head and peeked over the bulwark. "Lin," he whispered, "there is something wrong. We're not where we were when we went to sleep. God, we must be aground." I shot upright and tried to suppress a nervous giggle as Larry pointed out the huge earth-moving equipment on shore. "That must be where they are building the new naval station. What kind of prankster could have moved us five miles while we slept?"

Larry pulled on his swim trunks, reached into the cockpit locker, and got out the lead line, then rushed to the bow. "You won't believe this, Lin, but we've dragged the mooring all the way here with us." Larry sounded all the way around the boat while I got out our chart of the river entrance. When we figured out exactly where we were we realized that *Seraffyn*, the mooring buoy, and several hundred pounds of heavy chain had left the mooring block during the night, meandered past sixty anchored work

Seraffyn tied to the gypsylike mooring.

boats and ferries, then finally fetched up five miles later, slowed down by a nine-foot-deep sandbar. The strange motion we felt was caused by a riptide welling over the bar.

By the time we'd inspected the whole boat and found no scratches or dings, the whole incident started to take on a more humorous aspect. Then we remembered Irene. We quickly set sail to beat back toward our rendezvous. Unfortunately, the current kept us from any hope of being on time. Larry and I felt pretty bad, because she had been very excited about our planned excursion. Then, as we approached the main town square, we saw Irene running down the main street waving at us. I rowed ashore in *Rinky* and she called, "The old shrimp fisherman said he saw you anchored by the river's mouth early this morning. Why did you go there?" By the time we'd rowed everyone out to *Seraffyn*, then beat up to the shipyard to ask the owner to send a launch for the wayward mooring, our midnight promenade faded from the conversation. But later that night, when we were alone, we marveled at the close call we'd had. That mooring could have parted during the fifty-knot onshore squall we'd had two days before. That would have sent *Seraffyn* into the rocks and pilings in front of the shipyard. We resolved once again that we'd never hang on anyone else's mooring unless we could inspect it ourselves.

One of the joys of cruising, of bringing your own home with you as you visit foreign countries, is the chance it gives to reciprocate the hospitality that seems to be waiting in every port. Irene and her family had included us in their lives. Larry and I had spent a morning in their thatch-roofed kitchen making Chinese New Year's rice-flour cookies with ancient iron molds laid over a charcoal fire between bricks on the concrete floor. We'd each folded several hundred of the paper-thin pastries while they were still hot and flexible, then packed the perfect ones carefully into the traditional gift tins that lined one wall of the room. We'd snacked on the broken pieces and gone with Irene on some of her New Year's Day calls, where we'd bowed and accepted pieces of the traditional sticky, sweet good-luck candies each host or hostess offered. We'd shared the excitement of anticipation when a touring Chinese opera company from Canton began to assemble a prefabricated wooden stage and tent to shelter 400 viewers from the rain. Then Irene and her mother, who spoke five Chinese dialects, Malaysian, and German, but no English, tried to explain the story behind the six-hour-long productions that seemed to give their small-town audience as much pleasure as a Barnum and Bailey Circus. We never did understand the meaning of the operas, but we loved watching as the ordinarily quiet town center took on a country fair atmosphere. Even half a mile away on board *Seraffyn* we could hear the gongs and cannons, the firecrackers, the wailed songs of the jilted opera characters. We tried to bring along the appropriate gifts to show Irene our appreciation. We even tried asking the shipyard owners for ideas. But nothing seemed to work as well as this day of sailing, swimming, and an American-style lunch on board.

As our writing project drew to an end, the northeast monsoon began to loose a bit of its power. Half a dozen cruising boats trickled in from Singapore bound north toward Thailand or west toward Sri Lanka. Soon there were three or four boats anchored in front of the Perak Yacht Club most of the time. The skippers of two of these boats helped us solve our only problem. When we'd been in Penang we'd sent a check to Lam Sailmakers in Hong Kong along with instructions to build us a new mainsail and lapper. They'd sent us a receipt and a completion date plus a note asking for shipping instructions. Now we had written and gotten no reply. We'd tried a long-distance call and found no one in Lam's front

Sally Khor, Irene's sister, demonstrates proper fortune-cookie baking.

office who spoke English. Our local operator didn't speak the proper dialect of Chinese to get through to someone who did. We wanted those sails sent before we left Lumut, but to avoid customs fees they had to be shipped in bond labeled, "For the Canadian yacht *Seraffyn* in transit." Ray Triplett arrived first on his Hong Kong–built forty-six-foot ketch *Morning Star.* "Let's see what the ham net can do for you," he said after we'd spent an evening together. Within a day, ham radio operators from Papua New Guinea to Thailand to Hawaii were in on our problem. I don't understand the routing, but someone somewhere knew someone who lived next door to Lam's loft. That person was contacted, actually walked in and looked at our finished sails, and took over from there. (Thank you, whoever you were.)

The next morning Brian Merrill sailed in on a thirty-eight-foot cutter called *Starry Night.* "I heard all of the broadcasting. I have a friend in Singapore who loves to fly up this way. Let's see what he can do," Brian said. The matter seemed to be out of our hands. While we continued to write in the morning, afternoons became a round of boat hopping, socializing, and occasional bits of work. Then, on the fifth morning after Ray had started the ham net buzzing, a Cessna 185 buzzed the anchorage, scaring the hell out of us as its wingtips passed less than a dozen yards from our mast. A small bag fell from its window onto the club parking lot. "That's him!" Brian yelled from *Starry Night.* "That's Mel from Singapore." All three of us dove into the water and swam ashore to read a note that said, "I've got them. Let's have a party. I'll be back in thirty minutes if I can find a taxi."

By the time we'd showered and gone out to the boat for fresh clothes, a battered taxi arrived from the big village of Sitiawan, five miles inland. All six feet four inches and 250 pounds of Mel Nelson unfolded from between two bags of sails. The only explanation we got about this bit of magic that saved us over a hundred dollars in freight charges and introduced us to the man who was to become our playmate and guide during the next two months was that someone connected with Mel's Singapore-based, American-owned minerals-exploration company had been in Hong Kong two days before. They'd carried our sails back to Singapore and left them in customs. Mel had them transferred in bond to his plane and used them as an excuse to spend the weekend flying across Malaysia visiting friends. "Come on, let's get up in the air where it's cooler," Mel said in his deep, laughter-filled voice as soon as we'd opened our mainsail and fondled its clean white folds. "I flew over Michael's house on my way in. He's

Larry paints the outside of the bulwarks as I paint the inside.

there. Let's hit him for some lunch!" Brian and his crew, Susan, joined us for an afternoon of airplane joy riding, an experience that was completely new to me. I didn't have time to be apprehensive, since the partylike atmosphere kept up every minute until we took off from the fenced-in pasture where Mel had landed. We flew low over the dense jungle and across three rivers. It was only with Mel's guidance that we were able to pick out the slightly different green of rubber trees laid neatly over five square miles of riverside land. We roared low over a rambling white house, then came to land on a strip only twice as wide as the Cessna's wingtips, after Mel flew along the field to check for animals. "Had to buzz an elephant to clear a strip up near Kota Bharu last week," he explained.

Our visit seemed a welcome break in Michael's quiet life as manager of this huge plantation. Larry and I were intrigued by the lingering remains of English colonial life. Several hundred ex-patriots managed plantations for major companies, living quiet lives in palatial homes surrounded by servants. Whole villages worked and lived on these estates; as many as 4,000 people depended on this single source for their income. Yet each plantation manager, each wife we met, longed for the day they could retire home. Their children were sent to schools in England. Their social life consisted of a closed community of other ex-pats who often commuted by airplane for weekend house parties. During the four months we spent in Lumut, then in Singapore, we heard as many strange new stories about this self-isolated life-style as we'd read in two volumes of Somerset Maugham's short stories.

On the way back to the grassy field near Lumut we flew down the Dindings River at about 400 feet. The airborne view showed how the jungle seemed close to invading the fragile villages. The thick overgrowth, the tangled vines were impenetrable; each tiny ribbon of road looked ready to be strangled if man turned his back for a week. I began to understand why the villagers planted no flower gardens, no decorative trees or lawns around their wood homes. They wanted the safety and comfort of open space to help them forget the ever present jungle.

As we finished up our writing project and mentally prepared ourselves to leave the haven Lumut had offered over the past two months, we took time to get to know the suit of sails we'd ordered. We were pleased with the handwork the Hong Kong loft had done. The seaming was accurate and well stitched. We couldn't fault the accuracy of the measurements for both sails. The fabric, a Japanese variation of Dacron called Tetron, was a bit coarser to the touch than the American and English cloths we'd used previously but stood up just as well. The loft had followed our instructions to the letter. The only problems were that we'd forgotten to ask for a full-cut mainsail, since a beamy boat like *Seraffyn* needs the extra draft to keep her moving in a chop. Our mainsail had been cut very flat, and no amount of adjusting made it set to our satisfaction. We'd also forgotten to indicate that our boat was an exceptionally heavy twenty-four-footer. The reef patches on this mainsail would have been sufficient for a twenty-four footer that displaced 4,000 or 6,000 pounds. They were too small for one that weighed 10,500, as *Seraffyn* does. We eventually had the reef patches enlarged before we crossed the Pacific. But we accept complete responsibility for these problems. We'd seen other oriental-built mainsails with beautiful shapes and good reef patches. Our lapper was cut to our satisfaction. If we'd been more careful on our order form we'd have ended up with a mainsail on a par with any of the others we'd owned. Considering that the two sails cost us less than half of what we'd have paid by the time we shipped similar sails from the United States or England, we had no complaints at all.

If you are willing to deal with the possible problems of mail-order sail making, it is definitely worth considering Hong Kong sailmakers once you are out cruising and can avoid the customs duties. But do be sure to give the sailmaker you choose a complete sail plan with any changes you may have made to your rig, plus as much information as you can on items that could affect sail design, such as displacement, tack cutbacks, out-haul arrangements, and slide arrangements.

As February drew to a close, we rounded up the last made-to-order (for two dollars) shirt from the local tailor, paid farewell visits to Irene's family and our favorite shopkeepers, had one last weekend in Ipoh, settled the running tab we'd kept at the shipyard, and of course enjoyed the farewell racing day our yacht-club friends arranged.

Then, one day, our work list was down to inconsequential, easy-to-do-underway items. *Seraffyn* glowed under fresh topside paint and fresh varnish. Our book advance arrived, so our cruising fund was topped up. We slipped out of Lumut feeling wonderfully rested and in control of our lives. But as we meandered down the river-indented west coast of Malaysia, we began to dream of the wonders of Singapore. "Mel's told me they do great stainless-steel work for almost nothing. Maybe we can get a new stove top made up," I said as I got out our growing shopping list yet again. "Good idea, and he told me there is a marine company that has a surplus of bronze fittings. If we're going to build a new boat someday it might be worth

The seventy-six-year-old boat builder next to the club finished one of
these fourteen-foot Sampan dories in just three days.

looking at them," Larry added. This daydreaming was easy to do as we drifted along this friendly coast. But when we actually arrived in Singapore, the reality of what turned out to be the biggest spending spree of our lives made me wish for the peace and quiet of that bit of paradise we'd left in Lumut.

CHAPTER 17

Singapore Spree

An electrical charge seemed to fill the air around Singapore. From the moment we passed the first light buoy, marking the mouth of Johore Straits, and left Malaysian waters, we felt the throbbing pulse of this strange island nation. We reached through the warm, clear night, clinging to the very edge of the well-marked channel, as deeply laden oil tankers filed by, demanding the deepest water with their special staff of three red lights. An oil-drilling platform rumbled past us, guided by two huge tugs. We shaded our eyes from the white glare of welding torches as workmen scurried over the jumble of steel on the island-sized platform. Huge dredges sighed and gulped just outside the shipping channel. Hundreds of lights showed their chain of buckets pulling sand from the bottom of the channel. Lines of barges waited to carry the sand away. As dawn slowly changed the scene around us from a bobbing display of lights to an impressive panorama of trade, we found that neither of us really wanted to go below and sleep. There was just too much to see. We reached across the shallows south of Singapore toward the anchorage off Pasir Panjang, and the traffic was pruned by draft limitations to pilot boats, fishermen, raggedy trading canoes from Indonesia, and high-speed chandlers' launches bound for ships just approaching this commercial hub of the Far East. Barges lay alongside mammoth floating steamshovels at the shoreward edge of the channel, their cargo of sand being lifted overboard to keep Singapore literally growing at the rate of four acres a day.

Cruising sailors approaching Singapore have some important decisions to make. In 1978 there were no good anchorages that were safe, easy to use, close to shopping areas, and free. If you anchor off the main city with the big ships, the racket of passing bumboats and pilots will keep you awake twenty-four hours a day, you'll worry about ships running you down, and you'll find little protection from squalls that can kick up a nasty sea. If you go inside the customs port and tie to the dock, you'll be harassed by a constant parade of official boats rushing in and out to service the 500 commercial ships that lie in the roads and make up part of the 40,000 ships a year that clear through this unbelievably busy port. If you go to the Singapore National Yacht Club, you'll find pleasant facilities but the worst infestation of mosquitoes we've ever seen, plus unbelievably hot, humid nights, especially during the northeast-monsoon season. That leaves Pasir Panjang, where we first anchored, or the Changi Yacht Club, where we moved two days later. Pasir Panjang is a protected spot with good holding ground, little traffic, few mosquitoes, and no harbor charges. Unfortunately, to get to the main road, you have to cross a half mile of newly reclaimed foreshore. On normal days this means a scorching walk across the shoe-filling sand. On rainy days, it's a struggle across acres of swampy mud. Then there is a thirty-minute bus ride to reach the main shopping areas of the city. Half a dozen interesting cruising boats lay here. But the people on board warned us, "If you have a lot of stores to buy and carry across the sand, you'll hate it here."

After we'd bused to town and cleared our papers, we called Mel Nelson. Within an hour he came to get us for a ride out to Changi. The beautifully situated club lay on the northern shore of thirty-mile-wide Singapore. Lovely tropical trees edged its manicured lawns. An open-verandahed clubhouse offered inexpensive meals from 0800 to 2330 every day. Clean showers, friendly workmen, and a busy launch service added to the modern-yacht-club feeling. We saw a notice on the board, "Lady skippers race, all visiting cruising sailors welcome." We felt the cool, fresh breeze across the open waters, inspected the heavy-duty gear that workmen were setting out for new moorings, then forgot about the six-dollars-a-day fee and forty-minute bus ride to the city and decided to get here in time for the race. Mel encouraged our decision by telling us, "You'll meet a lot more local people by being here at the club. Besides, I have a spare room in my house. My wife has asked you to be our guests during the week, so you can shop more easily. It's no extra work for her, since we have an amah [housekeeper]." After several urgings we took Mel and Sharon up on their offer. Then we found that most cruising sailors stocking up for long voyages here come up with similar arrangements. They choose the comfortably but slightly expensive Changi Yacht Club for their boat, then either meet some club member who offers them a room or rent one of the abundant hotel rooms that can be had for about eight dollars a night in the shopping districts of central Singapore, and spend Monday to Friday in town going wild in the supermarkets and emporiums that are like a child's dream of Christmas.

A few words of warning about entering Singapore on a foreign cruising boat. Listen to any suggestions made by people who have just sailed from here. This is the only port we visited during eleven years of cruising where the officials seemed set on trapping unwary visitors. We'd been warned to get a deratification certificate before we reached Singapore. The official who signed us in was incredulous that we had one. In fact, he'd already pulled out a sheet telling about the fines for vessels entering without proper papers. We'd been warned to prepay the port garbage fee of ten dollars per month as soon as we entered. We had to ask for the proper papers to do this. It was a bit of a hassle but saved us almost seventy dollars U.S., since the daily rate, charged unwary yachtsmen at their departure, is three dollars a day. (You get no garbage pick-up service for this fee, just the right to land garbage at designated garbage cans.)

The politics of this crowded, business-oriented nation left us a bit confused. The president seemed to be elected, yet he ruled like a dictator. Racial prejudice on radio and television, in political speeches or in print was forbidden. Drug-enforcement rules were carried out to the letter. Anyone caught selling even a gram of narcotics was sentenced to jail, and several times during our stay, these drug sellers were executed. Drug traffic ground to a virtual halt under these tight rules. This strict law-and-order concept was even extended to traffic control. Five days after we arrived a new law forbidding jaywalking went into effect. We didn't know about it. We got stopped by the police as we ran gaily across a street. They put a note in our passports and warned, "Do this again and it will cost you two hundred fifty Singapore dollars." That's a hundred-five U.S. dollars, and he was serious! We saw absolutely no jaywalking after that. As attractive as certain aspects of this strict law-enforcement policy seemed, as safe as it made us feel when we wandered down back alleys of the city, it did seem unfair in many cases. We saw families forced to leave their traditional thatched-roof homes, their gardens and chicken pens, as the government relocated them in concrete apartment buildings, then razed their land to build more offices and high-rise apartments. The results may have been more sanitary, more land efficient, but they definitely were less interesting or personalized. On the other hand, business was thriving under Singapore's president, Lee Kuan Yew. An international community of prosperous businessmen added their exuberance to the vastly mixed population. The yacht club at Changi was like a social center for many of these foreigners.

Unfortunately for me, we didn't arrive at the club until 2000 the night before the lady-skippers race. We went ashore and put our name on the list. But we could find no crew in the quiet club that evening. In the morning Larry offered to scrub *Seraffyn*'s bottom while I went ashore to get the race instructions and look for crew. A dozen other ladies and their crews were getting ready and all were sympathetic, but it seemed that crew was in short supply that month because it was late in the racing season. I didn't think to go and ask on some of the cruising boats that lay nearby. So, when I got back to *Seraffyn* twenty minutes before starting time, I was ready to call it all off and watch everyone else sail. Larry would have none of that! He'd just finished spending an hour and a half diving with his snorkel to scrub off barnacles and slime. "This boat is rigged for easy handling, let's go!" he insisted. I felt flustered as we rushed around, securing the dinghy to our mooring, unfolding our big genoa, marking the race course on our chart. Over twenty boats were already milling around at the starting line, 200 yards away from our mooring. Two knots of tide ran against us, and Larry was just hanking on the genoa, I was leading the sheets, when the five-minute warning gun went off. "That's it," I said. "We couldn't even make the starting line in five minutes." But Larry pointed at the line of boats jockeying to get to the line. With only five knots of wind against a two-knot current, they just weren't making it. In fact, sitting tied to our mooring we were actually leading the race. That put a whole new light on the affair. When the starting gun blasted, Larry flung the bow line loose and I reached out from the moorings to join the fleet.

I learned some important lessons about sailing and racing that day. The wind freshened; the fleet reached off with the tide now behind them. I felt confident and enjoyed steering while Larry eased and tightened the sheets at my request. We both began to catch our breath after the rush to get ready. But three miles on, I saw a fish trap blocking our way. This stick-and-thatch shack stood on stilts guarding a half-mile-long line of pilings. Usually, nets stretch all along the length of pilings, so I said, "Ease the sheets, I'm falling off."

I shouldn't have. The whole fleet charged right through a gap they knew about, halfway down the line of pilings. So, on the next leg we had to sheet in snugly while everyone else was on a close reach. "You should have followed the fleet," Larry remarked. I bridled at what I assumed was criticism and snapped back, "How did you expect me to know that!"

"You're pinching," Larry snapped right back.

"If you're going to nag, you can take the helm!"

"Can't, it's lady helmsmen only."

During the next hour and a half I felt something slipping as smaller boats gained on us. I began asking Larry for suggestions, and he started taking charge until soon he was sailing the race and I was only steering. The heat of the humid tropical day grew intense; the glare of two and a half hours of watching the mainsail and the sparkling water began to make my eyes ache. Only two or three boats seemed to be anywhere near us as we beat toward the final mark. I was tired from trying to manage a race with only two of us on board; I felt defeated, sorry we'd come out, and angry at Larry. Then, as we neared the mark and prepared to run the last four miles to the finish line, I saw half a dozen boats converging. We were right where we belonged. A Folkboat lay a dozen yards ahead of us; a superlight twenty-footer passed the mark with us. My spirits started to pick up. Then Larry said, "Now, we'll reach up and . . ." For some reason I cut him off. "Sorry, Larry, this is my race and I want the genoa set on the pole. I'll run wing and wing, then blanket that blue boat."

"Good idea," he agreed.

All of a sudden we fell into the groove that we'd been missing all day. We worked like a well-oiled team, barely speaking a word, as Larry eased sheets just when I was ready to ask, or I headed up just as he pointed to a wind shift. I got really brave and gained a place by falling down on a well-handled twenty-four-foot sloop until *Seraffyn*'s bowsprit rested less than three feet from the helmswoman's shoulder. Our vast spread of canvas blanketed her sails; we slipped by and got an invitation to share a drink after the race.

As we sailed back to our mooring and cleaned the boat, we began to analyze the difference between the first three hours of the race and the last one. In the end it became obvious. I'd taken Larry's first comment as criticism rather than as just a friendly comment. Then I'd become afraid of making another mistake. Like too many less experienced sailing partners, I began stepping back, wanting Larry to take over so that he'd be responsible for the results. Then my resentment showed, and he began feeling angry at my lack of confidence. When I finally woke up and realized, "This is just a game. I'll learn only if I make my own mistakes," Larry willingly stepped back and let me take charge. During a race there's no room for two skippers. So, as soon as it was clear who was in charge, life lost its tension. From that day on, I began looking for other chances to make my own mistakes and learn from them. Although racing and cruising seem worlds apart, the close-quarters sailing, the course planning and short tacking are a wonderful, quick way to learn about your boat and how to handle it. Half a dozen races as skipper of your own boat will give you the confidence to be a full working partner on your cruising boat.

It was late when we left the after-race party. In the morning we'd move to one of the new moorings we'd watched being set the first day we'd seen the club. Then we'd head into Singapore City to begin our three-week shopping spree.

At first our shopping was like a game. We split our four-page list into galley stores, boat stores, Larry's list, Lin's list. Then we'd set off on our own separate ways each morning, scout out the best prices, the best sources. I'd tour each of the major supermarkets making notes, visit the chandlers and compare lists, contact the wholesalers for more prices. Meanwhile Larry dickered with the sheet-metal shop over the design and cost for a stainless-steel stove top to replace the rusted iron one we were using. He visited half a dozen tailors until he found one he trusted to make a blue corduroy blazer, toured the back streets looking for a bookbinder, oil-lamp lenses, fishing supplies, bronze screws. When we rendezvoused at Mel's air-conditioned apartment each evening we were footsore and weary but full of stories to share. Mel and Sharon would take us out to sample some of the wonderful local foods, the best of which we found at little streetside stalls that appeared almost miraculously after the regular shops closed down. Sharon would go over our list for the next day and suggest new places to check out, new ways to get around in the crowded, hot city. Then, on Friday, we returned to *Seraffyn* and a relatively quiet weekend of exchanging visits on board the dozen cruising yachts assembled here from Indonesian cruises, Indian Ocean voyages, and trips to Thailand and Borneo.

Then, the second week, the real shopping started. What had been a game of look and scheme became a serious matter of buy and pay. Every day I seemed to cash another three- or five-hundred-dollar check. Then, to my financial horror, Larry found a deal. He dragged me out to the far reaches of Singapore's industrial zone and we spent the afternoon looking at huge teak timbers. Since Singapore is one of the transshipment ports for Burmese teak, the prices were reasonable, less than half the cost of the same wood in the United States, but even so, after searching and scrounging, we would be spending close to $4,000 for enough timber to build a boat we hadn't even decided to build yet. Even with our book advance we had only $7,000, and the stores we'd ordered already would take at least $1,500. But Larry was like a miner who sees his first gold nugget. He wasn't going to leave without some of those golden brown timbers. "If we don't build a boat they'll still be a good investment," he insisted as we arranged for a transfer of funds. By the end of that week I was almost in a state of shock. Then the seventeen-year-old Chinese girl who worked as amah for Mel and Sharon showed me what shock really is.

We'd given her an envelope with $400 in cash to pay for a shipment that would be arriving at Mel's seventh-story apartment that morning. Since she could not read English, we didn't think to leave her a list of what we'd purchased. When I came back to the apartment to have lunch, the amah didn't come to open the door. I set my packages down and found the key I'd been lent. When everything was stacked in the guest room, I went looking for the girl, who should have been busy scurrying around the kitchen or cleaning the house. She was sitting on the edge of her bed surrounded by crates and cartons of food and stores. She was crying. Her red eyes and soaking handkerchief showed she'd been crying for a long time. When she saw me she wailed, "I sorry, I sorry." Fortunately Mel arrived home just then and took over. The conversation lapsed into a Singaporean patois and Mel began to roar with laughter. "Chen was sure she made a big mistake. She fought with the deliverymen because she just couldn't believe you'd want ninety-six rolls of toilet paper."

The amah was shaking her head and pointing at the huge box that sat on top of her tiny bed. "You say very small boat. No room for box that big! I no have four hundred dollars to give you. They no leave without money!"

We did our best to reassure the shaken girl. In fact, we cooked our own lunch and gave her money to run out to her favorite noodle shop for a treat. But I could understand her worry as she imagined paying for her error out of a twenty-five-dollars-a-week salary.

When we called two taxis to begin our trek back to *Seraffyn,* the case of forty-eight rolls of paper towels and the case of toilet paper wouldn't be squeezed in. Mel offered to bring them out the next morning, when we'd planned a day of sailing together. "I can't believe they'll fit in your boat either," he joked.

But within an hour of Mel's arrival the next morning, the last plastic-wrapped two-roll pack of toilet paper slid into its cubbyhole next to the water tank. The last of twenty-one cases of canned food fit into their proper lockers, and we showed an incredulous Mel the spaces left for twelve dozen eggs, forty pounds of fresh vegetables, and some snack foods.

By the end of our third week in Singapore, *Seraffyn* was down an inch below her normal-load waterline. She had new stainless-steel bread pans and a new shortwave radio receiver; our favorite hardback books had been rebound; Larry's handsome new sports coat was packed carefully away; three new sets of bed linens stuffed our locker; a shopping bag full of good paperback books crowded the clothes locker. We'd been warned that this was the last place where we could be sure of finding a good variety of reasonably priced stores, so we'd taken advantage to the utmost. At the time it seemed a bit like overkill, but as usual we learned it pays to keep the boat well stocked.

Our last two days in Singapore we spent leaning *Seraffyn* against the yacht-club pier and waiting for the tide to go out. We both scrubbed and scraped, then applied a thick coat of quick-drying antifouling paint as the tide came back to tickle our feet.

Seraffyn's ice chest was full to the brim; her fresh-stores locker overflowed into three plastic shopping baskets that lined the quarter berth. We

Seraffyn is sitting on driftwood timbers we staked in place on the previous low tide.

went ashore that last Wednesday evening for a party hosted by Mel. We missed saying a personal good-bye to his warm, beautiful wife, Sharon, since she was in the hospital with their three-day-old daughter. As we joked about our rush to leave the next morning to avoid the possible bit of bad luck that leaving on a Friday can bring, the sea stories began to flow. One long-term Far East cruising sailor began to tell us of the Ming pottery he'd found when he was diving for dinner near an island in the Gulf of Thailand. Another told us about the fantastic bays of New Guinea. The beautiful girls of Bali came in for glowing reports that turned the men's eyes glassy. The reefs of Australia's eastern shore made me remember the kind of bay hopping I love so much. As the evening wore on, we both began to realize we were giving up something special by continuing on our way directly toward Canada. We lay awake for a long time that night talking about how we could spend another year just around Indonesia and Borneo. But we both knew we were just talking. When the alarm went off at 0700, we rushed to catch the strongest of the ebb tide out of Changi and down the Straits of Johore toward our goal of Brunei.

A large Danish freighter passed, inward-bound. "I'll bet that's the ship our teak timbers will go on," Larry commented. I shook my head as I thought of the boat we both refused to openly commit ourselves to building. But I knew we'd never sell those twelve teak logs that weighed close to five tons. Both of us were reluctant to commit ourselves to three years of working and boat building when we still had three ocean passages ahead of us. But after that? I could see our future slowly forming as we close reached toward the South China Sea. The land fell away and we got out our voyage-planning chart. Then we began to fall into that hard-to-describe routine of ocean voyagers. The sea became our reality, the land only a dream, a pit stop for stores and refreshment along an unmarked highway toward our destiny.

CHAPTER 18

The South China Sea

At first it felt good to be at sea after three hectic weeks in Singapore. We enjoyed putting our little world back into shape. Larry rinsed the last of the shore dirt off the decks; I settled the last of our stores into secure spots. We relaxed into the routine of watches, sights, and quiet cocktail hours. I've always loved those first days at sea. Once we cleared the land it was too late to worry about what I'd forgotten to buy; we'd either have it on board or do without. It was too late to worry about whom we forgot to visit, call, or write. There was no reason to rush, no reason to keep busy. Decisions were behind us, our route chosen; now only the changing wind or sea conditions affected the pattern of our days.

I felt particularly content about our planned voyage from Singapore to the Sultanate of Brunei, on Borneo's northwestern shore. The pilot charts showed predominantly light southerly winds and absolutely no record of typhoons or even storms during this time of the year. We had close to 3,400 miles to sail in order to reach our final Pacific-crossing jump-off port of Yokohama, but we didn't want to sail from there until July 1, and it was now only March 30. If we averaged anywhere near one hundred miles a day, we could spend six weeks on shore exploring in Brunei, the Philippines, or Japan. That sounded great to me.

I was sound asleep, oblivious to the early-morning light, secure in the knowledge that Larry was on watch and we were moving along nicely. I think I remember hearing the radio go on for the 0500 VOA world-news report. But when Larry grabbed my shoulders and blurted out, "Quick, Lin, out of the bunk, we're taking on water. Must be that butt block we've been watching," I woke with a start. I *was* worried about that damned butt block. For two years I'd been noticing a little line of salt forming just where the two planks joined under the oak reinforcing pad. That was the only hint of a leak anywhere in *Seraffyn*'s hull, and Larry kept promising to recaulk it. Now I was lying on the cushion above it, and I didn't pause to think. I scrambled out of that bunk, smashed my elbow on the overhead, caught my feet in the sleeping bag, and ended up in a heap on the cabin sole, the sleeping bag tangled around my knees.

Larry's look of concern faded into a triumphant grin. "April Fool!" he crowed. I couldn't feel angry. Instead I lay on the floor convulsed with laughter, wishing I'd had a chance to plan a practical joke that worked as well.

We were headed almost directly east toward the Borneo shore to pick up a back eddy in the generally southerly current. Our winds had grown lighter and more flukey each day. Five nights out, we were absolutely becalmed ten miles north of a cluster of tiny islands. There wasn't a decent anchorage anywhere in the group. The current was setting us south at close to a knot; the high, steady barometer and clear, star-studded skies didn't hold any promise of wind. We didn't want to lose any of the northing we'd worked to gain. Larry came out at change of watch and said, "Let's anchor."

"Here?" I asked grumpily.

"Why not, there's only two hundred fifty feet of water under us, the chart shows a mud bottom, we haven't seen a ship in two days. Besides, I'd like to sleep with you. How about it?"

The idea began to sound interesting then. Larry switched our twenty-five-pound CQR anchor from its all-chain rode to the second bower. We eased out thirty feet of chain and 300 feet of five-eighths-inch nylon, then made a bowline in that line, lashed its tail securely with a piece of nylon twine, secured our 300-foot-long three-eighths-inch stern anchor line in place with a second bowline, lashed that tail securely, and eased the line overboard. As soon as Larry snubbed the line off, *Seraffyn*'s bow started to swing to stem the current. I stared at the tiny bow wake our flashlight revealed, fascinated by the idea of being anchored in the middle of the South China Sea. Larry set the anchor light in place and blew out the running lights; then I joined him in the cushion-padded cockpit for a night without watches.

Time started to drag as flukey winds, occasional squalls, and intermittent calms cut our average daily runs to fifty miles noon to noon. I grew more and more impatient as I checked our calendar and calculated that each extra day at sea meant one fewer on shore. At this rate we'd already lost a week. In our minds, that July 1 Yokohama departure date was a fixed point. Later than that, and we risked a typhoon near Japan, higher incidence of fog near the Aleutian Islands, and increased chances for autumn gales as we approached Canada. Apprehension led to tension, tension to boredom, boredom to occasional frayed tempers. It all followed a pattern. Whenever we were making at least two and a half knots, we were the best of friends, eager to talk, joking, planning, even working on boat-maintenance projects. As our boat speed dropped to one knot, we began to hide behind our books, go our separate ways. When the boat stopped, which seemed to happen for about five or six hours every second day, we'd start to grump. I'd snap if Larry asked for more salt on the salad. He'd grumble if I took the pillow he'd been planning to lounge against. We'd rarely fall into a real quarrel, but until a breeze came to start us moving again, we'd hover close to the brink.

Then, one evening just after we'd spotted the lights of Tanjong Sirik, on the shores of Kalimantan, one of us, I've forgotten who, said, "Why don't we just reach off and head into the river that leads to Kuching? Mel said it's a great place to visit. We could be in tomorrow." That led to a discussion of the discontent that had been growing between us.

"We both decided it was time to get back to Canada and California at least for a visit," Larry commented. "We knew it would mean hard work and a lot of time at sea. What's bothering us?" His question launched a searching conversation that followed a dozen paths and collided with a dozen dead ends. Over and over we kept asking each other, "What's really bothering you?" The early-evening stars reached the horizon and disappeared. The moon rose to illuminate the line of hills on the horizon ten miles away to starboard. *Seraffyn* glided smoothly along on a seven-knot breeze. We talked about why we were headed for Japan, why we'd gotten short-tempered. Finally, answers began to surface. Both of us had secretly been harboring fears of going "home," of giving up the unfettered life we'd led over the past ten years. We'd learned the tricks that make a cruising life enjoyable. Now the uncertainties of life ashore had us worried. We'd kept abreast of inflation news; we'd had letters from too many friends telling of divorces and separations. We both remembered the 4,000 hours of hard work we'd put into building *Seraffyn*, the three and a half years we'd spent earning the money to finance materials, food, and shelter while we built her.

It was long after midnight when we decided to tack north straight for Brunei, and both of us finally made a commitment. We'd work together to find ways to really enjoy building our next boat, because it was the most logical project for the next few years of our lives. When we'd built *Seraffyn* we'd planned only to take a six- or nine-month cruise to Mexico. We'd never dreamed we'd make her our home year after year. We'd never dreamed we'd want to live a floating life. We'd only set off for an adventure, for as long as it was fun. Now we'd learned that this was our life—roaming, exploring, meeting new people and new ideas. Now we needed a real floating home, one we could afford but one that could make us a bit more self-contained, with room to carry stores for half a year if we wanted to, room for our own shower-bathtub so that we'd be less dependent on costly yacht clubs and marinas, room for a conveniently stored, decent-sized typewriter so that we could expand the writing life we'd started.

"If we earn the money to build this new boat as we go along, we can eventually sell *Seraffyn* and use the money for an insurance retirement fund," Larry suggested. "Right now, all we own in the whole world is this boat and three thousand dollars. We've never paid into any retirement fund. No one is going to bail us out when we're sixty-five."

I sipped my glass of sherry and imagined our freedom slipping through my fingers like grains of sand as Larry talked of finding a place to build a boat shed, of buying a pickup truck. Thoreau's admonition to "use the land but own it not" buzzed through my mind as I suggested, "We'd be wise to buy an acre of land somewhere and find one of those houses they move when they build a freeway. That way we'd be investing our money instead of throwing it away on rent." Then I was caught up in the adventure of planning how we'd build the new boat, where we'd like to live, the skiing and riding we'd like to do on weekends, the friends we'd get to know again. "Remember, Lin, if we stick to a simple thirty footer we know we'll be under way again within three and a half years, and look what we'll have gained." Larry used logic to calm my fears when I reminded him of half a dozen cruising friends who had gone home to build a bigger cruising boat and were either divorced or still building and landlocked seven or eight years later. "Every one of them has tried to build a forty- or forty-five-foot boat. We know we could never afford something like that, not on the salaries we can earn. I can't think of many average working people who could. But look at the people we know who chose to build thirty footers. They all got under way in five years or less. With two of us working, we should be able to cut at least a year off that."

Once our deep-seated fears were out in the open, the reasons for our tensions seemed to disappear. "We'll just have to work at keeping busy when we run out of wind," Larry said.

"Let's try and get the boat in perfect shape so when we reach port there's nothing to do but buy stores and play," I added.

The days moved faster then, even if the winds didn't blow as we'd hoped they would. It took us nearly thirteen days to reach the oilfields lining the shallow waters off the coast of Brunei, a distance of only 700 miles. But as we reached between drilling platforms and flaring wellheads, we finished yet another on-board project. The dinghy now had a new cover on her rubber fender; we'd refastened the wood rub rails along her bottom. The lifelines had new chaffing guards at each stanchion; all of my shoes had new heels, courtesy of Larry's stash of rigging leather. We'd even written an article and outlined two others.

It's a good thing we were so caught up when we finally reached into this strange little country and anchored in the main port, just five miles down river from the capital city of Bandar Seri Begawan. One family owns this oil-, lumber-, and silicon-rich wedge of northern Borneo. The British government slowly backed out of control as the sultan trained his own family to take over. By 1978, when we sailed in, only foreign affairs were

Downtown Bandar Seri Begawan. The dome is gold-plated.

supervised by Britain, with full independence slated for 1983. Since fewer than 200,000 people live in this resource-rich country and over 35 percent are related to the ruling family, the standard of living is very high, with money left over for extravagances such as a fleet of 160 new Cadillacs for the sultan's family. The extravagance we noticed most was the British navy. The sultan had rented a 500-man contingent to teach his countrymen seamanship and defense. This community of transplanted Brits decided to make sure we were well entertained.

Within eight hours of our arrival our life was booked for the next seven days: dinner and dancing at the commander's home, water skiing, picnics and barbecues, a foray into the jungles with the flying doctor on board a jet-powered helicopter, shopping tours. It was hard to find an evening free to plan a party on board *Seraffyn* so that we could take just a few of our new friends sailing. Yet underlying all of this sheer fun was the serious business of moving on, plus hours of soul searching over the decisions that come when you try to combine cruising with being part of a family.

There was a telegram waiting for us at the port captain's office when we cleared our entry papers. My family had sent it to our last known address, at Mel Nelson's home in Singapore. I was in an absolute daze as I finished reading the two lines that could mean my father had died. The only place where we could make an overseas telephone call was in the city. The time difference meant we had to wait at least three hours to be sure we'd reach someone who was awake. Larry tried to keep my mind occupied. We went to the bank our friends from Singapore had recommended and found a fat mail package waiting. Unfortunately the banker's draft we'd ordered from California hadn't arrived. This added to my apprehensions, especially when we found that the $600 cash, which was all we had with us, would just cover the air fare on the twice-a-week flight from Brunei through Guam to California.

We sat in an air-conditioned café toying with our food and discussing what we should do. "If you want to go home, you should," Larry said. Then when we finally placed our call, a low cloud cover and a tropical disturbance to the east made the radio-transmitted call garbled and unclear. The operator in Brunei finally reached another operator in Honolulu who relayed our questions to my mother, then back to us. Thank God, my father was out of danger. The massive coronary he'd suffered two weeks previously had not left any permanent damage. The doctor had declared him definitely on the mend. My mother relayed her final wishes and freed us from further worry. "Your dad is really looking forward to meeting you when you sail into Victoria. We're going to fly up there and wait from August fifteenth on!"

I still wondered if it would be a good idea to fly home and see my folks. But after some more careful thought we decided to telephone again when we reached Manila. If I did fly home now, it would mean another year in the Orient waiting for the right season to cross the Pacific. If Dad continued to improve, a sailing reunion would be more enjoyable for everyone. Several cruising friends have told us that we chose the very best time in our lives to go off cruising, before our parents reached the age when health problems would create concern. We must agree. We've watched the painful debates that occur when a family member back home becomes ill and there are no really safe places to leave your boat, no easily affordable ways to get back home. We've watched potential grandparents torn between cruising even farther afield and being there to experience the joys of their first grandchild. Considerations like these must be reckoned with. Some cruising sailors feel a ham radio would be a solution. But in fact, the radio might create more havoc than peace of mind, as family worry when you miss a transmission. There really seems to be no solution to the problem of family back home and offshore voyaging, and this is one of the major compromises you have to mull over before you cut your ties and leave.

When we set sail eight days after our arrival, we'd received our banker's draft; we'd been well entertained by Brunei's imported navy. *Seraffyn* was again full of fresh stores, including two dozen two-and-a-half-pound watermelons, a local specialty that lasted all the way to Japan in newspaper-padded nests, on top of the anchor chain.

We grabbed the first of the ebb tide to sail clear of the quiet port. Larry joked as we set the boat on its course due north toward the Palawan Channel, "It's almost easier to be at sea. Do you realize we've had only one meal on board since we arrived?" I had to agree. Now that we were voyaging instead of cruising, our life had fallen into a pattern we'd read about in other people's books. Get ready for sea, sail, celebrate your arrival, have some parties, get ready for sea. We both missed the time to become part of the communities we visited. We missed the half-day sails to explore yet another cove or anchorage and the quiet days walking onshore with no real destination. But we'd made our choice, and now it was reinforced by our desire to make that late-August family reunion a reality.

CHAPTER 19

~~~~~~

Palawan

The voyage from Brunei, on Borneo's northwest tip, to Manila, on the island of Luzon, is one we both faced with trepidation. To the west of us, scattered across the whole South China Sea almost to the Cambodian and Vietnamese shore, lay hundreds of just submerged, ever growing coral reefs. These reefs were so poorly charted, the currents so irregular, that each chart, each navigation book warned, "It is unwise for any vessel to wander into the dangerous area," or "the foul grounds." To the west of us lay the reefs and rocky shores of Palawan Island. The only route open toward Manila lay through the Palawan Channel, but we read confidence-eroding warnings in the *Ocean Passages for the World:* "There may be less depth than charted off the west coast of Palawan . . . Furthermore, off the northwest coast of Borneo and in the Palawan Channel between 2°N and 11°N, currents may set in any direction throughout the year; they have caused the stranding of vessels on either side of the passage." We had carefully chosen April as the time of year to make our dash up this 400-mile-long, 30- to 40-mile-wide channel. Winds would be light but largely favorable, visibility better than at most times of the year, and typhoon chances low, with only two recorded during this month over the past fifty years. Yet no amount of careful logic made me relax as we picked up a fair current and headed north in light, flukey winds.

The magnificent volcanic peaks of northern Borneo made navigation easy. We could see 9,000-foot-high Victoria Peak for almost three days as we short tacked with winds that seemed to pick up in the late afternoon and die to complete calm by 1000 each morning. Then the heat would set in as we lay becalmed, nothing around us—no sea life, no birds, no passing ships. The motionless, humid air seemed hostile; the reports we'd read of revolutionaries raiding oil-rig-tending boats in the Sulu Sea began to force their way into our minds. Those so-called pirates, Muslim tribesmen who'd been fighting the Catholic settlers for almost 400 years, had some of their strongholds only 100 miles east of us. What was to prevent them from heading our way? Then, when we were seven days out of Brunei, our fickle winds seemed to wear out and quit completely. We'd made good only 200 miles during all of that time. We were still 500 miles from our goal, and now we lay in the middle of the Balabac Straits. Our last sight showed us being set west into the dangerous grounds by a three-quarters-knot current.

I was on watch at 0030, sitting in the cool of the cockpit, reading a book by the light of a kerosene cabin lamp I'd carried out and set on deck. The flame didn't flicker in the still air. *Seraffyn* seemed to be dead as she lay on the flat sea. The nearest reef was still forty miles east of us according to our afternoon fix, and I kept calculating, "If the current runs at three-quarters knots we'd have to be completely becalmed for two days to be in danger. It's been only twelve hours since our last sight . . ." But still I was edgy. Then I heard the sound that confirmed my very worst fears. Through the still, clear night I heard the faint whisper of waves breaking. I tried to remain calm. For nearly half an hour I listened with increasing dread as the sound grew clearer, closer. I went below and checked our charts. A note next to the first set of reefs said, "Position reported to be off by three miles." It didn't say which way, just "off." That could put the steep-to mass of hull-ripping coral even closer to us. With depths of 2,000 feet right next to the reef, we'd never have a chance to anchor. No one lived or worked in this forbidding sea. There would be little chance of being rescued if we got stranded. I couldn't stand to be alone one minute longer. "Larry, get up, quick. I need help," I said as calmly as I could. He didn't hesitate. "I hear breakers," I told him as he climbed into the cockpit.

"Holy shit," he whispered when he caught the swishing, gurgling sound. He ran forward and grabbed our fourteen-foot oar, got it in place, and started rowing with a vengeance. The sound grew louder no matter how hard he shoved on that oar. I held the tiller, terrified to look astern. After twenty minutes the glow of our stern light reflected off the sweat running down Larry's nude body, and still he kept stroking with that oar. Then it happened. The sound enveloped us and we had to look astern. The bright moonlight, the glowing phosphorescence of the tropical water illuminated the foamy breaking waves growing ever closer. We watched in horror until all of a sudden we were surrounded by hundreds, maybe even thousands of dolphins. They filled our horizons. They played in the tiny wake *Seraffyn*'s bow made as she moved under oar power at about a knot and a half. They jumped and splashed in undulating lines on all sides of us. Then they were past us, moving toward the east like an ill-disciplined army. The two of us collapsed against the cabin sides in a state of nervous exhaustion. We teased each other about our overworked imaginations. We laughed as I helped Larry bathe off the sweat he'd worked up. Then I sent him below to continue his off watch as I hauled our nylon drifter up to catch a hint of a breeze. "Wake me up for the next reef," Larry called as he blew out the cabin lamp and burrowed into the forward bunk.

Our morning sights showed we'd been set away from the reefs, not toward them, and it wasn't until a day later that our first real wind filled in. Even though this wind rarely stayed favorable, we kept on the move for the next nine days until we finally neared the entrance to Manila Bay. We'd had to work hard to gain our northing. For two days we'd tacked into heavy swells that were annoying to us, but since we were moving toward our goal, the skies were clear, and the barometer was steady, we ignored them. A week later we found that those swells had come from a ferocious typhoon that passed between us and our goal, devastating local shipping and destroying over a dozen Manila Yacht Club boats on a holiday cruise to a resort sixty miles south of their home port.

When we finally reached toward the yacht-club basin, near the center of Manila harbor, after sixteen and a half days, we were both feeling relieved to have what we felt was the worst part of our homeward voyage behind us. A fresh following breeze had us skimming toward the crowded-looking shore at close to six knots. The afternoon was perfect, and as we prepared to round up between the stone breakwaters that protect the club basin I said to Larry, "Bet there's no one here we know." We joked about how far off the beaten track we seemed to be sailing. Then a motor launch approached us, and its uniformed skipper pointed to a mooring next to a green forty-foot cutter. We were busy for the next few minutes, maneuvering into position to sail up to the mooring, dropping and furling our sails, securing the mooring lines. We didn't even see the fellow standing on the cutter watching us. When we'd finished securing a safety line to our mooring he called, "Hey, Lin, hey, Larry, how you been?" We couldn't believe our eyes. Ron Amy! We'd last seen him in Baja California nine years before. Different boat but same, unchanged guy. Ron had been in Manila for a week now. He'd sailed over from Hong Kong, where he'd outfitted the boat he'd designed and built in his own yard in Taiwan.

The next morning that "small world" cliché became even more worn as we watched a natural-wood fifty footer work slowly into the anchorage under sail alone. On board was a man who'd deeply influenced our lives. Peer Tangvald had sailed around the world during the 1950s in an engineless thirty footer called *Dorothea*. His book *Sea Gypsy* persuaded us to try sailing *Seraffyn* without an engine. We'd known Peer was sailing his engineless fifty-foot schooner *L'Artémis de Pythéas* somewhere in the Orient. We'd hoped to meet him.

Peer had been working with a Taiwanese boat-building company as a consultant. So, between Ron and him we heard some interesting stories about Chinese-built yachts, as we lounged on the breeze cooled verandah at the friendly club, drinking tall glasses of iced calamancy and rum. (Calamancy are a delightful Ping-Pong-ball–sized citrus fruit, sort of a cross between tangerines and limes.)

Both Peer and Ron agreed that the woodworking skills of the Taiwanese builders were excellent. Bronze castings also tended to be good. "Their problems are with modern stainless-steel fittings and hardware. I

Peter Tangvald sailing into Manila.

always told people to import their stainless fittings from the U.S. or take their boats to Hong Kong for outfitting," Ron said.

"Are there any real bargains in Taiwanese-built yachts?" Larry asked both men. Their final consensus was that if you arrive in Taiwan and ask a builder for a $25,000 forty footer, he'll build it for you and it will be lousy. Few Chinese builders will turn down a contract at any price, and that's what has given the industry a bad name. But if you come to Taiwan and ask for a carefully built boat, the builders will figure out a fair price that's probably 25 percent lower than U.S. prices. The woodwork will be finer and more detailed, but the quality of the hull construction will depend on the person you hire to supervise the construction. Just as in any other country, there are good yards and bad yards. The best solution is to handle the purchase of your yacht just as you would any other $100,000 investment. Investigate the different yards, talk to people who have had their boats built there, and ask how the final costs worked out, what changes those people would make. Then don't rush the builder, and allow ample time for completion of your boat. According to Peer, time overruns frustrated most of the people who flew out to take delivery of their own boats in Taiwan. The average delay was about two months. If you have only four months of summer holiday to outfit your boat and get it back to the United States that delay could be worse than frustrating.

Some real problems do exist for people who want to sail their own boats home from Taiwan. Because of governmental regulation and the fear of invasion from Red China, you cannot day sail your boat for sea trials. When it is launched you can leave the harbor only once.* There are only limited supplies available for general outfitting and language difficulties can be frustrating, since English is not so prevalent here as it is in other countries of the Orient. That is why so many people get their boat launched and rush directly to Hong Kong to continue outfitting and sea trials. But in spite of these difficulties, it may be worth delivering your own boat home from Taiwan. The shipping and duty costs you save could cover the expense of your living in Taiwan while you supervise some of the construction on your boat.

Peer Tangvald found the Chinese builders difficult to work with and did not enjoy living in Taiwan at all. Ron Amy, on the other hand, had experiences that encouraged him to set up a business in Taiwan. Now he

*Reports in early 1982 say the Taiwanese government has eased restrictions to allow for some sea trials, but we have not met anyone who has actually tried this yet.

is taking his boat on toward San Francisco, where he planned to set up an American office to distribute the bronze hardware his Taiwanese workers made.

A smart-looking forty-nine-foot black wooden schooner was the only other foreign visitor at the Manila Yacht Club. *Styx* had been built by her owner in Southern California during the same years we built *Seraffyn*. Don Johnson, a professional yacht-delivery skipper, had modified a Chappell-designed Tancock Whaler by adding a pinky stern. Now he and his crew, Linda Balser, were on a fast voyage from Hawaii to Singapore, then back to Hawaii. Linda had spent two years voyaging in the South Pacific as skipper of her own thirty-four-foot ketch. Don had thousands of miles of sea time on race-boat deliveries, including one voyage on George Kiskadin's *New World*.

We've rarely been in a port with such a variety of experienced voyagers. The only person among the four cruising couples who hadn't sailed at least 10,000 miles was Ron's girl friend, Lois Farrington. Her only

Don Johnson on *Styx*.

offshore experience was the 300-mile voyage from Taiwan to Hong Kong, then 650 miles on to Manila. Linda and I spent several hours answering Lois's questions about provisioning for her next passages from Manila to Southern Japan, then on to Hawaii. We kept reassuring her, "Don't worry, you'll do okay." But Lois had her notebook constantly open, asking each of us for suggestions on which vegetables to take along, what kinds of canned goods, how to store them. Her barrage of questions ultimately led to one of the most pleasant aspects of our north Pacific crossing.

Fortunately for all of us, Manila was an excellent place to shop, and several members of the club decided to make sure all of us had a good time while we got in our stores. Tony Wee persuaded us to take off two days to go touring. "My wife and her friends will help you make up the time you lose by driving you on your shopping errands." With the help of these gracious women, we found the best prices in town for our stores, and I filled *Seraffyn* to the brim with exceptionally low-priced canned vegetables, fruits, and juices, excellent coffee, and a wonderful treat—dried banana chips. Locally produced rum ranged in price from fifty-six cents a bottle to $4.50 for the aged-twelve-years variety. The yacht-club bartender fell into the mood of our four-boat shopping spree by holding a rum-tasting party for us one evening. He lined twelve different brands along the bar, and after much careful consideration all of us settled on the medium-priced seventy-eight-cents-a-bottle brand, and four cases of it were ordered to fill *Seraffyn*'s bilges.

We'd been warned about Japanese prices and filled every empty storage spot we'd made during our slow passages from Singapore. Then, on the day before we planned to leave, Larry and I set out to buy souvenirs to use as gifts when we reached Japan. We'd been told by Malaysian friends that gift giving is a ritual part of everyday Japanese life, and the finest gifts we could offer were the polished agates and exotic shells of the Philippines. While we wandered through the tourist market in central Manila, Larry spotted some nice-looking guitars. "Let's buy one for you," he said. I wasn't the least bit interested. I didn't play the guitar. I couldn't imagine where I'd store it in a small, stores-laden boat like *Seraffyn*. But Larry had a bug in his ear. "Let's buy one and try to figure out how to play it. That will fill up some time while we're at sea." Unfortunately, Larry didn't like any of the guitars he saw in the marketplace. So, he wrote down the addresses of each guitar maker and hired a taxi driver for the afternoon, then dragged me off for a tour of guitar shops. Even more unfortunately, I had an upset stomach from one party too many or one strange dish more than I should have sampled. All I wanted to do was go back to the boat and hide. I probably could have enjoyed our crazy search, otherwise. We ended up at the far side of the city, where rough board shacks on dirt roads seemed to be home for millions of children, goats, and chickens. The contrast to central Manila was shocking. Our taxi driver finally located the shack we'd been told held the workshops of one of Manila's good guitar builders. We were welcomed into a dirt-floored room surrounded by guitars in all states of construction. A wood fire burned in the center, with mahogany guitar sides arranged carefully next to it so that they could be heated in preparation for their careful bending into complex curved shapes. With Larry's eye for woodwork and my somewhat trained ear, we finally choose a thirty-five-dollar guitar that we later learned had the quality and tone of one that could have cost four times as much in another country.

So, the next morning, when we ran out of Manila, a guitar lay nestled among the fresh stores that filled five plastic bins on top of our forward bunk. Once again I was glad to be out of port. As much as we enjoyed the partylike atmosphere of evenings on the yacht-club verandah or in the

Stores coming on board.

homes of our Philippine friends or on one of the visiting boats, seven days of full-time shopping, list making, and rushing in the tropical heat had been just plain hard work.

Larry and I spent a lot of time discussing the voyagers we'd just said good-bye to. We'd all promised to keep in touch, and as we sailed onward and finally settled into building our new boat, we did exchange letters. Within two years, tragedy had struck two of the three couples we'd so much enjoyed meeting.

Don Johnson and Linda Balser left Manila a few days after us, bound for Singapore. Late one afternoon near Vietnam they spotted an overladen-looking vessel. The people on board were waving and obviously trying to attract their attention. Don decided to approach with extreme caution because he'd heard stories of local fishermen turned pirate, since so many Vietnamese refugees were trying to seek asylum using any boat they could find. As the boat got closer, Don and Linda were appalled to see forty-three refugees lined along the sides of a rickety thirty-foot launch, children in the first row, women next, men behind them. The spokesman for the refugees asked for some diesel fuel and water, explaining that they had less than a gallon of fuel left and no money to pay, since they had been robbed twice during their two-week voyage. Don insisted on inspecting their boat and came out to tell Linda, "This tub is barely afloat. It probably won't last the night." He turned to the refugees and announced, "I'll take you on board *Styx.*" Linda later told us, "The most heartbreaking thing I ever heard was when the spokesman asked, 'How many of us?' do you know, they'd decided among themselves who should live and who should die." but Don told them, "I'll take everyone on board."

Life during the next five days of squally weather was far from easy, with forty-three extra people on board a boat with little more interior space than a Cal 40. Linda said, "During rain squalls everyone could get below decks if we all stood up."

The worst ordeal came when *Styx* reached Thailand. The officials refused to let the refugees land. For six days Don sought our every official he could find, while *Styx* lay at anchor with an armed guard, watching and the forty-three Vietnamese tried their best to keep the boat livable.

Each day Linda would go ashore and buy the refugees twenty-five pounds of rice and forty-three of the cheapest fish available. Linda told us, "That's all they would eat even though I wanted to buy more fresh things. They insisted they didn't want us to spend the extra money." On the day their release actually came through, Don offered the group two hundred dollars cash to help them while they waited for resettlement. As he finally ferried his refugees ashore, the women insisted on staying on board. They cleaned *Styx* from stem to stern, bilge to overhead. "She's never been so clean, not even when she was new," Don told us when we saw him a year later in San Francisco. "Not only that, but I get envelopes from all sorts of strange places now. Each one has a dollar or two in it from those resettled refugees."

That was the last time we saw Don. He set off soon afterward to deliver a large racing boat across the Pacific via Singapore. Don was on watch late one night; the autopilot was set as the boat powered across a windless South China Sea. He didn't wake the next watch on time. When the crew came on deck, Don was gone. The genoa was partway up the head stay, which led the crew to believe that Don had gone forward when a light breeze filled in. He'd possibly tripped and fallen overboard; Linda wonders if maybe he had a heart attack. No one would have heard his shouts over the noise of the engine. A careful search didn't turn up any trace of this fine sailor.

Peer and Lydia Tangvald were not sure where they were going after they left Manila a week later than we did. Their boat had been badly damaged while it lay inside a Taiwanese shipyard shed during a typhoon. The roof had collapsed on it, crushing the bulwarks, shattering much of the deck, and splintering the mainmast. Peer had replaced the deck before he set sail, but his impatience with Taiwan persuaded him to leave with only the foremast standing and absolutely no rails, no stanchions. He and Lydia and their two-year-old son, Tomas, were brushed by the typhoon that had passed north of us as we sailed between Brunei and Manila. That convinced them they should not sail much farther until they rerigged the boat. Peer's next letter spoke of the village they found, two days' sail south of Manila, where wood and basic supplies were available. "We will have the boat rebuilt soon and Lydia wants to sail for Australia and then Cape Horn. But I think I would like to sail to Canada and the United States."

About two months later another letter arrived saying, "Lydia is dead." We read on and found that Peer and Lydia had for some reason decided to sail into the Sulu Sea, an area the pilot books, the yacht-club members, and even the port captain of Manila had warned all of us against. "Especially you two," he'd said to Peer and Larry. "The winds are not dependable there, and you have no engines, so you cannot rush through quickly as powered boats do. You would be in grave trouble if those revolutionaries spotted you."

Peer, Lydia, and Tomas Tangvald.

Peer and Lydia had been sailing slowly south near the northeast coast of Borneo when a fish boat came toward them. Lydia said she was going below to get the shotgun they carried. Peer told her, "No, it is too late to use a gun. They are already too close." But as the fish boat pulled alongside Lydia rushed below, grabbed the gun, came out through the forehatch, and fired a shot at the intruders. Someone inside the wheelhouse returned fire immediately, and Lydia fell overboard, dead. The intruders came on board and took Peer's ready cash and the shotgun, then left without in any way harming Peer or his son.

We have often wondered if Lydia would still be alive if the Tanvalds had carried no gun at all. Peer himself seems unsure. In his latest letter to us, written from France, where he is working on a book about his adventures in the Far East, Peer writes, "Lydia was not killed due to the possession of a gun; she was killed due to its improper use."*

Sometimes in the late evening, when we dream impatiently of going cruising again, we talk about those two vastly different tragedies. But as we compare them to the horrid stories we hear of freeway crashes, of senseless murders in the cities, we are reminded of how few of our cruising friends have come to grief during the eleven years we spent voyaging.

When we set off from Manila, we learned again that voyagers can often make mistakes and still survive. It's not like falling asleep at the wheel of a speeding car, where ten seconds can lead to death. In our case, we made a major mistake, but the slower pace of the sea gave us time to think and react, time to claim a second chance.

*For a further discussion of guns and cruising see *The Self-Sufficent Sailor,* W. W. Norton, Chapter 37.

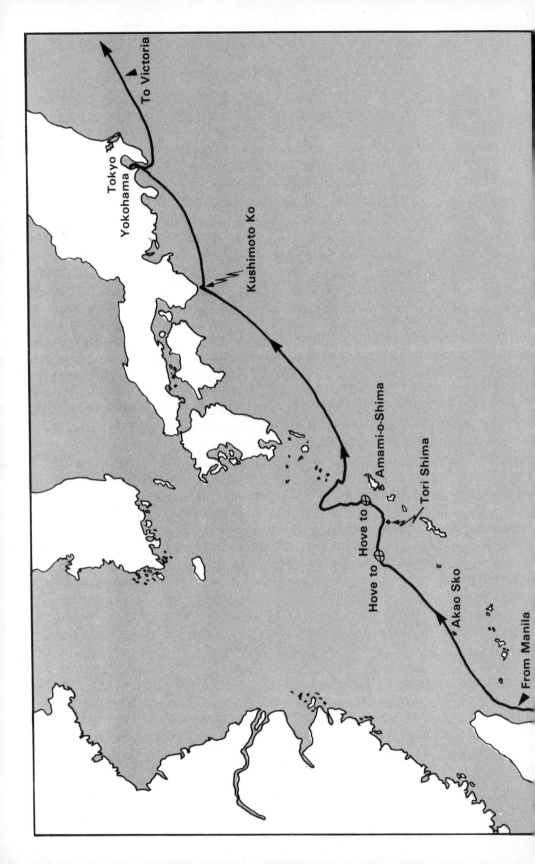

CHAPTER 20

~~~~~~

East China Sea

A wise man once said, "Intelligent people learn from other people's mistakes; normal people learn from their own; fools never learn." The way we chose our route from Manila to Japan made us wonder whether we even deserved to be in the "normal" category. We had two basic routes open to us. We could head north alongside Taiwan, inside the Ryukyu Islands and through the East China Sea, then make a right turn when we came near the Japanese mainland and head into the Pacific Ocean toward Yokohama. Along that route lay chances to visit some of the volcanic island outposts of Japan. We'd rarely be out of sight of some island or another, and we'd be in the axis of the Kuro Shio current, which could give us up to two and a half knots of free progress every hour. That could add sixty miles a day to our runs. The only drawbacks we noticed at the time were a chance of fog and a slight increase in the chance of typhoons. But we minimized those by saying, "Five or ten percent chance of fog, that's less than three days a month. And there have been almost as many typhoons during this time of the year outside the islands as there have been inside."

Our other choice was to make a right turn soon after we cleared Luzon and head out into the open Pacific, where there were few interesting places to stop and only a half to three-quarters of a knot of current to help us on our way north.

It was now the seventeenth of May. We definitely wanted to be prepared to leave Yokohama on July 1 so that we'd be out of the Orient before the typhoon season started in earnest. We chose what looked like the fastest route to cover the 1,900 miles that lay between Manila and our goal.

Life seemed to be going along quite well as we worked north along the west coast of Luzon. At night we'd sail through fleets of outrigger fishing canoes with huge propane-powered lights hung over their bows to attract squid and small fish. Sing-song greetings rang across the breeze-rippled water as we glided past. The first hint that we were leaving the tropics came when Larry asked where his sweatshirt was stored before he came on deck for his 0200 watch. So, when we were three days out of Manila he suggested breaking our voyage by sailing behind Hermana Mayor Island to anchor for the day so that he could check *Seraffyn*'s bottom for growth. "The water is going to be too cold if we go much farther north," Larry said. The lovely sand island, the coconut palms, the crystal-clear water, the colorful shells crushed by our anchor, the rugged coral heads astern of us were a final glimpse of the tropical world we were leaving behind. While Larry scrubbed the ever present slime off *Seraffyn*'s bottom, I rearranged our clothes locker so that jeans, sweaters, and turtleneck shirts were at the front, and bikinis, T-shirts, and shorts at the back. Then, just before sunset, I joined Larry for one last tropical swim. As we moved farther away from *Seraffyn* to get a final glimpse of her anchored in this paradiselike setting, Larry pointed down toward a huge coral head that lay less than ten feet below us. "Our chart showed a minimum of twenty-four feet of water in this anchorage. Must be a pretty old survey." We swam back to the boat and took a freshwater rinse-off. Then, while I waited for dinner to simmer, I checked the date on our chart. This anchorage, which lay fifty miles north of the American navy base at Subic Bay, had been surveyed only four years before. The coral heads had reached toward the sunlit surface at close to three feet per year. The next morning, as we sailed on toward Japan, Larry commented, "It will be kind of nice to be back in northern waters again. At least there the rocks don't grow."

The guitar Larry had forced on me in Manila did add a special note to our voyage north. Two or three times a day we'd get it out and thumb through the "how to play a guitar in ten easy lessons" book we'd bought. We took turns hanging Tom Dooley, we ruined "Three Little Indians," rowed Michael ashore thirty times in three days. The lovely varnished guitar back got its first scratch when a quick wind shift caught us in mid song and I had to sheet in the luffing genoa while Larry readjusted the wind vane. Within a week we began looking for a permanent storage place for this new addition to our sailing life.

Everything seemed under control as we caught the first lift from the northbound Kuro Shio current and cleared the tip of Luzon. Then we got a warning sign that should have made us reconsider our voyage plan while

Larry filleting a mahimahi or dorado.

we still could change it. We were running fast, the current was helping us with a half-knot push, and that night I'd noticed thin cirrus clouds around the moon. By morning, heavy swells from the north made the boat buck and lunge, shoved by a fresh south wind. Rain squalls kept us below for most of the day. Larry caught enough water to fill our tanks. We did check the radio to see if we could find out what was causing the oddball swells. Radio Manila reported nothing unusual; WWV did not include any warnings for our area. Besides, the barometer was rising and stood at a very normal-looking 1006, so we ignored the signs that a typhoon had passed to the west of us, and continued on. By late that afternoon the weather cleared and we spotted Taiwan. Bearings confirmed the promise our sailing directions had made. The Kuro Shio, or black current, was giving us a free ride, one and a half knots per hour, and just like addicts, we were hooked.

Now, even when changeable light winds kept us from sailing well, we were still on our way toward our goal. The current picked up speed as we neared the north end of Taiwan. It ran at almost three knots. Back eddies, whirlpools, and tide rips reminded us of its presence. Our sights confirmed its speed. But as we entered the first part of the chain of islands that stretch from Japan almost to Taiwan, we began to realize we'd made a mistake. Fog patches began to drift with us for two or three hours. Riptides would appear out of nowhere and shake the boat the way a dog shakes a bone. Minutes later, three-foot overfalls would be replaced by smooth waters. Two days north of Taiwan, the Kuro Shio showed us the depths of its fickle, mischievous ways. Our noon sight showed our northern rush was just what we'd hoped for, but when Larry got ready to take an afternoon sight to confirm our longitude, a fog patch moved in. When it cleared, five hours later, we got the scare of our lives. An island lay four or five miles astern of us. We'd seen no island when we'd taken our noon sight. The only island near us on the chart was a three-mile-long, 1,000-foot-high volcanic tip called Akao Sko, and it should have been about eighteen miles west of us. We dug out the *British Sailing Directions* for this area, and there was a diagram showing the outlines of Japan's southern islands. That damn current didn't just run north; it eddied and twisted. It had set us west over twenty miles since our last sights and pulled us along the wrong side of Akao Sko. Only luck had kept us from hitting that steep-to island, and we realized we had truly lost control of our fate. Now we began to worry, and for six days the tension grew worse.

The wind strengthened and backed as the current pulled us north, until we beat close-hauled over a foggy, shrouded sea. A light drizzle filled in on my 2100 watch. I remember spending the first hour studying our chart and our pilot books, looking for a safe escape route from this foggy, island-cluttered sea. The only safe chance was 300 miles north of us, near Amami Island, where navigation lights could guide us past just submerged rocks and reefs out into the open waters of the Pacific, where we belonged. Until then we'd have to worry about a current that could set us where it wished, about fog that obscured the steep-to islands, about shipping that grew ever heavier as we moved north, and about typhoons that know no season in this treacherous inland sea. I think it was those steep-to islands that worried me most: no place to anchor, no chance to hear breakers before we were driven ashore. Altogether I was in a lousy mood, when a strong gust of wind heeled *Seraffyn* until her leeward deck gurgled with foam. "Have to get that stupid lapper down," I thought as I pulled on my wet-weather jacket. Our routine for getting sail down quickly worked well. I reset the wind vane so that *Seraffyn* headed closer to the wind and began luffing but didn't quite tack. I eased the lapper sheet just a bit so that it would come down the head stay easily; then I went forward and let go of the jib halyard. The jib down-haul worked a treat, and soon I had the lapper down and secured around the bowsprit, the bulk of the sail stuffed in the jib net. Without the drive of that head sail, *Seraffyn* slowed right down until she lay quite comfortably. Spray stopped flying across her bow. The damp, foggy night seemed less ominous. But I wasn't in the mood to take chances, so I decided to get the lapper off the bowsprit and bagged before I set the staysail to get us moving again. That's when things began to get to me. I took the flashlight out of my wet-weather-jacket pocket and set it against the windward side of the forehatch so that its beam lighted the bowsprit and sail. Then I slid out toward the head stay. My boot caught in the jib net and I stubbed my toe. A jib hank didn't want to open, the wet sail wouldn't behave, and that damn flashlight got loose and began rolling up and down the deck, its plastic casing thumping first on the bulwark, then on the forehatch. I let out a howling string of frustrated curses as I debated, Should I get that stupid flashlight or get the sail off first? Larry appeared on deck just then. "What the hell's going on out here?" he called from the companionway as he zipped his jacket.

"I'm trying to get the f---ing jib off the bowsprit," I yelled back.

"What can I do to help?" he asked in a very easygoing tone of voice that infuriated me because I'd just ripped a nail on the halyard shackle.

"Grab that damn flashlight," I growled.

"And what shall I do with it?" Larry teased.

I wasn't in the mood for teasing and I barked, "Throw it overboard for all I care."

He did.

I couldn't believe it. I sat on the bowsprit, the bundled-up sail between my knees, and watched the light bobbing fifty feet from the boat. Then I demanded, "Why the hell did you do that?"

"You told me to," Larry said with an innocent smile on his face. Then I began to laugh. We both did. I climbed in from the bowsprit and stood with Larry watching that flashlight slowly fade into the East China Sea. Its beam winked up through the depths for an incredibly long time. When we finally set to work together bagging the lapper, setting the staysail, getting *Seraffyn* moving again, we felt grateful to have forgotten the tension of the previous two days for even a little while. But the Kuro Shio slowly made the tension build again.

For two more days we beat into winds that blew almost gale force part of the day, then dropped to less than force three for most of the night. It was all we could do to keep the boat moving through the leftover seas. Rain squalls poured over us half the day; fog drifted through between squalls. When there wasn't rain or fog, clouds covered the skies, so we didn't get a chance to take a sight. But by keeping a constant watch, Larry spotted the distinctive shape of Tori Shima through a rift in the clouds. Bearings showed that the current had started to slow down a bit. Now it drew us north inside the island chain at only one and a half knots. But soon after we got those bearings, the wind increased to a full gale that shook our last bit of confidence. We could no longer make headway against the built-up seas. So, for forty hours we lay hove to in dense fog while heavy rain pelted against our deck and the barometer dropped steadily down from 1008 millibars to a low of 998. For Friday, June 2, the noon entry in our log says, "Sure wish we knew where we were. If the current stays steady we're safe as can be. But visibility less than one mile." We knew that because a huge compressed-gas ship had come close to us early that morning, possibly attracted by the internal radar reflector in our wooden mast. The ship had slowed down as it passed, and even at this slower speed it disappeared, rolling and lunging into the fog in only minutes. We hadn't really needed that reminder of the dangers that lay shrouded in this wind-whipped fog. We stayed inside the boat, hiding from the weather. Most of the time I lay in one quarter berth, Larry in the other. We read books, tried to cheer each other up. We made shopping lists for Yokohama, talked about the interior we'd like if we ever built a bigger boat, worked together trying to make interesting meals to fill the time, as *Seraffyn* lay hove to much more comfortably than our minds did amidst the jumbled seas, confused by wind against current.

Then we got the break we had prayed for. The gale winds fell off as quickly as they'd started. The clouds cleared, and by noon Larry had the sights he needed to fix our position. If luck and our new southwest breeze held, we could sneak through a gap in the island chain and be in the safety of the wide-open Pacific before another blow came through. But the last six days had shaken our confidence. Even though we were sure of our sights, even though the channel we were sailing through was twenty-five miles wide, we grew nervous when we didn't see any islands by nightfall. "They should be only ten miles away. We should see some lights," I kept telling Larry. "There might be fog near the islands even though it's clear here," he suggested. "We've got to trust our sights." But just before midnight, as we reached along smooth seas at five knots toward the south end of Tohara Jima, Larry called, "Hey, Lin, come on up with our chart. There are lights in the wrong place!"

I pulled on warm clothes as quickly as I could and came out to see what was worrying Larry. A string of lights lay to the south of us. The lighthouse at Tohara Jima should have been north of us. The only seaside village shown on our chart was next to the lighthouse. "Current must have set us north again," we both concluded as we set *Seraffyn* on a close-hauled course to go around the lights. I brewed up some hot chocolate as the lights grew brighter. Then, when I came out the companionway to hand Larry a steaming cup full, I saw it. Dead over our stern. The flash of a lighthouse. The lights to the south weren't in a village. They were on a fishing fleet. We had been right on course. We should have trusted our navigation, but that damn current and the past six days had spooked us. Fog had obscured the beacon at Tohara Jima. We were already free, in the Pacific again after seven years. Now, only clear, open water lay between us and Yokohama, 600 miles northeast of us.

Later, when we were able to get more information about the local weather, we learned that two typhoons had passed within 300 miles of our course from the time we left Manila until we cleared Tohara Jima. The center of one went south behind Taiwan; the other ran due west along the southern tip of Japan, 300 miles north of our hove-to position.

We've often tried to figure out why we made such a bad choice of routes. The only answer we come up with is that we relaxed our guard.

When we'd planned our voyages from the Med, we'd been most concerned about the Red Sea passage, the Palawan Channel, and our Pacific crossing. Those were voyages other cruising sailors had written about, so we studied every note we could find on those areas. But we'd heard of no other voyager who'd chosen this inner-island route. In fact, only half a dozen cruising sailors had gone to Japan before we did. No one had warned us to be careful—no one, that is, except the people who compiled *Ocean Passages for the World*. For, now, as I read the copy we used to carry on *Seraffyn*, I see a whole page of warnings in the powered-ship sailing-directions section that we somehow missed because we'd become too sure of ourselves.

It is amazing how easy life became when we were once again in clear water. We began to enjoy the cool days; the changeable winds became a challenge. Even when one noon sight seemed completely out of whack and we spotted a headland a day before we should have, there was no tension, no deep-seated worry. Now we had sea room. Our afternoon sight showed that the Kuro Shio current had played one last trick on us. It had reversed its course and set us northwest sixty miles in twenty-four hours. The headland we saw lay over the fishing village of Kushimoto. It was only twenty miles away, so we decided to try and get in for a quiet night at anchor.

I'm glad we had this chance to glimpse the other Japan. It's one of the reasons we hope to sail back one day and spend a year exploring this fascinating country. We worked into a shallow, protected spot next to a minuscule fishing port just before dusk and spent a lovely, undisturbed night at anchor. Just at daybreak we got up to watch half a dozen fishermen loading their nets into flat-bottomed dories. A light haze covered the water; green-clad hillsides made a perfect backdrop to the wooden piers. Fisher-men's wives in loose-fitting pants, tunic tops, and white-stockinged feet carried woven baskets full of baited lines down the narrow catwalks. Each fisherman waved as he sculled by, and we hated to leave this quiet spot. But we did need to enter Japan properly before we could legally go ashore. So, we lifted our anchor and skimmed three miles deeper into Kushimoto Ko, where we tied at the exceptionally clean commercial docks next to the main town. Our arrival caused quite a stir. The port captain spoke just enough English to inform us he was sure there'd never been a foreign yacht in his harbor before. An hour later he returned with a very serious customs official who had driven over from a much larger port. "You may not enter here," he sternly told me. "But you may," he said to Larry as he stamped his passport. "You may go ashore. She cannot until you go to Yokohama and get her proper papers." It seems that Canadians do not require visas to enter Japan. Americans do. We were in a bit of a daze as the customs officer rushed up the steps to the top of the pier. Larry teased me about being confined on board the boat while he was free to roam. Then he saw the port captain sitting on the steps next to us. He chose his words carefully and asked if I was really restricted to the boat. The relaxed local official looked over his shoulder as if to make sure the customs man had driven off. Then he put his hand in front of his eyes while he shook his head up and down. We both began to laugh as he waved good-bye and walked into his dockside office, then sat down facing away from his window.

We quickly gathered a shopping bag and some traveler's checks and ran down the docks to find fresh food for a special dinner. We'd made it. We were in Japan, safe and sound. We had three weeks to cover the last 250 miles to Yokohama, then prepare for the longest voyage of our lives. *Seraffyn* was in fine condition. We'd learned some new lessons, and we felt we well deserved the bottle of Suntory champagne we found and drank that night, even though it did set us back almost all of a twenty-dollar traveler's check.

CHAPTER 21

<center>~~~~~</center>

Japanese Manners

From the moment we sailed outside the quiet of the hill-surrounded bay of Kushimoto Ko, we were caught up in a rushing crowd of shipping. We've never seen so much traffic: huge oil tankers, tiny inter-island steamers, cargo ships, fish boats, tugs, and barges. There were literally hundreds in sight during all of our two-day voyage to Yokohama. Yet discipline and manners prevailed. Each ship stayed in its proper steaming lane. Each signaled as it overtook us, then passed on the proper side. After the first twenty-four hours among this industrious flood of ships, we began to feel relaxed as we ran along at full speed, wing and wing on a ten-knot breeze with two and a half knots of current under us. Efficiently arranged, meticulously maintained navigation lights marked each headland. Beautiful steep hills held necklacelike concrete roadways decorated with charmlike little villages. The huge volcanic cone of O-shima, guarding the outer entrance to Tokyo Bay, stood clear and visible from sixty miles away. Occasional rain squalls seemed to materialize out of nowhere, cascaded through the peaks, forced us below decks to wait until the boat was washed clean, then passed to leave blue skies overhead, the sea smoother, the sailing better. We were thoroughly enjoying the short voyage, when a taste of the Japanese manners that lay ahead scared the hell out of us.

It was just after 2300 our second day out when I noticed a medium-sized freighter's lights. Our courses seemed to be converging. We were running fast, the main vanged out, the lapper set on the whisker pole. Everything looked completely under control. If I fell off just five degrees and ran dead downwind, the ship could easily pass ahead of us. But the captain ordered his big searchlights on, saw our sails and probably the Canadian flag that we'd left flying on the backstay, then decided to be polite and alter course to go astern of *us*. We both seemed to make our decision at the same time. We both changed course, and now we were headed for a collision and closing fast. We both again made the same decision. We altered course back to original, and I figured if he kept moving at the same speed we'd clear his stern quite nicely. But the extreme politeness that Japanese seem to reserve for visitors took over. The captain ordered his ship stopped to let us sail in front of him. I heard the clanging of engine-room bells even though I was 400 yards to windward. "Larry, get up here quick," I yelled. He'd already been wakened by the churning noise of the ship's propellers, and he was through the companionway before I finished. "Grab the tiller and gybe her quick," I ordered as I ran forward. Larry pulled the tiller hard to windward when he saw that wall of steel rising in front of us. I did my best, hauling up the inboard end of the whisker pole so that I could release the sheet. Larry grabbed the tail of the boom vang and jerked it free. The mainsail flew across with a bang, filled, and heeled the boat just as I ran back to sheet in the flogging lapper. In spite of the Chinese fire drill, we had the sails in and pulling on a beam reach within seconds. That got us clear of the ship's stern just as her captain saw his error and ordered full steam ahead. The wash of churning propellers only fifty feet from our side twisted *Seraffyn* from her reaching course. But we were clear and safe, and somehow we even remembered to wave to the seamen bowing and shouting greetings from the ship's towering stern.

The next morning, as the tide rushed us into Tokyo Bay, we searched our charts and sailing directions for a place to land. There wasn't one yacht club mentioned. The only docks listed were huge shipping piers. So, we used the friendly following breeze and coasted along the indented shores of the bay, looking for the masts of some local sailboats.

Every inch of the waterfront was lined with industrial buildings, docks, ships, and giant mooring buoys. We sailed past ten miles of closely packed city until we finally spotted three sailboats inside a quiet cul-de-sac almost filled with cable-laying ships. We reached in and dropped our sails, then tied up temporarily alongside a barge. There wasn't a person in sight, and Larry went searching for someone while I stayed on board. It took him almost twenty minutes to find anyone, and when he returned he was chuckling. "We've just landed in the security area of the American naval base. This is Yokosuka. Those sailboats belong to American officers stationed here. But there's a small Japanese yacht club about three miles farther on, just beyond those fuel tanks, in Yokohama."

We short tacked along the huge tank farm, past loading ships and long lines of factories, and there in one of the most unattractive settings we've ever encountered lay the most warmhearted yacht club in the world. A tiny gray-haired lady in a bright kimonolike dress scurried down the steel ramp to bow as we sailed slowly up to the empty dock in front of the clubhouse. "Welcome, welcome," she said in heavily accented English. Then she skillfully helped us secure our lines as a young man rowed quickly ashore from one of the 200 small boats that lay tied to double moorings amid the innermost line of fuel docks. Uyro bowed and introduced himself in English that was sometimes not quite adequate for the situations we later found ourselves involved in. After a brief discussion with the tiny lady, who turned out to be the manager of the club, he said, "It is illegal to sail into this club. You must next time use your motor."

"We have no motor," Larry said.

This caused a very animated discussion. Both of our new Japanese friends looked concerned. Finally Uyro said, "We won't tell any of the officials. You are the very first foreign visitors ever to come to the Yokohama Shimin Yacht Haven and we want you to stay!"

Within an hour, customs and immigration officials were mingling with friends of Uyro's who'd come to welcome us and offer their assistance. Larry stayed on board, giving tours of our little home, while I sat inside the yacht club filling out form after form, patiently explaining to three different officials why I had not gone to a Japanese embassy to get an entry visa two weeks before I arrived.

In eleven years of voyaging to thirty-five different countries, we'd arranged for visas only before we sailed into Mexico and Poland. Mexico had been the first country we'd sailed to, and local sailors had warned us that the normal nine-dollar fee could be increased to fifty or a hundred dollars by unscrupulous port captains if we waited until we arrived in Mexico instead of going to the consulate in the United States. Poland was such a strongly regulated Communist country that we didn't want any unpleasant surprises once we arrived. So, we got our visas before we sailed from England. In every other country we visited we just sailed in with current passports, up-to-date immunization cards, and our ship's registry papers. We'd been treated like big-ships' crew. Our clearance usually came through immediately; fees were rarely more than a dollar or two. We did not, however, visit Indonesia, where, we were warned by the American embassy in Malaysia, a visa and cruising permit were vitally important and could take up to six months to arrange.

My Japanese interrogation was more pleasant than I thought it would be. Lovely tea cakes and hot, fragrant green tea appeared like magic. Between questions and phone calls, the customs agents kindly answered as many of my questions about their country as they could. Meanwhile I could see out to where Larry was the center of attention, surrounded by eight or nine young Japanese small-boat sailors. When I finally got my passport stamped, three hours later, I was amazed at Larry's plans for the next morning. "Uyro is going to bring us a map of the city, and he's already arranged to have stronger reef-point patches sewn in our mainsail. We take it in tomorrow. The shipyard just down the street is going to spray-galvanize our butane tank tomorrow. Uyro arranged that too."

Late that same evening, Uyro, a young mechanical engineer who raced a Lazer dinghy and was one of six partners in a syndicate that owned a twenty-five foot cruiser-racer, arrived dressed in an elegant black suit, a tie, and highly polished leather shoes. He'd brought along a friend who was even more elegantly dressed. We of course asked about their formal clothes, and that's the first time Uyro's English broke down. He tried every word he could, then finally resorted to a wonderful two-man pantomime in our cockpit. He took the female part; his friend replayed the part he'd

One of our weekly visitors.

performed in earnest only two hours before. Amidst giggles and mock seriousness we watched a complete reenactment of a formal Japanese wedding betrothal. No scene could have been more bizarre. Here we were surrounded by oil tanks and factories that could have been in any industrialized country in the world, while two extremely modern-looking young men knelt and bowed until their heads almost touched in our cockpit, then carefully passed imaginary ceremonial cups of tea to each other in a ritual that reached back thousands of years.

It wasn't until we had our mainsail off and our empty propane tank loaded into the folding wheel-away shopping cart we'd bought in Singapore that we opened the map Uyro had brought us the evening before. Every single street and town was designated by Japanese characters, not one word of English, nothing we could understand. Uyro had carefully written our destinations on a sheet of paper in English, then the best equivalent he could come up with so that we could try to say the Japanese words to passersby, and finally in characters so that we could show them to people. But we didn't even know where we were on the map, let alone where to start looking for streets we needed, and I must say the hugeness of this city that seemed to stretch thirty miles from Tokyo through Yokohama to Yokosuka left us dazed. Fortunately, Moma-san, as everyone called the club manager, drew *X*s on the map and gave us a note to show any policeman or train conductor if we had trouble. We laughed when we learned that her note ended with this admonition: "If all else fails, call me and I'll tell you how to send them home."

We were absolutely amazed at the fine quality of craftsmanship we found in Japan. The sailmaker, a bright young Japanese named O'Hara, did an excellent job of adding patches to our sail at a very fair price. The shipyard manager didn't understand a word we said but still did a first-rate job of sandblasting the rust off our eleven-year-old tank and respraying it. Every item we purchased, from fruits and vegetables to a music book, was of the highest quality. Prices for food were extremely high, in fact, shocking. Seventeen dollars for a pound of ground beef, a dollar fifty for an apple, five to nine dollars a pound for fish. But every item was perfect, each piece of fruit individually wrapped and displayed. We were glad we'd stocked up before we arrived, because the idea of paying two-fifty for a small chocolate bar was beyond my scope. Mama-san helped by calling each of the big ship's chandlers and arranging for their duty-free price lists, and there we found affordable prices.

Meanwhile, we had two and a half weeks to enjoy and our work list required only three or four days of that time, so we gladly accepted two very special invitations. Uyro brought down a new group of friends one evening and asked us to join them the next day for a sail out of Enoshima, the harbor the Japanese had built for the summer Olympics a few years before. Thank God, someone came to get us and guide us through the maze of Japanese trains and monorails. I'll never get over the press of humanity that surrounded us everywhere we went. Even on the handsome forty-five-foot ketch we sailed that day there were sixteen eager guests.

Just as we began to wonder how people kept their sanity in this crowded land, we met Jim Parker, an American from Arizona who'd come to Japan with the navy and stayed to marry a lovely Japanese teacher. Now both Jim and Sanea worked as English teachers for a local language school and saved for the boat they hoped to buy some day. To keep their expenses down, they lived the purely Japanese life-style that was so natural to Sanea. Jim felt we'd understand his adopted country better if we came and stayed with him and Sanea for a few days. We spent the first afternoon and evening in their ten-foot-by-eighteen-foot home on a noisy side street lined with identical paper-doored houses. We sat and watched the street life go by until dark, when Sanea closed the screens and the sounds seemed to fade away. She served a lovely banquet dinner for eight on a low table while we sat on cushions scattered over sweet-smelling rattan mats. The real treat for the Japanese sailors Jim had invited was grilled hamburger patties the size of half dollars, two per person. Raw fish and prawns were the main course, rice balls of all types the filler. Desert was half of a small watermelon, sent as a gift from the principal of the school.

As soon as the last guests departed, Jim and Sanea rearranged the room as if they'd done it hundreds of times. Bedrolls and screens appeared from cabinets built into the walls, and the banquet room became two private bedrooms. Just as Jim had promised us, we forgot the outside noises; the lovely wall hangings and warmth of the tiny home were enough to shut off any thoughts of crowds. The smell of grass mats was my last memory as I fell off to sleep that night.

We toured all the way to Mount Fuji and along the seaside in the car Jim had borrowed. The rain that fell most of one day seemed to add a special flavor to the tiny roads, where bullocks still pulled woven-basket carts. We watched women planting rice and men plucking tender tea leaves from the plants on the terraced slopes of the rugged countryside. Sanea used all of her persuasive powers to get us into a small hotel normally reserved for only Japanese people. The manager asked the twenty other

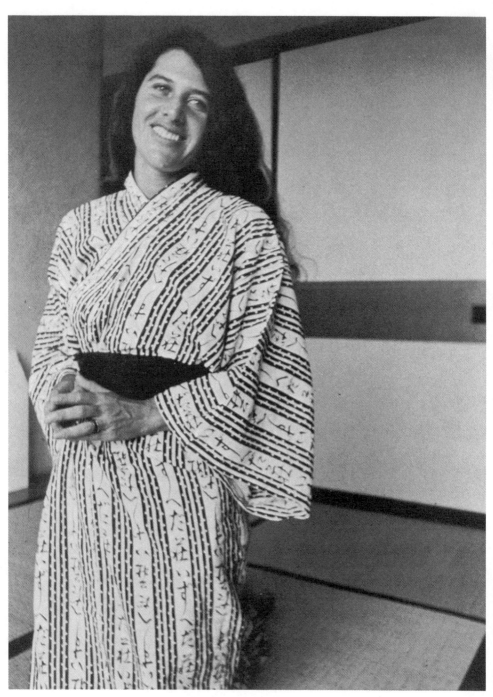

Lin pretending to be a dutiful wife.

guests if they minded before offering us the kimonos worn by all visitors to hide distinctions of wealth and position in the common dining rooms and baths of the meticulously clean hotel, nestled among pines and ferns above a restless bay.

We were amazed at the desire the Japanese people seem to have to learn English. During our short stay, we were offered seven or eight different jobs as English teachers, with serious promises of salaries that started at fifteen dollars an hour, just to converse with people in their homes. So, we tried to return Jim and Sanea's hospitality by spending a morning at their school, conversing with a class of seven women who wished to learn English in order to help their upper-management husbands by being hostesses to foreign visitors.

After a hilarious morning of showing photo albums and explaining the simple puns we carelessly use, the women insisted that we be their guests at the best new restaurant in Yokohama. We both tried to hide our disappointment when we walked through the doors of the largest department store I'd ever been in, turned the corner, and entered Denny's Restaurant. But the food and service were like no "Denny's" we'd ever been in before. After lunch our hostesses took us to a kimono shop. I was amazed to find that even the most modern of Japanese girls needs two or three of these ceremonial dresses in order to meet the social demands of civilized life. The beautiful fabrics and design that went into these five-layered outfits explained their high costs. Even a simple one started at $300.

The day was capped off by tea at the home of one of the women, whose husband was manager of the largest bank in Yokohama. Much of the lovely quarter-million-dollar house was like any midwestern U.S. two-story, three-bedroom, 1,500-square-foot house. But in the center was a special room, raised a foot above the rest of the house. As our hostess slid open the paper doors to this room, we stepped out of Western civilization, with its overstuffed chairs, piano, and china cabinets, into the quiet, uncluttered graciousness of Japan. One low lacquered table, one exquisite watercolor, and a single branch of blossoms in a china vase were the only furnishings in the mat-floored room. It was here that our hostess spent an hour each evening with her husband, forgetting the outside pressures of modern life.

We felt very much part of the yachting scene we found at the Yokohama Shimin (people's) Yacht Club. Most of the boats were small; only a few were close to thirty-four feet in length. Their owners were usually syndicates of young working people. In the back of the club, a taxi driver was finishing a thirty-foot glass hull, and a shipyard welder was rebuilding a wooden boat during his evening hours. This was the first Far Eastern country we'd been in where sailing wasn't the private reserve of very wealthy people or foreign businessmen. Within three days we'd met almost two dozen young sailors, and once or twice a week they'd return with new friends to meet us and spend the evening. Each time they'd bring Japanese delicacies for us to taste. Some of these, like the delicate rice cookies, we loved. Others, such as strips of dried seaweed, didn't quite strike our fancy. But we tried them all.

One of our immediately favorite people was Tadami Takahashi. His English was even more limited than that of Uyro, who'd come with him. Fortunately, Tadami had brought along some samples of his artwork. His comic illustrations for various magazines fascinated us, as did his excellent guitar playing when he discovered our Philippine acquisition. After he and his friends left that evening I said to Larry, "Wouldn't it be great to have cartoons like those in the book we're talking about writing?" Ever since we'd left Manila we'd been discussing the idea of writing a book that answered the questions we were always being asked about provisioning and crew care at sea. A few weeks before we reached Japan, Larry came up with a good suggestion. "Why don't you keep a diary of our trip from Japan to Canada? That's a real long passage that should remind you of all the things seagoing cooks want to know. It'll also give you something to do. I know you'll need that."

Now Larry goaded me on. "Offer to buy some drawings. Then you'll be committed." So, when Tadami came by three days later, we tried to explain our idea, and he seemed more than pleased but insisted that a translator was necessary before we went any further. Two days later, I had a list of eighteen captions for possible cartoons ready when Tadami arrived with Ryoki, a young translator for a large Tokyo bank and the female Laser sailing champion for all of Japan. Tadami was as delighted as we were to find that our original negotiations hadn't been too far off. Final prices and terms were easily agreed upon; then the fun began. Ryoji tried her best to translate our captions for Tadami. In most cases we had to resort to pantomime. All was going smoothly, if somewhat humorously, until we came to "Sometimes the cook feels like she's buried under an avalanche of stores the first few days at sea." Ryoji had never heard of "avalanche." The dictionary she carried didn't list it. We couldn't pantomime "avalanche" to people who didn't have a rugged mountain peak full of snow anywhere on their island. Finally we said, "Cross that one off." But seven months later, we saw the results of Japanese persistence when twenty lovely blue-

and-black cartoons arrived. We were amazed that Tadami had been able to capture our expressions, almost our whole personalities, from only four evening visits and two photographs we left with him.

We'd set a definite departure time the day after we sailed into Yokohama: Saturday, the first of July, 1978. On Friday, June 30, everything we'd ordered during our three-week stay began to arrive. The first ship's chandler we'd visited telephoned early. "Where is your vessel lying?" he asked. We again told him, then handed the phone to Mama-san. She covered her mouth to hide a giggle as she hung up. "His deliveryman was already here once, but all he saw was your little boat and he was looking for a ship!"

We'd ordered two hundred dollars worth of fresh eggs and produce from a vendor in the local marketplace, and I was a bit disappointed when every bit of it arrived loaded on one motorscooter. But as we transferred things from the double-stacked cartons over its rear wheels and out of the basket hanging from the handlebars, I was definitely impressed with the high quality of each item.

By 1700, when Mama-san came down the dock for her usual evening farewell, you couldn't see *Seraffyn* for the cartons loaded along her decks. We bowed repeatedly and gave this sweet, patient lady a perfect venus's-comb *(Murex)* shell we'd brought from the Philippines. Her eyes glowed and she started the bowing we never figured out how to stop politely.

When she left I panicked. "Larry, Uyro and his friends will be here in less than an hour. We'll never be ready."

"Calm down. You go take a shower. I'll stack everything on the side deck and cover it with our canvas. Then I'll help you make dinner."

So, when Tadami arrived, carrying his own guitar and banjo, things were somewhat under control. We'll never forget the party that grew on the dock next to us and cascaded over *Seraffyn*'s decks and into her tiny cabin. Each of the people who'd become regular visitors brought some kind of exquisite gift: a lacquered music box, a handmade set of ceremonial porcelain teacups signed by the artist who'd painted them, Mount Fuji tea in a pottery jug, a pair of happy coats, bottles of twenty-five-year-old Suntory whiskey. The small pieces of agate we'd brought from the Philippines seemed inadequate in return. But all eleven of our guests seemed more than pleased and laughed in delight as Ryoji translated the name of the hot American-style "sloppy Joe" sandwiches we served. Then the music began. Out came two guitars, a banjo, and a fiddle. The harbor rang with some of the best bluegrass sounds I've ever heard. "The Gleen, Gleen

Uryo arriving for our farewell party.

Glass of Home" brought tears to my eyes. Then our guests started playing a real hoedown. Jim Parker, the only other non-Japanese there, jumped onto the floating steel dock next to us and began a real country stomping dance. I joined him, lifting the skirts of my long Malaysian dress; Larry began hooting and yelling; the music grew wilder; and when we'd all danced and played to exhaustion, Jim waited for a moment of silence and put a real capper on the evening by letting out with a full-voiced, traffic-stopping, two-mile hog call that stunned us all.

Someone noticed the time. Panic ensued. "The last train leaves for Tokyo in fifteen minutes," Uyro explained. It was only then that we learned all of these lovely young visitors had been taking an hour's train ride once or twice a week just to visit us. We bowed until we were almost dizzy and promised to return someday, a promise we both intend to keep.

The sound of rain woke me minutes before our 0730 alarm went off. "Departure. The big one starts today," I thought. Then I remembered the stores all over our deck. "Get up quick, it's raining," I said as I rushed into the main cabin. Together we tossed everything below just as Jim Parker arrived with a farewell cake that Sanea had baked after our party the evening before. We couldn't invite him below. In fact, we had to move everything in order to find our clothes. But the rain was turning to a light drizzle, and Jim didn't mind filling the six extra water jugs we intended to carry on the foredeck next to the bulwarks for this 4,500-mile voyage. I laughed as I stood on the settee and reached across a case of duty-free Mount Gay rum and two cases of Coca-Cola in order to light the stove. I laughed even harder when I managed to clear the top of the ice chest and found I couldn't open the lid to get the butter. The twenty-five pounds of dry ice we'd ordered to augment five pounds of frozen shrimp and twenty pounds of regular ice had been too much. The lid was frozen in place and stayed that way for another day.

When I brought out two cups of coffee for Larry and Jim, there were over two dozen yacht-club members on the dock. The commodore presented us with a crate of beautiful tomatoes. Mama-san had come thirty miles on her day off to give us six perfect ears of sweet corn, a gift we know cost her half a day's salary. Don Harrison, a college professor of literature from Tokyo, presented us with a shopping bag full of English paperback books he'd collected from among his friends.

Then, as we began to take off *Seraffyn*'s sail covers, our Japanese friends said a quick good-bye and seemed to disappear. Now only the two Americans were left, helping us untie our mooring lines. "Why don't you two sail out to the entrance of Tokyo Wan with us? You can catch a bus or train back," Larry suggested. In minutes all four of us were skimming away from the dock. We rounded the first corner, and four Japanese yachts converged on us, their decks crowded with our friends, their foghorns blowing. "Sayonara," we called. "Sayonara," they replied, and then *Seraffyn* picked up speed and heeled to a fresh breeze as we skimmed clear of the special yacht club hidden inside an oil-tank farm.

A heavy fog closed down about us just outside the fuel docks. We had little trouble negotiating the well-buoyed waters of Tokyo Wan, but the idea of trying to get safely through the maze of shipping at the entrance to the bay made us nervous, since we had only two or three hundred yards of visibility. So, four hours later, when we headed into a tiny fish harbor just inside the entrance to Tokyo Wan to let off our guests, we decided to stay for the night, get all of our stores out of the main cabin and into the lockers they belonged in, and have a good rest. Before we loaded the dinghy back on board, the two of us took one last row around our floating home. She'd carried us into some wonderful adventures, been our calling

The last guests depart.

card in hundreds of ports, served us perfectly for over nine years already, but now her biggest trial lay only hours ahead. She seemed so tiny sitting among fish boats with dories that were even longer than she was. She definitely was overloaded, with her waterline two inches lower than it should have been. But I knew she'd do her part just fine. As we lifted the dinghy on board and secured it for sea, I wondered how we would react to the confines of spending the next forty or fifty days at sea.

CHAPTER 22

~~~~~

Fog

W e've both said, "If that North Pacific crossing had been our first long voyage, we'd have given up sailing for good." We were as well prepared as any voyager could be, so we had no real problems, no gear failures, no personal tensions, lots of food and water. It wasn't the length of the voyage, the hard work of sailing with constantly changing winds, or the ten major depressions that moved past us during our forty-nine days at sea that made this such a difficult passage. What really wore on our nerves was the constant fog. For thirty days of that passage, our visibility was down to less than 150 yards. Our whole world became a drizzly, damp gray cocoon, its floor a dull green sea, its ceiling the same color as its walls. *Seraffyn* seemed to shrink as perpetually drying foul-weather gear cluttered her cabin. We'd put up with fifty degree temperatures half the day just to have her companionway boards open; then, when the fog began to make everything below decks damp, we'd reluctantly close up the boat and light the oil lamps and oven to warm ourselves.

Yet, two things made this voyage the most interesting one we've ever been on. First, we'd learned from our own experience during the previous year of sailing across six different seas, and now we'd arranged to have several projects to fill our sailing time. Second, the unusual weather that chased us across the Pacific gave us a chance to learn about storms and storm tactics in an intense training session that filled eleven days of the voyage.

We'd met only one other person who'd sailed along this route in a small boat. Dale Nordlund had taken his thirty-eight-foot ketch, *Aegean*, from Yokosuka to Victoria in thirty-eight days, reaching most of the time. He'd really enjoyed a fair-weather voyage, and we'd planned just as he did with the help of the pilot charts and *Ocean Passages for the World.* From the weather information they recorded, we expected to catch a fair current of about fifteen miles a day soon after we left Japan. Winds promised to be fair and not too fresh; nowhere along our route was there more than one day of gale-force winds shown during the average year. No typhoon tracks crossed our path once we were five hundred miles east of Japan. The charts did indicate a chance of fog as we neared the Aleutian Islands, but even there it was supposed to occur fewer than five days out of any one month. So, when we set off from Yokohama we were looking forward to the fast, comfortable reaching Dale had spoken of in such glowing terms.

Our first week at sea was a delight. We stood careful three-hour watches as the mountains of Japan fell slowly below the horizon. Shipping began to thin out, and the Kuro Shio current gave us a fantastic ninety-mile lift along our way, so our third day's run, noon to noon, was an amazing 185 nautical miles. We spent those first days getting organized, resettling the stores we'd bought, catching up on the sleep we'd missed because of having too much to see and do onshore. We rummaged through the paperback books we'd been given and chose the ones we wanted to read first. Warm, sunny days lured us topside most of the day, where I spread out swatches of the fabric I'd bought in Japan and began stitching the first of thirty flags we needed so that we could dress ship and fly one for each country we'd been in when we arrived in *Seraffyn*'s home port of Victoria. Larry got out his small carving tools and a scrap of teak from his secret stash and began making mountings for half a dozen wild boars' teeth we'd bought in Manila. "I'll make chains for them out of some sail twine. They'll make nice gifts for some of the friends we haven't seen in years," Larry said as he whittled away in the cockpit. My night watches flew by as I began outlining chapters for our "care and feeding" book. I'd write for twenty minutes, go out on deck, take a look around, then go back and cram myself into a pile of cushions I'd stacked in the corner of the settee and write some more. In the morning, after Larry finished getting his first sight, I'd read my night's work to him and we'd edit it together. Larry would add his suggestions and hints for the next chapters. Every evening just before sunset, we'd get out the guitar and take turns stretching our fingers to reach the awkward positions needed to make chords. Our private sing-songs just before Larry went below to fill the oil running lamps, then climb into his bunk, seemed to end the comfortable, full cycle of our twenty-four-hour days.

The *X*s that marked each day's run on our Western North Pacific chart

The first week.

began to inch away from the Japanese mainland. We had 2,700 miles, or forty inches, to go just to put our first mark on the same chart as our destination. A day's run of a hundred miles moved us an inch and a half. Eleven days out of Yokohama, our sun disappeared behind a heavy bank of gray clouds, a light drizzle began to fall, the barometer started to drop, and when Larry gave me the coordinates for our noon position from his plotting sheet, I marked an X on the passage chart that was only thirteen inches from Yokohama. I got out the adjoining chart and measured the distance we'd have to cross on that. "Do you realize we have over fifty-three inches left to sail?" I said, feeling depressed and impatient.

"What's that in miles?" Larry asked as he put away the dividers and parallel rules.

"Thirty-six hundred miles, thirty-six days if we move along okay. God, that's a long time," I said, staring at the vast expanse of white on the two charts spread the full width of our cabin.

"Nothing much we can do about it except sail the boat harder, keep busy, forget the time, and be glad we're finally clear of any typhoon zones,"

Twice-a-week egg inversion

Larry said as he climbed into the quarter berth for an afternoon nap. "I'm sure glad to leave the Orient for that one reason. I hate watching you worry about typhoons."

The drizzle slowly turned to fog. The southeasterly wind we'd had for five days slowly headed us until we sailed close-hauled, pointed at the Aleutian Islands one day, the Hawaiian Islands the next. Now the boat heeled and plunged over the fog-shrouded seas. Spray kept us out of the cockpit. Our log recorded eighty or ninety miles each day, but our position guesses put us only forty-five or fifty miles closer to our destination, since we were actually sailing at a forty-five-degree angle to our rhumb-line course as we took day-long tacks and prayed for a lift. During the five days these east winds persisted, Larry would do his best to cheer me up whenever I began to feel frustrated because my pen wiggled off the chart table, found the tiny slit between the floorboards and the hull, then ended up in the bilge, or a head of cabbage broke loose from my chopping board and scattered bits and pieces all over the cabin sole. Then, two or three hours later, it would be my turn to try and lift Larry's spirits when a burst of spray made him miss a sight he'd been waiting to get through the only break we'd seen in the clouds and fog in three days. I'm amazed that we never both seemed to feel "down" at the same time. I was also surprised at how the smallest bit of thoughtfulness would break the beginnings of a bad mood. Larry would tease me, "Let's try a game of cribbage. I'll beat the pants off you. I'll get the cards and board out." Or I'd see him getting frustrated and say, "There's a Milky Way bar hiding in the noodle locker. I'll give you a half inch more than I take."

We felt a definite change in the boat on our fifteenth day at sea. At first we couldn't figure out what it was. The frustrating east wind was still with us. The seas still sent spray across our decks every ten or fifteen minutes, so going out meant putting on all your foul-weather gear. The wind vane still steered steadily toward Hawaii or Alaska. Our world was still limited by the pressing fog. Then Larry said, "It's cold as H in here," when he got out of his sleeping bag. I leaned against *Seraffyn*'s hull as I reached into the forward clothes locker for a sweater and my arm came away damp. That startled me, and I began looking carefully around. The whole interior of the hull from the waterline down was misted with condensation. The only other time we'd had any condensation below decks had been during our winter in England, when temperatures fell below forty-eight degrees, and that had been on the upper part of the hull. "I think we've found the Oyo Shio current," I told Larry. In spite of the fifteen-degree drop in the water temperature this cold current brought with it, in spite of the condensation that I tried to wipe up each morning, we were glad to have the Oyo Shio with us, because our daily runs increased by seventeen or twenty miles a day.

Seventeen days out, the wind began to back until we could lay our course again. Then, late that evening, we sailed clear of the fog bank we'd been in and I saw one of the loveliest sights of my life. A full moon glowed over the undulating sea. The world turned into a study in silver, gray, and black. I was out enjoying the immensity of the fogless world when all of a sudden a perfect moonbow developed. The arch rose high overhead, glowing misty white and silver against the star-studded sky. Six carefully shaded bands hung there for a few moments, then began to fade as *Seraffyn* reached directly toward Canada, making a true five knots for the first time in six days.

The east winds never returned. Instead, fresh west or southwest winds kept us moving toward our goal. The fog was not quite so kind. It plagued us. The only time it wasn't there was when it turned to rain. Some days it would clear off for a few hours and we'd get a quick round of sights. But often we'd go for five days without being sure of our position.

The weather turned cold. On deck it was about forty-five degrees. Below, our three kerosene lamps burned almost all day to keep our living space at fifty-eight degrees. We slept in our jerseys and bundled up to go on deck or even to sit in the settees. Once each day I'd straighten up the interior of the boat and wipe it down with fresh water to keep it salt free and, we hoped, a bit less damp. Then I'd turn on the oven for a while to dry some of the socks and towels that lined the sea rail ever since Larry's sea boots developed a leak. But we had to conserve fuel and limited the oven use to an hour each day as we noticed the gauge on our butane tank dropping steadily toward the 50 percent mark. The eight-foot-wide, six-foot-long cabin seemed perpetually cluttered with navigation charts, my notebooks, wet-weather gear, Larry's latest rigging project, half-sewn flags. The forward cabin, on the other hand, began to grow less cluttered as our fresh stores diminished at a comfortable rate. First the fruit baskets emptied; then the tomatoes disappeared. Within three weeks, four of the six baskets were emptied and stored in a cockpit locker. Our dirty-clothes bag began to balloon as the time passed. We'd bought three extra sets of sheets for our sleeping bags, figuring we could each have a new set every 1,400 miles, then throw the four-year-old ones overboard when they got smelly. But when the time came to deep-six them Larry couldn't bear the thought of wasting such potentially useful rags. In spite of the abundant supply of water we caught off our mainsail, I couldn't figure out a way to wash these big sheets and dry them, so they got stuffed into the bag with our dirty towels, and we had to stash them all under the dinghy.

Twenty-three days out, our WWV radio report warned of a depression passing 400 miles north of us. By midday we lay hove to while gale-force winds cleared the skies and stopped our progress. "We may be stopped, but at least we know where we are," Larry said as he came below after taking a third round of sights from the bucking, spray-whipped deck. I lay in the quarter berth behind him admiring the persistence with which he computed each sight. "Gives me something to do," he said when he went out for an extra round of sights late that day. By the next afternoon the wind backed and dropped, so we got under way again, reaching over a rumpled sea with our double-reefed mainsail and staysail pulling us at five and a half knots. "Well, that should take care of the one day of gale-force winds per month the pilot chart shows," I said foolishly.

Small diversions make a tremendous difference on a fogbound voyage. We made the most of my thirty-fourth birthday which occured thirty-one days out. Larry offered to do all of the cooking, all the dishwashing. We'd been twenty days without a real shower, and I knew I could no longer stand having dirty hair. Our water tanks were completely topped up, since the heavy fog caused sweet water to run off our mainsail at a rate of four gallons a day. So, in spite of *Seraffyn*'s unpredictable motion as she ran along fast and bumpily through the fog, in spite of the outside temperatures, which rose to only forty-seven, we improvised our own Turkish bath house by closing up the boat, hanging a towel over the companionway into the forepeak to keep that area from stealing any of the heat, lighting the oil lamps, then warming big pots full of water on the stove top. We took some towels out of the laundry bag and lined the settees and covered the floor. I knelt down and leaned over our five-gallon bucket while Larry poured warm water over my head and shoulders. He steadied me as I sponged my body, then sudsed my hair and rinsed it. Then I did the same for him. Together we wiped up the cabin, changed the sleeping-bag sheets, and got out fresh towels 300 miles earlier than we should have. I leaned over the open oven and combed my hair dry, then lounged back in the corner of the settee, a blanket around my bare body, as I enjoyed watching Larry cook up a beautiful fish soup from the leftover meat of a ten-pound tuna we'd caught three days before. The fish had kept perfectly in the misty cockpit.

Later, Larry rigged up the double bunk he'd devised for the main cabin. It consisted of the table and some bunk boards laid across the settees, then covered with our quarter-berth cushions. It was small, only four and a half by five and a half feet, but it was far better than trying to lie together in the bucking cold of the double-sized forepeak bunk. As we cuddled together, savoring the special feeling of warm, clean bodies, Larry said, "This may not be the most comfortable way to travel, but it sure beats not going at all." I had to agree. The last month had been uncomfortable most of the time, but tomorrow we'd be on the same chart as Victoria. We were well over halfway to our goal, and I knew I could put up with the unaccustomed fog and cold better than I'd expected. In fact, the fog had its advantages. We didn't have to stand watches; there was absolutely nothing to see. A once-every-three-hours check on the gear and sails was all we needed. We'd stopped worrying about shipping. We were well north of normal steamship routes, and so far we'd heard no ships and of course seen none at all. Our food supplies were holding out well. The variety was definitely limited now, but I still had some treats hidden away: lots of raisins, some chocolate bars, cocoa to make our own fudge, a few canned camembert cheeses. We still had books we each wanted to read. I had another ten flags to sew, and our book project began to fill more of each day as it progressed. Larry's boar-tooth necklaces were beginning to line the tie rod above the chart table, and his rigging jobs had *Seraffyn* in amazingly fine shape. "Yes, crossing oceans in a small boat definitely beats staying at home," I said to Larry as we disassembled the makeshift double bunk, since the constant motion kept us from sleeping there together. We crawled into our individual sleeping bags in the comfortable quarter berths and enjoyed the luxury of sweet-smelling sheets and fresh, clean hair. Larry reached across the space between us and took my hand. "Good night, friend, wonder where we'll be this time next year," he whispered before he blew out the oil lamp and turned to go to sleep.

CHAPTER 23

The Last Leg

E ach morning at 0910 we'd listen to the WWV weather advisory for the North Pacific. I'd write down the latitude of the fog bank that seemed to stretch from Alaska to Hawaii and we'd both give a curse. Even if we altered course and dropped 200 miles south, we'd still be fogbound. Then I'd list the coordinates of any storm within a thousand miles of us. Four unseasonable depressions passed far to the north of us, marching from Russia's Kamchatka Peninsula, across the Bering Sea, and into Alaska. We could feel their progress as our winds slowly veered from south to west, then northwest, before settling back to south again. A fifth depression made a short swoop south of this track, and we'd been just inside its storm radius for a day. We'd felt sure that would be our last exceptional winds for this voyage. After all, it was midsummer.

Then, just after we moved our noon-to-noon position marks onto the Eastern North Pacific chart, a sixth depression developed that seemed to detour determinedly south and crawl along the Kuril Islands of Japan before rushing toward the tip of the Aleutian Islands. I'd been ready to turn the shortwave radio off when I heard, "All mariners stand by for further storm warnings." I waited impatiently through a minute and twenty seconds of time-tick recordings; then the announcer said, "Typhoon, speed nine knots, projected course east-southeast, radius of storm winds, 300 miles on southeast quadrant." The coordinates he read off put the center of that storm 600 miles behind and just to the north of us.

During the next hours, the wind slowly veered until it lay on our beam. The seas increased and their tops began to crumble. Spindrift streaked down the back of each towering, marching wave, and exactly one day after that first report, Larry went out on deck and rounded *Seraffyn* up to face the growing seas and shrieking wind. We lay hove to for less than an hour before the steadily increasing wind began to sail *Seraffyn* forward out of her protective slick, even though she carried only a triple-reefed mainsail and her tiller was tied to leeward. That's when Larry decided to set the sea anchor. I put on my foul-weather gear and brought the para-anchor out with me. Then we both tied lines around our waists and cleated them to the mast to protect us as we worked on the plunging foredeck. Larry rigged a bridle while I spread the parachute-type sea anchor out on deck. Once it was rigged we fed it slowly over the rail and watched it set to work holding *Seraffyn*'s bow fifty degrees from the wind. Now she lay hove to in the slick that the nine-foot parachute and her long keel created, as the force-ten winds shoved her to leeward. For twenty-nine hours we lay to the para-anchor, the tiny triple-reefed mainsail steadying the boat, only occasional seas crumbling ineffectively against her hull. Every six hours the WWV updates moved the typhoon along a track 300 miles north of us into the Alaskan Gulf. Then, as the seas started to lose their growl, as they began to stop cresting into tunnels of green-and-white foam, the newest WWV report downgraded the typhoon to a storm, but with that good news came some bad. Two more storms were following the same track; the first would be in our area in two and a half days, the storm behind it in four.

As soon as Larry felt the seas had lain down enough so that we could safely begin reaching again, he set sail to try and get more room between us and the storms. But they moved faster than our five and a half knots, and we lay hove to fifty-six hours later. This storm lasted only fifteen hours, and we began to run again for ten hours, only to get hit by the next storm, with new reports of two more depressions approaching. In all, five storm fronts blew directly over us in eleven days. We later learned that this was almost unheard of during the month of August. In fact, it caught the fishermen of Washington and Oregon completely unprepared, and twenty-nine large trawlers with close to a hundred crew were lost as we fought our own private battles several hundred miles off the rocky shores of Canada.

My reaction to this series of storms where we'd expected good sailing was anger. I shut the radio off and refused to listen to any more weather reports. "I don't want to know where the goddamned things are. We'll feel them when they get here," I said after six days of sail, heave to, wait, set a scrap of sail, run, then heave to again. So I stayed in my bunk most of the time, reading, writing. In the relative calm between storms I worked like a demon, baking bread and coffee cakes, boiling potatoes and dried beans for salads, cooking up anything I could so that we'd have something interesting to eat when the next storm hit.

Larry's knee-high, heavy-duty Sperry Topsider boots spent most of the day upside down over the oven as we tried to dry them out and figure some way of patching the newest leak. "Lousy pair of boots my brother gave me," Larry grumbled as he sanded around yet another pinhole and gooped it with contact cement. "Larry, your brother gave you those boots six years ago! They do have a right to wear out," I said as I dug out the last of our plastic shopping bags. Larry slipped a pair of bags over his feet, then used rubber bands to hold them in place to protect his limited supply of Norwegian wool socks. Those plastic bags made his feet sweat. The aroma that filled the cabin each time he pulled off the bags made me cover my nose with the sleeping bag. In between each storm I'd rinse his socks, but still the cabin began to remind us of a men's locker room.

During those five separate depressions we had to resort to storm tactics for over a hundred hours. While I spent most of my time in the relative comfort of my bunk and got up only to heat coffee or soup, Larry seemed to get excited by the series of storms. He spent hours on deck watching the para-anchor work, tossing bits of paper towel overboard to see how *Seraffyn* was drifting. "You should see how those waves crumble when they hit our slick," he yelled down. "Come on up out of there; get some fresh air, you lazy little mole." I'd be tempted then I'd hear another lashing of spray fly across the boat and I'd say the hell with all that wet. I think in reality I didn't want to be reminded how small our floating world really was. Below decks I felt safe; on deck the endless marching, towering waves, the scudding fog, the noise of hissing foam, and the occasional sight of the huge, silent brown albatross that had followed us for almost 2,000 miles left me feeling dwarfed and lonely.

When the second storm began to howl around us, Larry decided to try lying ahull instead of setting our triple-reefed mainsail and heaving to. Within three hours the gale-force winds WWV reported seemed to grow to storm force. It was night, but neither of us could sleep as the boat rolled and lunged. "This is the worst we've ever been in," I said to Larry. "Can the boat take it?" He listened to the waves crashing against our bow and said, "I hope so." Then we heard a roaring freight-train–like noise. The boat lurched sideways as that wave landed on top of us and seemed to force us down into the cold, storm-tossed sea. Squirts of saltwater found minuscule crevasses around the sliding hatch and drenched the inside of the cabin. "I don't like this; I'm going on deck," Larry said as he struggled to pull on his foul-weather gear. "You be ready to hand me the para-anchor if I need it."

I could hear him working near the mast while I mopped up saltwater from the countertops and settees and tried to dry the spots where it had drenched our sleeping bags. I heard the rattle of sail slides and the crack of a flogging sail. Then, all of a sudden, the boat seemd to fall asleep. She lay at peace, heeled about ten degrees. It was almost as if we'd sailed out of the storm into a mild gale. Larry came below about a half hour later glowing with reports of how well the boat was lying hove to. "Lying ahull gave the boat no protection at all. She kept sailing because of the windage against her rig and hull. The minute I got her stopped, she started sliding to leeward and her slick made those waves lose their force. You should see it. Waves are breaking forward and aft of us, but as soon as they hit our slick they crumble into foam."

Between each storm we rushed toward Canada. On our forty-fifth day at sea, Searffyn was running under triple-reefed mainsail and double-reefed staysail on the edge of the ninth depression. Larry was hand steering, helping the wind vane keep us stern-on to the largest of the growling waves in fifty knots of wind. "Give me a log reading," I called out to him. I plotted our "guestimation" and called back, "Only about four hundred miles to Cape Flattery."

"If this fog doesn't break we'll heave to at noon tomorrow," Larry called. "I'm not going any closer to the coast until I'm sure of our position." We hadn't had a sight for seven days now. Fog or low gale-driven clouds had hidden the sun from us, and I had to agree with Larry. It would be foolish to close the coast until we were absolutely sure of our position. Currents or miscalculations could put us closer to the rocky, foggy lee shore than we thought we were. With following winds such as we had, we'd never have a chance to hear the surf before we sailed into it. We remembered one comment from the letter we'd received when a friend ran onto a reef and lost his boat near Fiji: "The worst thing was when I realized I was in the surf. I didn't have time to get the whisker pole down, then shorten sail and sheet in to beat off." If this had been an offshore wind, I know we'd both have felt less apprehensive about going closer as we waited for the fog to clear.

Later that evening, whn the winds lay down and the sea became more regular, Larry unreefed the staysail and set Helmer to work steering full-time, then came below. I offered him a hot buttered rum, then dug out our second-to-last camembert cheese for a cocktail snack. For some reason Larry turned the radio band selector to broadcast and spun the dial. Richland, Washington, came in loud and clear. Local tidbits like "Rotarians meet tonight at seven P.M., Little League playoffs set for Saturday" filled *Seraffyn*'s tiny cabin. I got so excited that I started to cry; then, just as I became embarrassed, I noticed that Larry's eyes were glazed too. "We're on the other side, we've almost sailed *Seraffyn* home," he said as he made room for me to sit next to him. We listened to hometown news for an hour, then all during dinner we talked about finally reaching Victoria.

During the past twelve months we'd been at sea for over 185 days to cross seven oceans and seas. We'd covered 14,500 miles in that time. Before the almost insatiable urge to go home attacked us in Israel, we usually sailed four or five thousand miles a year. Now our goal was only a few days ahead, and we began to wonder why we'd done it.

The obvious answer seemed to be our desire to build a new boat, one that incorporated some of the ideas Larry had learned by wandering through boatyards all over the world. As *Seraffyn* ran closer and closer to Canada we realized we were having fun planning how we'd build the new boat, how we'd arrange her interior and deck. But we really didn't want to rush into a building project that we knew would tie us in one place for at least three years. "No, I'd like to explore the Gulf islands again," Larry said as he got out the chart and began to show me anchorages he'd loved as a nineteen-year-old. "Boy, I had some good times there when I was racing *Annalisa*. We could spend a year cruising within sixty miles of Victoria." He made my mouth water with his descriptions of fresh oysters and clams, salmon steaks, and bushes full of wild blackberries. That led to a discussion of the word *home*. Where was it? Vancouver held sailing memories for Larry, but I'd never been there before. Newport Beach held three and a half years of memories for both of us, because that's where we met and built *Seraffyn*. But neither of us wanted to spend the rest of our lives in either place. "That's why I want to build a slightly larger boat," Larry said. "I can't imagine a full-time life onshore. We need a boat that has room for a good, solid fuel stove and real bathing facilities, so that it's a real floating home we can take anywhere, not just to warm places."

The reason for our year-long dash finally became clear when I poured one last cup of tea for each of us, then asked, "What is it going to feel like to sail into Victoria?"

"I guess it's going to feel like we've finished something," Larry answered. "*Seraffyn* will be a fully proven boat; we will be a fully proven team."

For the first time I began to understand the urge that surfaces among most offshore voyagers after they've been sailing for a few years. One day the desire to write "complete" creeps into your mind, even if "complete" lasts for only three or four months before you start a new voyage. That explained why Eric and Susan Hiscock beat back to England three separate times, only to set off again within a year. It was as simple as the reason we loved making a landfall at the other side of any ocean. "To begin" implies "to search for some kind of ending." And for the ocean voyager, the perfect emotional end is to tie the knot of a circumnavigation.

We set normal watches that night despite the thick fog. A north–south shipping lane showed on our chart, and as *Seraffyn* ran over the undulating sea each of us heard the thumping sound of engines as ships passed somewhere nearby. "At noon we'll stop running," Larry reminded me as I got ready for my early-morning watch. "We'll be within 200 miles of the land, and that's close enough."

The sound of Larry stomping around over my head woke me at 0930. My eyes had a hard time adjusting to an unusual sight. Sun flooded through the port lights. Not perfect bright summer sun, but hazy yellow light such as we hadn't seen in weeks. Larry was on deck most of the next two hours, catching five morning-sun lines and a perfect noon sight. Together we plotted them on our ocean-passage chart. Our 132-mile noon-to-noon log reading and the bit of current we'd had put us over the line we'd drawn to show where our chart of the approaches to the Strait of Juan de Fuca started. We were on course, sailing along the imaginary border between the United States and Canada.

Clouds covered our sun before Larry could get an afternoon sight, but we got one more indication that our navigation was right on. At about 1600, as we crossed the edge of the two-hundred-mile fishing limit demanded by the tuna fishermen of each country, we sailed between two Coast Guard vessels, one flying the American flag, the other a Canadian flag. They sat dead in the water facing each other a few hundred yards on either side of an impossible-to-patrol boundary.

Now we didn't have to listen to WWV to hear about the last summer storm marching across the Pacific after us. Local announcers interrupted the broadcast stations to warn sportsmen and fishermen of expected gale-force winds from the west. We heard their announcements on every station as we twirled our radio knob and savored the wonderful variety of music and familiar accents we'd missed in the Far East. We soon lay hove to only 150 miles off Cape Flattery, and for the first time in our month-and-a-half-long voyage we both felt impatient at the same time. Larry stayed on deck watching for the first break in the weather, for the first sign that the breaking seas were lying down and losing their power. After four hours the wind began to get gusty, the first sign of a storm's end. But, better still, the seas slowly lost their overhangs and stopped cresting so powerfully. Larry dropped the reefed mainsail and set the staysail by itself, then steered off toward our goal. He was whooping and hollering like a kid as *Seraffyn* reared up on each foaming wave crest, then surfed down its back in a welter of white water.

After forty-eight days at sea we sailed between the protecting capes into the Strait of Juan de Fuca. The fog disappeared; the wind eased off until we trickled along at a sedate two and a half knots. We passed Port Renfrew and the seas began to die. For the first time in seven weeks we could move around the boat without holding on. Then the decks dried off, and for the first time in thirty days the air temperature went above fifty degrees, even under the layer of low clouds.

I flew into a frenzy of house cleaning. We had full water tanks thanks to our rain catcher, so I rinsed foul-weather gear and stowed it away, wiped the whole interior down, and polished the clock, barometer, countertops, and cabin sides. Larry unrigged our seagoing, shoulder-high life line, then inspected and unlashed our anchor gear. He teased me about my nesting urge as I scrubbed mildew off the underside of the white-painted cabin top with my toothbrush. "Who do you expect to meet you in Victoria? The queen?"

"My folks said they'd try to be here," I answered. "I've saved some camembert cheese and one can of Danish butter." Then I set to work baking a batch of fresh bread, just in case. Larry seemed to pick up my mood. He pitched in, inspecting the boat from stem to stern, washing the outside varnish to get the salt accumulation off it. He spotted a small motor yacht trolling along the Canadian shore. "Quick, get a note and put it in the plastic can we've been saving," he said as he unclutched the vane and altered course. I came on deck and waved until the people on *Altair of Astoria* noticed us and came close alongside.

"Could you call my folks collect?" Larry yelled. "We've just come in from Japan." The crew of *Altair* maneuvered to pick up the can we tossed, then gave us a long toot as they headed for home.

That last night at sea was a very special one for me. I was glad we were

Sailing into Victoria.

sliding along at such a sedate pace. In a way, I almost hated to see this voyage come to an end. Larry and I had grown so close as we endured the discomfort of constant motion, constant cold. The hustle and rush that lay just ahead worried me. All during my on watches I wrote a summation to the book that now filled three one-hundred-page tablets and had become such a comforting part of our daily routine. Then I strung the flags I'd sewn so that they'd be ready for our arrival in port. All during my off watches I lay wide awake talking with Larry. His mood seemed to match mine, yet when we approached Race Rocks, the final turning point on our voyage, we were fully awake and feeling great.

We spotted a sailboat heading directly toward us. We'd have recognized it even if we hadn't been able to see our parents jumping and waving from the cockpit. *Marie Rose,* the twenty-seven-foot cutter Larry's father built during his retirement, powered alongside. My father and mother were there with Larry's folks, yelling congratulations and questions. Fresh fruit came flying at us: plums, apples, a beautiful pear.

It seemed appropriate to be sharing these special moments with all our parents. I was delighted that mine had timed their two-week visit to Canada so perfectly, and pleased that our message reached the Pardeys at their island home, thirty miles north of Victoria, in time for this offshore rendezvous.

Seraffyn heeled and curtseyed as if to show us she loved that last bit of short tacking into the basin in front of the majestic Empress Hotel. As we dropped the lapper and eased into the customs dock, she seemed reluctant to stop. We had a few quiet moments to stand on the dock and survey our little kingdom. The only signs of her 4,500-mile voyage were goose barnacles hanging below the waterline and streaks of mildew under her transom. The decks glowed a uniform silver, bleached by the constant rubbing of salt spray; her varnish shone from Larry's careful wash-down. A bright new Canadian flag lifted to the sunny Saturday-morning breeze. Larry put his arm around me, and we didn't say a word as we silently thanked the brave little vessel that had served us so well.

Then a customs officer walked over and handed us a pink slip of paper. "Fill this out," he said. "Where you in from?" Larry answered, "Yokohama." The customs man walked down the dock toward a fifty-foot ketch that had just powered in from Port Angeles, twenty-five miles across the straits. Just as he began to hand her skipper a form he turned and called, "Did you say Yokohama? Like, in Japan?"

His amazement wasn't too surprising. *Seraffyn*'s name was followed by the words *of Victoria*. As we thought back to the day we set off, almost ten years before, we were just a bit amazed too. We'd never dreamed the voyage that began as a desire to spend six months, maybe a year, in Mexico would stretch into a wondrous world-encircling adventure.

Epilogue

~~~

Although our arrival in Victoria marked the emotional climax of our circumnavigation, it took another fifteen months to actually cross our outward-bound track and officially end what became an eleven-year cruise on board *Seraffyn*. We spent two summers wandering through the wonderful Gulf islands and northern Puget Sound. I bought a collapsible trap and became an avid crabber. This started the seeds of a dream that may someday see us retired on a fishing boat in the Northwest. *Seraffyn* made us a hundred new friends at the Port Townsend Wooden Boat Festival, where Larry talked to every boat builder he could to learn about supplies for the cutter we were now certain we wanted to build.

Then, late in 1979, we set off down the West Coast of the United States and met Lyle Hess in Redondo Beach, thirty miles north of Newport. It seemed right to have him on board for the very last leg of our voyage. He'd sailed on the first sixty-mile leg, eleven years before. Three boats filled with old friends came out to greet us, friends who had shared the champagne at *Seraffyn*'s launching. We all tied up at Gingerlee Fields's waterfront home for for a perfect welcome-back dinner. As the boisterous group began to quiet down Gingerlee said, "You must be a bit sad to see it end."

For that evening, we did feel a sadness as we pictured the next few years without the excitement of constantly new places, new faces. But within three days we'd started the move to the quiet canyon home where we began to build our new boat, and our thoughts turned toward the future.

A year later, when our thirty footer was no longer a dream but a towering reality of teak backbone and stem, locust frames, and bronze floors, we reluctantly sold *Seraffyn*. Two and a half years later, as I write these lines, the new boat still has no name, but now her rudder is ready

Seraffyn with her largest light-weather jib set and pulling.

to hang, we've got the deck beams fully varnished, the bronze deck straps are secured, and next week we begin laying her teak decks.

Now I'm starting to think of galley layout, supplies, and stores. Larry is dreaming of her launching and sea trials, which probably lie about a year ahead. Our friends ask us, "Where you headed this time?"

We answer, "East. We'd like to see Norway."

"Headed around the world again?"

"Not planning to," we say in all sincerity.

"How long you going to stay away this time?"

We give the only answer we can, the answer our years on *Seraffyn* taught us, "As long as it's fun!"

Lin and Larry Pardey
Bull Canyon, California
June 1982

When we'd been cruising on *Seraffyn* for four years, we approached a literary agent with the idea of writing a book about the adventures we'd had.

"Been attacked by any whales, eaten by any sharks, held hostage by any pirates?" he asked.

When we shook our heads, he snapped, "Then forget it. No one wants to read about having fun!"

Two years later, to our amazement a publisher felt differently, and the first book of this series, *Cruising in Seraffyn*, proved that many people felt just as we did, that the joy of being free to wander as we wished, to savor the people our cruising life helped us meet, the small delights of negotiating challenging canals, tricky sailing waters—all were worth sharing. Three more "story" books followed to close the circle of the eleven years we lived and roamed onboard 5-ton, 24-foot, 4-inch *Seraffyn*.

Then, as we built our new cruising boat, *Taleisin*, our writing began to take on a much more serious, purely practical aspect. Now people who dreamed of going off cruising kept asking questions, such as how much does it cost, what gear works, how do I fix it, how do I keep my crew satisfied? So we set aside "story" writing. Although five more books have been added, none is like the *Seraffyn* books. This, in spite of a wonderful twelve years of wandering and gathering story-like memories onboard her bigger sister, 29-foot, 6-inch *Taleisin*, another Lyle Hess cutter, that took three-and-a-half years to build.

Now, as I read through *Seraffyn's Oriental Adventure* to prepare for this new edition, the urge to again tell of the people we have been meeting, the lessons we have been learning, the special sailing days is almost irresistible. I look back at the people whose lives touched ours briefly back in 1977 and 1978 and am amazed at how many we are still in contact with.

In 1991, we sailed *Taleisin* into Sydney Harbour in Australia, past the famous Opera House to find work at a shipyard five miles upstream so we could replenish our cruising kitty. There we discovered Ross and Margaret Irvine, learned the details of their successful journey through three more years of adventures, and relived our days together in Rhodes Harbour. Their two sons, 11 and 14 when we first met, had come home to continue their education. One is now a successful doctor, father of two, and husband to a sailing woman. The other is boat-mad as ever and currently helping his parents finish the 36-foot steel boat that will replace *Girl Morgan*.

The friendship I formed with Lillian Jarmon in Rhodes was kept alive by frequent letters. She joined us in California while we built *Taleisin*. Her two years of wandering as a cook/mate on Mediterranean charterboats left her feeling ready to return to the research-laden atmosphere of university life. We have spent time with her and her husband, Steve Rhode, every time we return to the United States. Lillian has gone on to earn further degrees in social work and art history and is an administrator at the University of Michigan in Ann Arbor. Steve, like Larry, looks on in delight as Lillian and I fly off into our own private world, often acting as uninhibitedly as we had during those days of hum mums and retsina.

In 1980, I had the unique chance to revisit the Suez Canal as a guest of the Egyptian government. They were looking for ways to improve their water-based tourism. I spent a day with Ali at the yacht club where he had built a shaded, comfortable hospitality area for visiting sailors. (Now up to 30 yachts at a time lie where we had been). Ali's two sons proudly showed me the workboat they had just finished building. We learned of the work being done to make transiting yachtsmen feel more comfortable in obtaining clearance to transit the canal. But, in a quiet private moment, Ali did let me know that "baksheesh" is still the grease that smoothes the process.

The Firestone family, with their amazing tribal lifestyle, kept in touch as we headed for home. During our visits with them at their headquarters in Los Angeles, we watched their families grow, their joint businesses prosper. Bob Firestone has become famous for his family-interaction counselling as a psychiatrist. He has since written several books. The family, again working communally, soon owned a second, even larger schooner that saw each new generation of teenagers off on another tribal adventure.

Galle, in Sri Lanka, has become a much busier port of call for cruising sailors, but the Windsor house still offers a warm welcome and good, inexpensive meals to all. We kept in touch with Don and Prima until his death at the age of 63 from a heart attack. His son has continued his traditions.

The oddest adventure, and the saddest one of our cruise on *Seraffyn*, was the loss of *Crusader* with Don Sorte and his crew of five in the waters between Sir Lanka and Malaysia. When we sailed back to Canada, we were surprised to find that we were the center of attention among several of Vancouver's sailmakers and yacht-chandlery owners. They wanted to know if we felt he had truly been lost at sea. It seems Don had left Canada without paying many of these people. When the original edition of this book was published, Judy's husband wrote asking for more information, as did the parents of two of the paying crew. We also got letters from other people who had met or sailed with Don Sorte through the years. One of them has been working on a novel based on Sorte's life, as it seems that Don was considered one of the heroes of the hard-hat diving world.

We learned that he had been the only diver clever enough to take on a contract to remove live ammunition from a naval vessel that sank in Seattle harbor. He was responsible for the diving miracle that saved nine men from a tugboat that turned turtle and sank in the Straits of Juan de Fuca. To this day, we wonder about this amazing rogue and hero, adventurer and casual sailor.

Update 1996

Our guide to all things Chinese, Irene Khor of Lumut, graduated with honors and went on to get a nursing degree, worked in Switzerland, learned three languages, married a Swiss banker, and now lives with him and their two children in Japan. She continues to sail on Lasers, as does her sister Sally. They return frequently to Lumut and write that the heart of the lovely small village is still there even though the naval base has brought in several thousand more people and swelled the membership of the Royal Perak Yacht Club to almost 150 members and 30 Lasers. Such is progress!

Each of the four voyagers we met in Manila Harbor kept a close relationship to the sea. Peter Tangvald sailed on his engineless *Pythias d'Artemis* across several more oceans, several more traumas. He remarried twice more, losing the mother of his second child (Tomas' younger sister) overboard when she was hit by the boom during a gybe. He then went on to have another wife and another child onboard, bringing his family up to three children. Unfortunately, his last wife did not find this life to her liking and left him with his first two children to work under sail in the Caribbean. Peter met his untimely death when, late one night, he was towing 16-year-old Tomas' soon-to-be-cruising boat towards the place where they planned to repair and upgrade it. An error in navigation put both boats on the reef. Only young Tomas survived, managing to maneuver over the reef onboard a surfboard he carried on his boat. A book published posthumously earned the funds to help Tomas carry on until he learned the skills to continue the sailing life, the only one he knows, as he was born at sea.

Don Johnson, as told in this book, was lost at sea. Linda Balser, his partner, went on to start a company to make lovely bronze hardware for classic boats. Bright Star Marine was still going well when we last visited San Diego.

Ron Amy followed a line similar to Linda's. Using all of the contacts he made while he lived in Taiwan, he sailed to California and soon had a thriving business called ABI Marine, which makes bronze fittings and other parts for sailboats.

Then there is the delightful Tadami Takahashi. Although we couldn't communicate well, except with the help of an interpreter, he went on to do some wonderful cartoon drawings for our book, *The Care and Feeding of Sailing Crew*. Those drawings delighted American sailors, and soon his work began to appear in U.S. magazines. Tadami later married his translator, another eager sailor, and to this day is deeply involved in small-boat voyaging and racing out of Yokohama.

The storms that plagued us on our North Pacific passage also had a deep influence on our lives. As we built *Taleisin* and then began voyaging to higher latitudes, we learned not only that many people had forgotten the techniques of heaving to, but also that a popular misconception began to grow that discounted this age-old sailor's safety-valve. We listened in growing dismay to stories of small crews on cruising boats trying to run before storms, dragging warps or steering to keep their boats' sterns to the seas. Several friends described being rolled and capsized. Boats were lost and crew badly injured as gear broke loose. Otherwise strong crew grew exhausted and frightened as waves washed over their cockpits time and again as they tried to steer for 30 or 40 or more hours in front of a raging wind. Several of them abandoned their boats only to have them found serenely afloat after the storm abated. So we began doing research into ways modern boats could continue to lie hove-to using parachute-type sea anchors. This led to our expansion of the original appendix that had been at the end of *Seraffyn's Oriental Adventure* in the first edition. This information is now in *Storm Tactics Handbook*.*

And what about the real main character in this book, lovely *Seraffyn?* We were reluctant to part with a boat that had given us so much pleasure. For a year after we began building *Taleisin*, we kept our first love on a mooring in Newport Beach and spent alternate weekends cruising or racing along California's southern coast. Then one day, a young sailor drove into our boatyard and said, "You don't need *Seraffyn* any more, and I do." Tony wanted to go cruising right then, and *Seraffyn* was ready to be topped up with water and provisions, then set to sea. He left for Mexico three weeks after he became her owner. She has had three owners in the last fifteen years since we owned her. Our favorite has definitely been Tom Pattison, a San Francisco sailmaker and racing sailor who bought her because he liked her seaworthy looks even before he found she had had a successful cruising career. When we later met Tom, he expressed his pleasure and surprise at her exceptional light-wind performance. "My racing buddies teased me the first time they saw me out on the course with that long bowsprit. But when I got her tuned up and going well, I just told them, 'Don't think of her as a cutter. She's really a three-quarter rigged sloop with a light-air sail extension.'" She is now berthed back where she was originally launched, in Newport Beach, California. When it comes time to scrub and paint the bottom of her bigger sister, I become terribly nostalgic and remember the nickname a favorite sailing friend gave her, Small but Mighty. That she was, and the perfect choice for two young people who wanted to explore the world waiting just beyond the horizon.

Lin and Larry Pardey
Onboard *Taleisin of Victoria*, Falmouth, England, July 1996
* *Storm Tactics Handbook* is available from Paradise Cay U.S., 800-736-4509

The authors—
Lin and Larry